The Symbolic World of Federico García Lorca

The Symbolic World of Federico García Lorca

BY RUPERT C. ALLEN

Albuquerque
University
of
New
Mexico
Press

FIRST EDITION

© 1972 by the University of New Mexico
All rights reserved
Manufactured in the United States of America by the
University of New Mexico Printing Plant, Albuquerque
Library of Congress Catalog Card No. 72-80890
Designed by Bruce Gentry

For Emi

Preface

During the first half of this century Spain produced perhaps a half-dozen significant poets, and of these Federico García Lorca is the best known and best loved. His claim to fame rests mainly on the fact that he was both poet and dramatist. In a few short years he brought to the decadent, middle-class theater of Spain a fresh conception of what drama was all about, and a stark technique of characterization that continues to elicit from actors what can only be described as moving, fundamental performances.

Lorca's short life (1898-1936) was one of complete devotion to the arts. With extraordinary rapidity he discovered where his talents lay and placed his life entirely at their disposal. Andalusian by birth (he grew up in Granada), he was one of a group of talented young men who owed their final intellectual formation to the liberal atmosphere prevailing at the Residencia de Estudiantes in Madrid.

Lorca never ceased to be impressed by the pre-intellectual sources of poetic genius, and he gravitated naturally toward the mythic world of eros. This gravitation first found effective expression in the flamenco music festival of 1922, which he and Manuel de Falla organized in Granada, and in the children's music festival of the following year—though as early as 1920 his children's play *The Butterfly's Curse* had been produced in Madrid.

That same sensitivity to the unconscious as the source of creativity furnishes one of the reasons for the close friendship and sympathy between Lorca and Salvador Dalí, for whom the surrealistic mode of reality was nothing if not the projection of unconscious contents in the form of impossibly tangible symbols. And, indeed, Dalí was one of the principal organizers of a one-man show of Lorca's sketches in Barcelona in 1927.

In the late twenties Spaniards began awakening to the fact that they had in their midst a young new talent who was both a dramatic poet and a lyric poet of the first rank. By the early thirties, after a year in New York, Lorca was a national celebrity. Lorca premieres were newsworthy events; his strange "folk poetry," grounded in the legendary world of the Spanish Gypsy, became a classic in its own time; Lorca was somehow the incarnation of a collective unconscious carrying the stamp of absolute originality. He spoke with a voice as ancient as the myth, and yet we have the unmistakable impression that he was saying it all for the very first time.

Any reader of Lorca knows that he frequented by preference the world of artists, children, peasants, and primitives. The wisdom of hindsight makes it seem strange that anyone might have thought that his plan to live for a spell in New York City as a student at Columbia University could have been anything but a personal disaster. In 1929-30 he discovered Harlem, and saw (even then) that black "soul"—he called it *duende*—was being crushed by the megalopolis in a way that he himself felt crushed. He escaped with his equilibrium barely intact, and the net result of the visit was the apocalyptic, terrible—and terrified—surrealistic vision of civilization: the book of poems entitled *Poet in New York*.

Lorca treated his genius like the inheritance that it was—an inheritance meant to be used philanthropically. He sensed it as a *heritage*, belonging to the *pueblo*, the people. It was this that led him to organize in 1932 a university theater-on-wheels, *La Barraca* (The Hut), dedicated to the performing of Golden-age repertoire in the provinces of Spain—performances of seventeenth-century works which were received enthusiastically and with intuitive understanding by the people whose collective soul survived in them and who still did not differ substantially from their ancestors of three centuries before.

By the mid-thirties the days were fast running out for Lorca, as for many thousands of his fellow Spaniards. In July of 1936 the Civil War erupted, and a month later Lorca was dead at the age of thirty-eight, shot dead for reasons best known to his anonymous murderers.

This is a book about Lorca, but it is not a book about a foreign poet so much as it is about the world of symbols which all of us inhabit and the transformation of that world into poetry.

What is essential to Lorca transcends the limits of nationality. If one would have a finely tuned esthetic appreciation of Lorca—or of Rabelais, or Shakespeare, or Pushkin, or Leopardi—one must no doubt read him in the original. But at present we are concerned with something else: a *substantial* understanding of poetic symbolism, i.e., an understanding of the symbol as the *substance* of poetry —with Lorca as our principal exhibit (for how can poetry be studied apart from poems?). Presumably any gain in substantial understanding will be an important gain in esthetic appreciation.

It happens that I have chosen a modern Spanish poet because modern Spanish literature is my academic field of specialization. The preparation of this study for English-speaking readers, however, serves to point out the essential quality of the symbology being used; and this is, that a sound symbological explication of poetry ought not, and indeed does not, depend to any significant extent upon the reader's knowledge of the original text being discussed, just as the exegete explicating the Apocalypse (say) does not require the reader's knowledge of Greek. The essence of the poetic statement is the symbol—*the image to which the word refers*—and this material is not "foreign" to any of us. The dreams that you and I had last night are the same that Lorca had and wrote about in his day.

Acknowledgments

The author thanks these publishers for permission to reprint copyrighted material. William Golding, *Lord of the Flies*. G. P. Putnam's Sons, 1959. Federico García Lorca, *Obras completas*. Copyright Aguilar, S.A. de Ediciones. All Rights Reserved. Reprinted and published in translation by permission of New Directions Publishing Corporation, Agents for the Estate of Federico García Lorca. Kostís Palamás, *The Twelve Lays of the Gipsy*. Lawrence and Wishart Ltd., 1969. John Crowe Ransom, "First Travels of Max," from *Selected Poems*. Alfred A. Knopf, Inc., 1963. Wallace Stevens, "Mandolin and Liqueurs," in *Opus Posthumous*. Alfred A. Knopf, Inc., 1957. James Wright, "The Frontier" and "To the Muse," in *Shall We Gather at the River*. Wesleyan University Press, 1960.

Contents

Introduction

For many years now it has been apparent that any symbology, to be of value to the literary critic as an instrument of explication, must be based upon a sound theory of the symbol. The critic who seeks to analyze a literary text cannot well accomplish his aim without a working understanding of what a symbol might represent and how it might possibly have an autonomous significance and function transcending the personal consciousness of the writer using it.

It seems clear that any theory of the symbol must take into account the immense collective effort of symbological investigation that has been going on for more than half a century. It is a labor of scholars and field workers engaged in the study of man as a psyche; they include ethnologists, mythologists, folklorists, sinologists—the number of disciplines represented is varied; but certainly the one discipline which has progressively attempted to assimilate the findings of the others is depth psychology—that field of study which concentrates on the phenomenon inherent in its very name: the psyche.

To be a human being means to enjoy a peculiar psychic condition. What modern understanding we have of this condition has been determined to an incalculable extent by the evolution of depth psychology, beginning with Freud over seventy years ago. Freud's well-known theories of the dynamics of the psyche have not proved to be of much heuristic value when applied to spiritual problems beyond the domain of psychopathology. Certainly the use of psychoanalytic principles has long since been discredited as the tool of the literary critic, principally because Freudian theory postulates a limited, causal connection between the work of art and the artist himself. A psychoanalytic study of a poem ultimately becomes biographical; psychoanalytically the poem is little more than a symptom of the troubled psyche which produced it; and to discover this is to practice not literary criticism but biography—usually spurious biography at that.

Psychoanalysis was, of course, only the beginning of depth psychology—a necessary one, because it established the principle that the proper study of the psychologist is the psyche. And not only the psyche of the mentally disturbed—for it appears that depth psychology has come to be the primary humanistic discipline of our time.

This object of study, the psyche, has a dynamics observable in the form of images and ideas which in turn become an object of study for the symbologist. Now any deep study of these images and ideas must be of significance for the literary critic, for literature—and especially poetry—is nothing if not a profoundly *psychic* act. The psychological understanding of poetry (not poets!) is much more than just another approach, for we are concerned now with grasping the dynamics of the symbol, the very foundation of the poetic statement; and so it is that we must turn to analytical psychology in particular, for it is there that the most thoroughgoing study and sympathetic understanding of the symbol have been achieved.

The present work was undertaken in hopes of fulfilling a twofold purpose. First, it has been my intention to set forth the meaning and spirit of an extraordinary and significant symbolic world which has, for many years now, consistently been admired from a distance. Practically no attempt has been made to deal with the work of Lorca in terms of modern symbology, despite the fact that Lorca was intuitively as far beyond Freud as was the elder Jung himself, or Erich Neumann, or H. G. Baynes. Lorca's most elaborate drama, *As Soon As Five Years Pass,* is as "psychological" a statement of the problem of individuation as it is possible to make without abandoning altogether the world of imaginative writing. It sometimes seems that Lorca himself had a distinctly Jungian grasp of the inner world of man; but to think this is to see the matter turned inside out. It is not that Lorca had a Jungian grasp of psychic realities, but rather (of course) that Jung knew clearly that no psychology could be sound unless it be a rational declaration of facts already known intuitively in myth and poetry. He was not interested in explaining away the symbols of poetry and myth by trying to show what they "really" mean; rather it became a matter of understanding theoretically what it is that makes poetry and myth become what they become. The poem and the myth are not disguises for something else. Jung never tired of pointing this out about dreams; and the principle naturally extends itself, of its own impetus, to all other symbolic expressions of man's inner life.

Second, beyond wishing to make a contribution to Lorcan criticism, it has been my intention in this study to attempt a demonstration within my field of the substantial relationship between poetry and modern symbology. If this is the reader's introduction to modern symbology, he may well discover that what he learns extends beyond the works of Lorca—our example, but not our final goal.

The critic who sets himself the difficult task of characterizing Lorca's poetic world view will not get very far until he has come to terms with the manifold questions of psychology which confront him at every turn, for it is a fact that the complex dynamics of the human psyche are simultaneously the source and the goal of Lorca's creative activity. At bottom the psyche is always a world born out of the inter-workings of ego-consciousness and the unconscious, and so it is only a truism to declare that Lorca's poetic world was so born. But we have stated that this world is also the *goal* of Lorca's creative activity. His creativity is the result of a delicate adjustment between his conscious world and his unconscious world—but at the same time his great theme is precisely that delicate adjustment, and the dangers attending apathy toward it.

Lorca's concentrated interest in the dynamics of the psyche, then, requires a psychological commentary—which is to say a commentary based on the theoretical framework most relevant to the phenomena with which Lorca characteristically concerned himself. It is not a matter of demonstrating that psychological concepts are relevant to Lorca's poetry; to do this would be to commit a crucial error in emphasis, since psychological concepts are obviously relevant to anything done by human beings. Rather, it is a matter of demonstrating that Lorca's largest meanings *are none other than psychological.* If it is possible to demonstrate this, it is because modern depth psychology—thanks largely to the enormous contributions of Jung—has achieved a sophistication which enables us to undertake the elucidation of the complex symbolism of a poet like Lorca.

Indeed it was not until an adequate psychological theory of the symbol was developed that it even became possible to formulate intellectually statements about phenomena which Lorca himself intuited with the utmost clarity, and to which (we now see) he gave symbolic expression. Lorca apprehended in a profound way the relationship of ego-consciousness to the unconscious, the one as a relatively stable and limited system, the other as a seemingly limitless flux. He recognized that the substance of poetry derives from the images produced out of the unconscious—that is to say, *symbols* (though he was but little concerned with the question of nomenclature).

Lorca's feeling for the *vital energy* of the symbol implies (1) the realization that it carries an archetypal significance transcending the idiosyncratic individuality of the psyche in which it appears, and (2) a recognition of the creative powers of the unconscious mind. Lorca was, indeed, at one with Bergson in recognizing that originality and creativity can never have their source in the conscious mind. To bring something new into the world of spirit means nothing else than to *raise to consciousness* material upon which the conscious mind can set to work. No more than the factory can the conscious mind furnish its own raw materials.

"To grow" both as a man and as a poet means to expand the limits of one's conscious life by the process of integrating into it fresh material from the unconscious. It means, ultimately, to seek an identity with something other than one's ego-structure, to shift the center of one's conscious life from the ego to what Jung called the Self—a state of existence in which ego-consciousness comes to admit its own relativity. The world of nonego which I carry within is not alien to "me," so much as it is alien to "my" ego-structure; and spiritual growth lies in realizing that nonego is no less a part of "me" than is ego-consciousness. It is the ego-system which tells me that my dreams are insignificant—but it is also true that my dreams are often telling me that the ego-system is insignificant. The latter would like to think of the unconscious as a realm of "forgotten" material—a kind of musty basement—because such a conception implies that the unconscious is subordinate to ego in the same way that the basement is subordinate to the parlor. But the matter is not so easily disposed of. True, my psychical house does contain a basement filled with worn-out and obsolete personal belongings of every description; but to confuse that basement of mine with the earth out of which it is dug would be a grievous error indeed.

Conscious life itself represents in the beginning a "fragmentation" of unconscious elements. The child experiences from year to year a growing awareness; with growing success he learns to keep operative a continuity of consciousness or, to put it another way, *he learns to stay less and less unconscious.* Twenty years later, as an adult, he may well have convinced himself that the unconscious mind is nothing more than the sum of all that his conscious mind has forgotten—

while the merest reflection on the matter would tell him that his conscious life did not descend upon him from heaven, but represents the arduous climb out of an anonymous blackness.

Once ego has securely established for itself a place in the sun, once it has conquered the external world in its own little way, it may then view as obsolete a good many of those defenses with which it has depotentiated the disintegrative threats of nonego. The little child may not be at all convinced of the reality of his ego-structure; but the man who has successfully competed in the world at large generally has no need to be worried on that score, and may, with some confidence, address himself to the task of individuation, i.e., to the discovery of where his self lies, and what its lineaments are. He can, in short, discover what H. G. Baynes called the "mythology of the soul."

Such a mythology did Lorca seek, for he knew intuitively the secret of the myth as being the story of the god, or numen, that each of us bears within, beyond the threshold of conscious life and beyond the threshold of the personal unconscious.

The six chapters which follow reflect Lorca's threefold awareness that ego-consciousness and the unconscious may stand in different relationships to each other, which is to say that for Lorca the microcosm unfolds on three levels: (1) *the mythic,* (2) *the esthetic,* and (3) *the psychological.* Since the first four chapters are concerned with these levels as they are embodied in specific works by Lorca, the observations which follow may be useful to the reader.

The mythic level. Lorca's mythic apprehension of reality reveals itself in two ways, inwardly and outwardly. First of all, he grew up aware that the Spanish Gypsy lives in a strange world vulnerable to invasion by symbols, i.e., unconscious impulses raised to consciousness in the form of *experienced reality.* In this, Lorca is very much like Yeats, whose rural Ireland constitutes the world that he called the "Celtic Twilight"—the spiritual twilight merging a collective consciousness and the collective unconscious. If we call it a "mythic world," it is because myth, for the primitive, is surely the living experience of apprehending archetypal images; that is to say, the symbol is not a "thing," not an abstraction, but a personal event. Such was Lorca's own viewpoint with respect to the world of the Gypsies, and the poem we have chosen to exemplify this—*Preciosa and the Wind*—hardly leaves room for doubt.

5

Apart from this twilight microcosm in which consciousness and the unconscious are mingled, we must recognize Lorca's mythic apprehension of external reality as a world filled with mana. The biosphere which we inhabit is an energic unity; it is indeed the gigantic Dionysian web of life which has now achieved scientific recognition as an ecological manifold. And in this, Lorca belongs to the Children of the Sun, for to him the energic principle vitalizing the biosphere is nothing less than a solar myth, incarnated particularly in the youthful poem *Cicada!*

The esthetic level. It is a truism to say that Lorca's own poetic genius made him peculiarly susceptible to the dynamics of the mythic world, because by "poetic genius" we mean precisely that ability to deal creatively with the twilight world as a reality inwardly familiar to one. Lorca was quite aware that to be "inspired" means to experience a creative and self-fulfilling interplay between ego-consciousness and the unconscious. Frustration of the inspired state, on the other hand, means repression, the erection of a barrier between the two realms—which is the waking state in which most of us habitually live. This awareness of the phenomenon of inspiration is a familiar theme in Lorca, but its most impressive example occurs as the poem *Girl Drowned in the Well,* which concerns the shock suffered by the poet suffocating in what was to him the repressed world of New York City. At that point the only kind of poetry he could write was the "shock-poetry" of the dissociated state: repression, sickness, and death. To us, this may appear to be as "inspired" as anything else he wrote, but to him it meant a radical change in the relationship between his own ego-consciousness and the unconscious; and certainly there was no satisfying esthetic self-fulfillment. The poem is, however (for all its surrealistic agony), a remarkably clear statement by Lorca of the spiritual dynamics of esthetic creativity.

The psychological level. What we have said implies a concern on Lorca's part with the larger problem of spiritual growth, for he was not, finally, a poet, but rather a man who wrote poems. His need for the creative powers of the unconscious is, in the long run, a need for the instinctual realities of life out of which man's unconscious has evolved. Lorca's life is an attempt on the part of a civilized man to maintain in assimilable form a vital contact with the realm of Mother Earth built into us long before we learned the trick of imagining ourselves to be self-contained subjects separated from the natural world around us. This attitude of Lorca's is already apparent in his earliest work, *Book of Poems* (1921). It continues to remain always the "larger problem," and the "older" Lorca devotes to it an extensive and complex treatment, for it is the sole theme of his mature drama, *As Soon As Five Years Pass* (1931). Here it appears as civilized man's most pressing spiritual problem, and one which is, perhaps, not finally soluble within a context of civilization because civilization seems unalterably opposed to the symbolic apprehension of life. At any rate, it is this extraordinary and traditionally baffling work which we have chosen to present in the form of a résumé accompanied by a detailed commentary.

The "symbolic apprehension of life" just mentioned brings us to the last two chapters, which are concerned with the archetypal content of Lorca's poetic world.

The cosmos of any poet may be defined as a mythic structure reared on an archetypal foundation, a bedrock of one or two primary symbols adumbrating the shape of all that he will ever create. In Lorca's world these are the *ocean*, the womb of all life, and the *child*, the promise of man's continued renewal. The oceanic unconscious and the spiritual child ready to be delivered from its amniotic depths typify Lorca's symbolic grasp of the largest meaning for him that a man's life may have; and so a general description of Lorca's poetry must include a consideration of these two archetypes.

If the first four chapters may be said to deal analytically with the dynamics of Lorca's work, the last two constitute a brief but essential synthesis of its primary content.

PART I
EGO-CONSCIOUSNESS AND THE UNCONSCIOUS

CHAPTER ONE

The Mythic Perspective of the Microcosm

Preciosa and the Wind

Playing her moon of parchment
Preciosa comes along
an amphibious pathway
of crystals and laurels.
5   The starless silence,
fleeing the rhythmical sound,
falls where the ocean roars and sings
its fish-filled night.
On the mountain tops
10   the carabineers doze
guarding the white towers
where the English live.
And the water-Gypsies
construct, by way of amusement,
15   bowers made of conches
and green pine branches.

Playing her moon of parchment
Preciosa comes along.
The wind that never sleeps
20   has risen at sight of her.
Naked St. Christopher,
a giant of a man,
full of celestial tongues,
playing a sweet, absent flute,
25   looks at the girl.

"Girl, let me lift
your dress to see you.
Open in my ancient fingers
the blue rose of your belly."

30   Preciosa throws down the tambourine

11

and flees without hesitating.
The wind-giant pursues her
with a hot sword.

The ocean puckers its roar.
35   The olive trees grow pale.
The flutes of darkness play,
and the clear gong of the snow.

Preciosa, run, Preciosa,
the green wind is catching up with you!
40   Preciosa, run, Preciosa!
Look, there he comes!
A satyr of lower stars
with their shining tongues.

Preciosa, full of fear,
45   goes into the house
of the English consul
up beyond the pines.

Startled by the screams
three carabineers come,
50   their black capes around them,
and their caps about their ears.

The Englishman gives the Gypsy girl
a glass of warm milk
and a drink of gin
55   that Preciosa leaves untouched.

And while she sobs out
her adventure to those people,
the wind gnaws furiously
at the slate shingles.

Preciosa y el aire

Su luna de pergamino
Preciosa tocando viene
por un anfibio sendero
de cristales y laureles.
5   El silencio sin estrellas,
huyendo del sonsonete,
cae donde el mar bate y canta
su noche llena de peces.
En los picos de la sierra
10   los carabineros duermen
guardando las blancas torres
donde viven los ingleses.
Y los gitanos del agua
levantan por distraerse,
15   glorietas de caracolas
y ramas de pino verde.

Su luna de pergamino
Preciosa tocando viene.
Al verla se ha levantado
20   el viento que nunca duerme.
San Cristobalón desnudo,
lleno de lenguas celestes,
mira a la niña tocando
una dulce gaita ausente.

25   Niña, deja que levante
tu vestido para verte.
Abre en mis dedos antiguos
la rosa azul de tu vientre.

Preciosa tira el pandero
30   y corre sin detenerse.
El viento-hombrón la persigue
con una espada caliente.

Frunce su rumor el mar.

Los olivos palidecen.
35 Cantan las flautas de umbría
y el liso gong de la nieve.

¡Preciosa, corre, Preciosa,
que te coge el viento verde!
¡Preciosa, corre, Preciosa!
40 ¡Míralo por donde viene!
Sátiro de estrellas bajas
con sus lenguas relucientes.

Preciosa, llena de miedo,
entra en la casa que tiene,
45 más arriba de los pinos,
el cónsul de los ingleses.

Asustados por los gritos
tres carabineros vienen,
sus negras capas ceñidas
50 y los gorros en las sienes.

El inglés da a la gitana
un vaso de tibia leche,
y una copa de ginebra
que Preciosa no se bebe.

55 Y mientras cuenta, llorando,
su aventura a aquella gente,
en las tejas de pizarra
el viento, furioso, muerde.

Lorca's awareness of the unconscious as the source of mythological material has crystallized very dramatically in his narrative poem *Preciosa and the Wind* which dates from the midtwenties when the ethos of the Spanish Gypsies constituted for him a major source of inspiration.

Because the protagonist of the poem is a young Gypsy girl, we would do well to state at the outset that the whole question of gypsiology is, in Lorca, more relevantly dealt with from a psychological rather than an anthropological point of view. That is to say, Lorca is not a folklorist-poet, a kind of ethnic spokesman for the *gitanos*, and it would be inaccurate to think of him as a Romany rye. Rather, the *gitanos* (like other cultural elements of the Iberian Peninsula) were basically grist for his mill. This was his own view of the matter, as he points out in a letter to a friend:

> My reputation as a gypsy-poet is beginning to annoy me. . . . The *gitanos* are a theme. And that is all. I could just as easily be a sewing-needle-poet, or a hydraulic-landscape-poet. Besides, the *gitanismo* makes it sound as if I were untutored, primitive. . . .[1]

The important word here is *primitive* (*salvaje*). "The *gitanos* are [only] a theme," says Lorca, meaning that he does not consider himself to be a "Gypsy at heart"; they are primitive, but he is civilized. By virtue of their noncivilized world view they illustrate for him certain elemental properties of the human psyche. The *gitanos* are useful to Lorca because they are an example familiar to him of a cultural group lacking the highly differentiated, rigidly structured ego-consciousness of civilized man, and so more responsive to the realities of nonego.

What consciousness the primitive man does possess tends to coincide with the collective consciousness of his cultural group. The concept of *personal* property, for example, is much more subtle and complex among primitives, precisely because they cannot say purely and simply, "This belongs to *me*."[2] The primitive "me" is not easily separable from the life of the group in which it shares. The ego-consciousness of the individual member is constellated to an overwhelming degree by the collective world view in which he is reared; and the spiritual similarity of one generation to another is remarkable when contrasted with the differences between generations taken for granted in civilized societies. This means that, for the primitive, continuity of the individual ego-consciousness is heavily dependent upon continuity of contact with the collective ego, whereas separation from the group implies a weakening, or temporary loss of conscious stability; and continuity of consciousness is more like a task than a habit:

> This state has often been reported of primitives, who, if they are not actively occupied with something, drowse off and are easily tired by conscious effort. Only with the progressive systematization of consciousness is there an increase of conscious continuity. . . .[3]

These considerations are of elementary relevance to the poem *Preciosa and the Wind,* which is concerned with a breach of continuity in the ego-structure of the protagonist. We might say that her very name, *Preciosa,* is the label which identifies this ego-consciousness, whereas *Wind* is the form taken by the unconscious material which erupts, to be projected as a numen, an external and transpersonal procreative force in nature seeking fulfillment in the person of the Gypsy girl.

The poem tells us that Preciosa is walking by herself along the seashore one night, playing her tambourine. Suddenly a wind comes up—a wind which the narrator identifies as a naked St. Christopher, who heads lustfully for the girl, quite like the gods of old who were given to pursuing nymphs. He casts lewd remarks at her; she is panic-stricken, throws down her tambourine, and runs as fast as she can, till she reaches the house of the British consul. Alarmed by her screams, three uniformed "carabineers" come running. Preciosa gains admittance to the house, where the consul, in an effort to calm the girl, offers her gin and milk, which she leaves untouched. And while she hysterically sobs out her story, we hear the Wind howling angrily, tearing with his teeth at the shingles of the roof.

The entire episode comes about because the girl succumbs to the combined effect of her activity and the natural setting:

> Playing her moon of parchment
> Preciosa comes along
> an amphibious pathway
> of crystals and laurels.

Lorca, by calling the tambourine (*pandero, pandereta*) a "moon of parchment," bestows an increased significance upon an object which is already heavy with symbolic meaning. The tambourine (like the drum) plays an important role in shamanistic rituals the world over as the means whereby the hypnotic trance is induced.[4] When Lorca calls the tambourine a "moon," he gives full recognition to the lunar symbolism with which the Gypsies themselves have invested it, in obedience to the universal belief that a natural sympathy exists between women and the moon.

The moon, the sun, and the horse are the three symbols preeminently used to decorate the shamanistic drum and the tambourine, because they are all symbols of libidinal power, just as the drum and the tambourine are instruments thereof.[5] An instrument so decorated, and used to accompany (or induce) the emergence of unconscious forces in the form of ecstatic and (to us) lascivious dancing, is inseparably associated with the liberation of eros.

This meaning and usage of the tambourine may sometimes be explicitly recognized, as gypsiologist Clébert points out:

> In the Basque drum, or *pandero* of the Spanish Gypsies (the use of which is reserved for women) these have the portrait of their lover pierced with an arrow.[6]

It is relevant to mention here, in connection with the compound woman-moon-tambourine symbolism, that maternity is generally held to constitute the Gypsy woman's supreme value and that the moon plays an important role in her fertility spells.[7]

The poem tells us that Preciosa is coming along an "amphibious" path of crystals and laurels as she plays rhythmically upon the "moon." This places her upon a symbolic threshold separating consciousness and unconsciousness. The seashore—specifically the intertidal zone—is the threshold between ocean and land, between the great womb and the stable land realm whereon man finds his conscious orientation. I take "crystals" as a reference to the effect of the moon shining upon the rippling surface of the water, which is broken up into a coruscating interplay of light and dark.[8]

"Laurels" is quite evidently being used here as the symbolic counterpart of "crystals" (since these are the two elements of an "amphibious pathway"), and so by deduction means "land." This meaning of "laurels" is not, however, dependent upon textual deduction alone, since the laurel has important associations with the Sun God Apollo, Lord of man's consciousness which has emerged from the depths of the oceanic unconscious.

Our principal clue to the appearance of the laurel at the beginning of *Preciosa* must lie, of course, in the fact that the best known legend concerning this tree is that of Apollo and Daphne (Gk. *daphne,* "laurel tree"). Apollo fell in love with Daphne and pursued her; she fled, praying that Mother Earth might save her. Her prayer was answered, for by the time Apollo had overtaken the object of his lust, the chthonic metamorphosis had begun. Daphne was transformed into a laurel tree and was thenceforth held sacred to Apollo. Lorca himself alludes to the story in his poem *Manantial* (*Wellspring*): ". . . like Daphne . . . who flees affrighted / from an Apollo of shadow and nostalgia. . . ."[9] It is not difficult to see in *Preciosa and the Wind* an Andalusian version, as it were, of the Apollo-Daphne story.

Apollo, as the Sun God, is opposed to the chthonian Dionysus, since he is the god of ego-consciousness, of ego differentiation, which orients itself in the world by the light of day. In the poem *Your Childhood in Menton* (from *Poet in New York*) Lorca describes himself as an Apollo who has reached a psychological impasse because his ego-consciousness has lost contact with the creative unconscious; he is "stuck," as the analytical psychologists say, and he actually applies to himself the Spanish equivalent of this term: he is an *Apolo detenido,*[10] a "stuck," or "arrested" Apollo, an ego-consciousness trapped in the mechanics of its own stereotyped behavior.

But it is in the poem *To Carmela, the Peruvian,* where Lorca gives the greatest evidence of his intuitive understanding of Apollo as a psychological symbol. *To Carmela* is an erotic poem in which the speaker describes how his archaic surge of primitive, animal lust is rechanneled by his conscious ego-structure, which he identifies as Apollo:

> An Apollo made of bone obliterates the inhuman channel wherein my blood plaits rushes of springtime. . . .[11]

As for the *daphne,* or laurel, it possesses an ambivalent symbolic meaning, for merely by virtue of being a plant it lends itself as a fertility symbol,[12] and by virtue of its association with Apollo, it was used anciently to crown the victors in the Pythian games celebrating Apollo's defeat of the chthonian serpent (Python)—i.e., in remembrance of the Apollonian "obliteration" of the "inhuman channel": the "triumph" of ego-consciousness over unconscious instinct.

In Lorca, the most detailed representation of the laurel is to be found in his *Invocation to the Laurel*, a telluric poem in which the speaker enters the "ancient, dark forest" to learn secrets from the vegetative world. There he intuited, he says, the rhythm of the forest. Every form of vegetation spoke sweetly to his spirit—with the sole exception of the laurel, which he describes as formed from the body of Daphne, and carrying in its veins "the potent sap of Apollo."[13]

This identification of Apollo with the "blood" of the plant seems to contradict the notion of Apollo as symbolic of ego-consciousness, for if he represents "blood" (libido), does this not make him a kind of *de facto* Dionysus? It would seem so, until we recollect that the paradox stems from the fact that the very sun itself actually contains the two principles of libido and ego-consciousness: libido in the form of solar energy, or heat, and ego-consciousness in the form of solar illumination. As libido, the Sun God constitutes the vital principle, the driving force of all *materially* differentiated terrestrial forms; as ego-consciousness, he represents *spiritual* differentiation.

In the poem *Invocation to the Laurel*, the laurel is depicted as unique among all plants. The speaker apostrophizes a number of trees—the cedar, the rose, the cypress, the olive—and in each he sees symbolized some given aspect of his own psyche, whereas the laurel represents *wholeness*: Mother Earth energized by the Sun God; a materially differentiated form vitalized by the illuminating spirit. And, after all, the story of Apollo and Daphne tells us that the laurel stands for the abrogation or frustration of lustful instinct—which is precisely what ego-consciousness stands for, in the form of what is called "sublimation."

We have tried to show, then, how the laurel is intimately bound up with the phenomenon of life rooted in the land masses and so launched on the evolutionary journey culminating in the appearance of ego-consciousness—a rechanneling or "sublimation" of the vital impulse towards noninstinctual ends; a conversion of libidinal heat into libidinal light. In *Preciosa and the Wind* the "crystals" of the sea (the result of tidal motion illuminated by the moon) reveal only the presence of a vague and undifferentiated surge; whereas the laurels on the other side of the "amphibious" threshold represent the differentiated growth of land-rooted forms harking back to the abrogation of the purely lascivious impulse of the enamored Sun God.

The fact that the solitary Preciosa is treading a threshold and that she is playing a tambourine by the light of the moon suggests at the very outset of the poem that Lorca apprehends his subject matter as a psychological phenomenon, the key to which is the hypnotic effect of Preciosa's rhythmic activity:

> The starless silence,
> fleeing the rhythmical sound,
> falls where the ocean roars and sings
> its fish-filled night.

Prolonged rhythmic activity of any sort, whether it be dancing, chanting, fire making or drumming, has a hypnotic effect, for conscious attention flags, and the production of associative thought is encouraged until at length the level of consciousness is reduced to such a degree that its cohesive structure collapses.

The text insists on the duality of Preciosa's "amphibious" situation, for we are told that on the one hand the ocean is filled with fish, whereas

> On the mountain tops
> the carabineers doze
> guarding the white towers
> where the English live.

Perhaps it is worth pointing out here that the ocean, as symbolic of the unconscious, is apprehended as depth, not as extension.[14] In the opening lines of the poem attention is called to the *surface* of the sea, dappled by shiny "crystals" of moonlight—an image of lowered consciousness glimmering here and there with dim flashes of thought; but now we are made to descend into the night sea (a deep night full of fishes), whereas on the other hand the uniformed carabineers doze on the mountain tops.

These "carabineers" have been posted to guard "the white towers where the English live," and while it is not appropriate at this juncture to discuss the role played by the English, the "carabineers" deserve a few explanatory remarks.

Carabineros are primarily soldiers armed with carbines, of course. But their role in Spanish culture is rather more specialized, for they are used as "revenue agents" (akin to the "revenuers" of the American hillbilly and his illegal distillery). So much have they been used in Spain for the control of traffic in contraband that the word itself—*carabinero*—has, by metonymy, taken on a special meaning. Thus the Dictionary of the Spanish Royal Academy gives, as the second meaning of *carabinero*, "a soldier assigned to the control of smuggling."[15] This, in turn, means that the *carabinero* is what we would call a border guard, intent on preventing the illegal entry into Spain of articles outlawed or prohibitively taxed.

It is worthwhile emphasizing this connotation, since it attaches to the symbolic idea of the threshold with which the poem opens. Preciosa is engaged in a rhythmical activity which is characteristically related to hypnosis or ecstasy—and we are told that the "border guards" are sleeping on the job. Now it will actually happen that Preciosa, caught with her defenses down, will allow unconscious "contraband" to cross the threshold into consciousness. The sleep of the guards is symbolic of revery, or of what is called (after Pierre Janet) "*l'abaissement du niveau mental.*"[16]

Quiescence on the landside is accompanied by a good deal of animation on the waterside:

> And the water-Gypsies
> construct, by way of amusement,
> bowers made of conches
> and green pine branches.

These Gypsies who live in the water and who amuse themselves by the building of their own fantastic constructions are evidently water spirits in the form imagined by Gypsies; i.e., they are Gypsies who live in the water (just as the fairies, whom the Irish consider to be mound-dwellers, are conceived of as "Irish folk who live in mounds").[17] Water spirits, as a matter of fact, play an important role in Gypsy witchcraft, and they are called, in Romany, *nivashi*. A *nivasho* has, for example, the power to cure hysterical weeping by "taking away" (i.e., down into his watery realm) the impulse to weep which has broken into consciousness.[18]

Preciosa, as the member of an ethnic group, possesses an ego-system structured in the image of a collective consciousness; and by the same token her unconscious behavior finds expression in forms characteristic of her ethos. In this sense her behavior may be said to be controlled by the "Gypsies who live in the water."

The constructions with which these Gypsies amuse themselves deserve special commentary. Though we have rendered the word as "bowers," Lorca uses *glorietas*: the water-Gypsies are building *glorietas de caracolas*, "*glorietas* made from conches."

Glorieta is a diminutive derived from *gloria* and means, variously, "arbor," "summerhouse," "public square," and "traffic circle." The idea underlying all these meanings of *glorieta* ("little glory") is that of "radiant center"—i.e., the center of a circle at which the radii meet. The *glorieta* of a formal garden is the center at which all pathways converge. Similarly a traffic circle (e.g., the Place de l'Etoile, Paris), frequently containing a monument or fountain, is the point at which a number of streets meet.

Lorca, in his poem on Silverio Franconetti, a flamenco singer, uses *glorieta* as a psychological metaphor when he says that Silverio was a "gardener" who created "*glorietas* for silence,"[19] or when he says, in another context, that "frogs and crickets make the *glorieta* of the Andalusian summer."[20] In other words, we have to do with a form of the "magic circle" whose center functions as an organic nucleus. When a number of elements, whether physical or spiritual, constellate around a common center, that center is metaphorically a *glorieta*, the one point to which all paths lead. Thus Silverio is depicted as a creator of "*glorietas* for silence," because flamenco singing depends to an extraordinary degree upon the timing of pauses pregnant with dramatic meaning; so the great performer builds a "circle of silence" full with meaning because at its living center we hear a tragic voice crying in the wilderness created by that silence.[21] Similarly, when Lorca says that the frogs and crickets "make the *glorieta* of the Andalusian summer," he means that the singing of these creatures forms the "radiant center" of the summer night, turning it into a living darkness.

Consequently the constructive activity of the "water-Gypsies" indicates that the protagonist has fallen gradually into a state dominated by her unconscious; therefore her behavior will now be constellated by an unconscious tendency. She is at the mercy of "water-Gypsies" who amuse themselves by constructing thematic centers out of elements from both water (conches) and land (green pine branches).

These *nivashi* are hardly different from the mythical water sprites

known to us as nixes, and it is instructive to recall an analogue
from the Grimm brothers. The young man in the story entitled "The
Nixie of the Mill-Pond" faces the same danger as does Preciosa, for
his father

> . . . never let the boy himself go near the water. "Beware," he said
> to him, "if thou dost but touch the water, a hand will rise, seize
> thee, and draw thee down.[22]

The alien realm ruled over by the water spirits is always dangerous—
and not for young people alone; as one authority tells us, "There is
still a belief among the Greeks that the . . . Nereids . . . can render men insane."[23]

And so Preciosa is "drawn down"; the hypnotic state is induced,
unconscious patterns are taking shape, and suddenly

> The wind that never sleeps
> has risen at sight of her.
> Naked St. Christopher,
> a giant of a man,
> full of celestial tongues,
> playing a sweet, absent flute,
> looks at the girl.

The Saint's name appears here not as *Cristóbal* (Christopher),
but rather with the augmentative attached—*Cristobalón*—whose
meaning I have tried to suggest by the addition of the line "a giant of
a man."

Cristobalón is a popular concept of the Saint, frequently depicted
on the walls of Spanish churches as a gigantic figure perhaps ten or
more feet high. He is traditionally a hulking, primitive rustic, who
appears here as a lascivious male figure towering over the protagonist, and playing a flute.[24]

The flute played sweetly by *Cristobalón* is said (somewhat enigmatically) to be "absent"—an idea typically Lorca's for he alludes
with some frequency to the notion of psychological proximity to,
or distance from, ego-consciousness. In the poem *Wellspring*, for
example, he characterizes the "secret song" of the living waters of
Mother Earth as a sweet melody "yonder" or "beyond" (*más
allá de*) us; that is to say, the song of the Earth is characteristically
absent from our day-to-day consciousness.[25] In *Nocturne*, love sounds

from "very far away," and appears to us as the wind beating against our windowpanes[26]—a notion which is really not dissimilar to the activity of the wind in the closing lines of *Preciosa.*

But it is in the *Ode to Salvador Dalí* where the psychological value of *absence* appears with the greatest clarity. There Lorca makes the point that Dalí's surrealistic paintings, though depicting events occurring in the unconscious, are nevertheless executed with an extraordinarily precise draughtsmanship. Dalí's surrealistic structures are not typically vague, or shadowy; as one critic puts it, "everything is vividly real"; "every detail of every explicitly represented image is undeniably *there.*"[27] Dalí's hallmark is his "accurate photographic realism."[28] And yet the architecture of his paintings is reared upon the stage of the unconscious. It is solidly there, like an architectural presence—in a realm which Lorca can only describe as "the Absent": "You love [he says to Dalí] the architecture which builds in the Absent."[29]

The realm of the unconscious is "absent" to ego-consciousness, involved as is the latter with the world of empirical reality "present" in the form of a physical environment. And so Preciosa, on the threshold, "hypnotizes" herself through the medium of her tambourine and finds herself confronting a numinous being who plays a duet with her in the land of "the Absent."

From this point on, Preciosa believes herself to be pursued by a kind of gigantic satyr which rushes upon her like the wind, and is called by Lorca a *viento-hombrón*, a "huge man made of wind":

> "Girl, let me lift
> your dress to see you.
> Open in my ancient fingers
> the blue rose of your belly."
>
> Preciosa throws down the tambourine
> and flees without hesitating.
> The wind-giant pursues her
> with a hot sword.

It has been pointed out by Jung[30] that our most obvious example of the symbolic identity of "wind" with "fructifying spirit" is afforded by the Greek word *pneuma,* which means both these things, since the underlying notion is that of the "breath of life." In Greek, the beginning of Genesis tells us that the *pneuma* of God moved over the waters, by which we must understand that "the (fructifying) spirit of God moved over the waters in the form of a wind."

Among Occidentals the symbolic identity of *fire* and *passion* seems to be so obvious that it virtually excludes the notion that the other volatiles, air and water, could be used in the same way to represent the generative or libidinal impulse. And yet we know that the three volatile elements are interchangeable for this symbolic purpose. We have but to think of the comparison between the river and the stream of libido (one of Lorca's commoner symbols) to understand why people should believe (as Pliny reports) that "drinking the water of the Nile causes fecundity."[31] Drops of water are like drops of semen, which is why it has been thought that insects were commonly born from dew,[32] or why Psyche, as the "new Aphrodite," is held to have been conceived when the earth was impregnated by a drop of heaven's procreative dew.[33]

The generative powers of the *pneuma* appear in a particularly literal form in the ancient rustic belief in the power of the wind to impregnate livestock. Pliny tells us about it,[34] as does Aelian, who also adds helpfully, that in the matter of impregnating sheep, "whereas the north wind tends to produce males, the south wind produces females."[35]

Lorca's use of the wind as a symbol for libidinal stirrings may be exemplified by the passage in his play *Yerma* where, toward the beginning of Act Two, the fertile body of a wife is said to be covered by a nightgown which is like the sail of a ship impelled by a coastal wind,[36] hence the fertile woman may sing that her husband brings breezes to her.[37] Wind is life itself, and so elsewhere Lorca contrasts it to the worms of death: in a poem to the Host he says that the Wafer expresses in one material symbol *la brisa y el gusano*—"the breeze and the worm."[38] Similarly, in his lecture on what Andalusians call *duende*—the instinctual power that any art form must have if it is to live, charged with a primal energy—he says that this kind of "inspiration" operates upon the body of a dancer as wind upon sand.[39] In a poem about a dead girl, Lorca says that her body is now "denuded of breeze";[40] and when libido is cathected in the form of a wish, it is like a maiden who marries the wind.[41]

In *Preciosa* the Gypsy girl represents the individual overwhelmed by the imperious demands of Mother Earth, who will not tolerate virginity and who floods her consciousness with the drive toward

25

defloration. The reproductive urge appears as a wind god, who tells her to open the "blue rose"[42] of her productivity, i.e., her sexuality.

> The ocean puckers its roar.
> The olive trees grow pale.
> The flutes of darkness play,
> and the clear gong of the snow.

The girl finds herself precariously fleeing on the threshold, and threatening to fall into the unconscious: landward the olive trees "grow pale," i.e., withdraw, or recede, while the surf rolls in. According to the metaphor used by Lorca, the incoming tiers of white-caps are like the puckered gatherings of a flounced skirt, undoubtedly of the kind traditionally associated with Gypsy costume. The ocean roars its *rumor,* the great sound of libido.[43]

Preciosa is overcome with terror. She has thrown down her tambourine, and the darkness is filled with the sound of flutes, and something described as "the clear gong of the snow."

In Lorca, *snow* is generally used in symbolic opposition to vitality, i.e., as "frozen vitality," whether physical or spiritual. Thus a dead girl is said to have a "body of earth and snow,"[44] and at the end of the tragedy *Blood Wedding* two dead men are said to have teeth which are like handfuls of hardened snow.[45] Elsewhere, an epitaph by Lorca calls the deceased *nieve tendida,* "snow laid out."[46]

"Psychic snow" appears frequently in Lorca. In the play *As Soon As Five Years Pass,* the protagonist can hardly remember what his absent sweetheart looks like: her devitalized, "dead" image seems to have "tresses of snow";[47] the protagonist himself thinks of his own spiritual potential as an inner infant waiting to be born; for the present it is a "snow baby,"[48] awaiting the warm blood of libido. Elsewhere an unresponsive woman is called a "sphinx of snow."[49] In a period of spiritual sterility Lorca characterizes his life as a deserted precinct (*campo,* "field") which is gradually being covered by falling snow.[50]

Snow then, generally functions in Lorca as a symbol of immobility, or vitality immobilized, and so may its use in *Preciosa* be understood. Before we assign a specific value to the "clear gong of the snow," however, we should note that the Spanish word *gong* which Lorca uses means specifically the Chinese gong, and that such a gong, which gives forth a loud, sonorous clang, is used (like the

26

fanfare) to call dramatic attention to a particularly significant announcement or event, or to usher in a personage of the first rank.

In *Preciosa*, the fact that we hear the "gong of the snow" would indicate (1) devitalization of some kind, and (2) the imminent appearance, or final arrival of some significant phenomenon. Now since the protagonist is terrorized precisely by her libido in numinous form, the concomitant presence of any kind of devitalization would have to be sought in what we may call psychic paralysis. It is a phenomenon known to us all as an element of the anxiety dream which, after all, represents to us a situation in which ego-consciousness finds itself trapped and under attack, powerless to act: we are "frozen" with fear, and our will to escape from the hostile force cannot be transformed into action.

Now Preciosa finds her mind flooded by archaic contents: "ancient fingers" reach out, and the "hot sword" threatens to deflower her. She flees hysterically, on the point of being drowned in the murky waters of the unconscious. She is panic-stricken, i.e., the darkness is filled with the sound of the music of Pan—and suddenly the "gong of the snow" clangs forth: she is paralyzed, gripped by terror. The crucial moment has arrived: it is now or never! And so the narrator urges her on: "Preciosa, run, Preciosa . . . !"

This form of hysterical paralysis is described from a different point of view in Lorca's lecture on *duende*, to which we have already alluded. We noted above that this *duende*, or "inspired, instinctive impulse," operates upon the body of a great dancer like the generative wind upon sand; but Lorca goes on to say that "with magic power it transforms a girl into a *paralytic of the moon. . . .*"[51] Obviously, such a girl, as a dancer at her vital best, cannot appropriately be called "paralyzed" in any physical sense; but of course we may say of her that when she is "inspired," she is not in her right mind. Like the poets of Plato, she is maddened—has been turned into a "lunatic." Her ego-consciousness is immobilized, held in check; and like a dervish, she is "possessed" by unconscious forces.

> Preciosa, run, Preciosa,
> the green wind is catching up with you!
> Preciosa, run, Preciosa!
> Look, there he comes!
> A satyr of lower stars
> with their shining tongues.

The "green wind" is, of course, the wind apprehended chthonically as a force of the vegetative realm, as we have discussed in detail in another place;[52] but what we have translated here as "a satyr of lower stars" (literally, *sátiro de estrellas bajas*—"satyr of low stars") needs comment, especially with respect to Lorca's own idiosyncratic vocabulary, for he was peculiarly "noncivilized" in his feeling for the natural world as a telluric phenomenon. In order to distinguish between his own chthonian attitude and the uranic, or "celestial" point of view associated with Christianity, he sometimes spoke of the *low* and the *high*, i.e., the earth-centered and the heaven-centered, respectively.

The moon in the sky, for example, may be contrasted to the moon reflected in a river or lake; as such, one is "high," whereas the other is "low." Not infrequently one notes the suggestion of an invidious comparison:

> Upon the water
> a round moon
> bathes,
> making the other one
> (so high!) envious.[53]

In a *Nocturne* the speaker gazes meditatively up at the moon. As the object of his celestial contemplation, it is "high": *Alta va la luna*, "the moon is high in the sky," or perhaps, "the moon is riding high." By contrast, the wind, blowing chthonically (i.e., in the troposphere— "*our* air," as another poet, Jorge Guillén, puts it),[54] draws his contemplation earthward: *Bajo corre el viento*, "the wind is blowing low (close to earth)." As he continues to gaze earthward, he hears the distant voices of two girls, and such is the impression made by their innocent and disembodied speech, that his attention is again diverted to heaven:

> . . . effortlessly,
> from the moon in the water,
> I went off to the one in the sky.[55]

In Lorca's narrative poem *Tamar and Amnon*,[56] the brother, aroused by an incestuous longing for Tamar, associates with her the moon as a chthonic attraction, the "earth-moon" of which his lustful instincts, no longer sublimated, tell him:

> Amnon was looking at
> the round and low moon,

and he saw in the moon the breasts
exceedingly firm of his sister.[57]

In *March Orchard*, the speaker is overcome with the libidinal
euphoria of oncoming spring, which appears in the form of a flourish-
ing apple tree full of birds:

My apple tree
has shadow and birds now.

What a leap does my dream make
from the moon to the wind!

My apple tree
gives its arms to Green.

How different, the white brow of January,
when seen from March!

My apple tree . . .
(low wind).

My apple tree . . .
(high heaven).[58]

Our instincts are bound to the cyclic phenomena of the "low" realm,
and it is they that have the power to infuse our entire mortal being
with a sense of birth and renewal. The "high" region (so distant from
instinct!) is the region that "spiritual" man likes to inhabit, for it is
far more appropriate to his unique dignity—until his instinctual
impulses, activated by the living transformations of the realm whence
they come, pull him back to earth despite himself.

The same thought underlies *Refrán (Proverb)*:

March
passes, flying.

And January stays on, so high.

January,
it stays on in the night sky.

And, down below, March is a moment.

January.
For my old eyes.

March.
For my new hands.[59]

Here it is evident that man's cyclic, instinctual side is tied to time and change ("March is [but] a moment"), and that it expresses itself through a sense of fleshly renewal ("my new hands"). Man's "spirit" dwells in the "upper" realm, removed from the possibility of rejuvenation. It is an intelligent ego-consciousness characterized by its visual assessment of the world around it ("my old eyes"). For intellect, the lower region is a thing apart, an object of study; for instinct, the lower realm is the very matrix of its own existence. Hoary intellect, like January, lives on forever, high in heaven, far above the earth, while instinct, like March, succors with cyclic renewal the mortal body of its own making.

One last example: in the poem *De otro modo* (*Otherwise*), the speaker is alone in the countryside. It is approaching sunset; the afternoon seems to be closing in, and the speaker senses that the natural surroundings are causing his ego-consciousness, his habitual experience of himself as a separate, human individual, to slip away from him. A powerful sensation thrusts itself upon him that he is but one more element of the ecological manifold. He says, "Llegan mis cosas esenciales," "the essential part of me comes on the scene," and he is flooded by a feeling of strangeness when he tries to think of himself as a differentiated ego-consciousness labeled "Federico":

> Among the rushes and the low afternoon [*baja tarde*],
> how strange that my name should be Federico![60]

The reader will recall that in our preliminary remarks concerning *Preciosa and the Wind* we noted that the girl's name might be considered a label, identifying her as the individual aspect of the psyche which the transpersonal aspect—"Wind"—threatens to possess. Now in the lines just quoted, we can see that an analogous psychological split has occurred. The individual, Federico, begins to disintegrate, submerged in and enveloped by the atmosphere of the "low afternoon," in a way not basically different from the threatened disintegration of Preciosa in the presence of a satyr of "low stars" (all this, while the "border guards" doze on the mountain tops "up there," high above sea level), the "low" terrain at which ego-consciousness is accessible to the reaches of the insistent, oncoming surf.

"Low stars," then, refers to a burning energy that shines forth out of the chthonic darkness, just as "high stars" would mean the

lights that twinkle in the vastness of the celestial vault. More specifically I would take it to mean the stars *as reflected in the ocean* (just
as in the lunar poem quoted above, the "high moon" has its enviable
counterpart in the round moon bathing upon the water). Out of the
oceanic unconscious comes a lewd image of instinct, the satyr of the
lower stars, the ones reflected in the sea.

Preciosa bolts hysterically up the hill toward the "high" region
where the British consul lives. Her screams arouse the guards. The
consul takes her into his house and tries to calm her. He offers her
gin and milk, which she does not taste.

> And while she sobs out
> her adventure to those people,
> the wind gnaws furiously
> at the slate shingles.

Preciosa, then, finds renewed security, not in the midst of her own
people, but in the house of an Englishman—which fact suggests that
Lorca is exploiting the stereotyped image of the English common to
Mediterranean people. For these, the English character is rigidly
self-possessed and lacking in spontaneity—an image which applies
especially to the representatives of British officialdom. Preciosa, a
"hot-blooded," "impulsive" Gypsy, falters on the threshold of the
ocean "down there," but finds safety with the British consul, en-
sconced in his house "up there," which the furious Wind God cannot enter, because the Englishman has effectively sealed himself off
from serious encounters with unconscious contents.[61]

It still remains to be discussed precisely why the numen appears to
Preciosa in the form of St. Christopher, the saint who is best remembered, of course, for the episode in which he carried the way-
faring Christ Child across a bridgeless river—hence the name Christopher," or "Christ-bearer" (Gk. *Christos* + *pherein,* "to bear").

Now if we consider that this "wind-giant" is a numinous projection
proceeding out of the unconscious of Preciosa, the reason for its
appearance as a giant *Christophoros* begins to grow clear; for that
numen, being at the center of her own inner tendencies (in the manner of a *glorieta*), constellates in the form of a venerated figure who
carries Christ. Though the numen appears in the form of a man, it is
not to be forgotten that it is, at bottom, a projection of Preciosa's
imagination, a Gestalt of her own psyche.

"Christ-bearer" is an epithet which applies not only to Christopher, in the form of a name recalling a legendary incident, but (quite obviously) to the Virgin Mary also, who was impregnated by the spirit or *pneuma* of God. It seems, therefore, proper to assume that Preciosa herself is a virgin whose own unconscious reveals itself to her in the form of a Christ-bearer. Preciosa herself, as an unschooled young Gypsy girl, need have no knowledge of the etymology of Christopher's name; it is enough that pictures characteristically represent him acting out the meaning of his name—a hagiographic charade, as it were.

The idea of parthenogenesis has a very primitive and very real mythical basis which Erich Neumann has linked with the *prepatriarchal* (i.e., matriarchal) experience of birth:

> Woman's primary experience of birth is matriarchal. It is not the man who is father to the child: the miracle of procreation springs from God. Thus the matriarchal phase is ruled, not by a personal father, but by a suprapersonal progenitor or power. The creative energy of woman comes alive in the miracle of birth, by virtue of which she becomes the "Great Mother" and "Earth Goddess."
> . . . it is precisely at this deepest and most archaic level that the virgin mother and bride of God is a living reality.[62]

Parthenogenesis, as a primitive hypothesis, is not nearly so "superstitious" as it might seem. Even though the primitive knows that sexual union can result in conception, he also knows that sexual union of itself is not *necessarily* fertile; and if it is not necessarily fertile, then the miracle of impregnation must be due to some cause not supplied by the simple fact of copulation. Since fertility is a primary value of all primitive peoples (who, needless to say, are never troubled by the problem of overpopulation), it is easy to understand that fertile unions would be ascribed to the benevolence of a higher power whose favor had been successfully courted: that is the crucial factor.

Such being the case, then, the higher power can impregnate a woman without the intervention of a human husband or lover. Until civilized science provides the knowledge that conception is related to the ovulation cycle, there is no reason to doubt the possibility of virgin birth. In this sense, the Virgin Birth traditionally recognized by Christians represents not an exceptional circumstance, but rather the "natural" possibility inherent in every mythology, because it is inherent in the fabric of prepatriarchal thinking.

Preciosa, being a Spanish Gypsy, is "Christian" and "primitive" at the same time. In the solitude of a moonlit night, rhythmically playing her tambourine as she walks along the seashore, she has placed her precarious ego-system in dangerous circumstances. Night, moon, ocean, tide, solitude, rhythm—all these converge to minimize her level of conscious control, to activate unconscious strivings, and to produce a terrifying symbol of what it is that the Earth Mother requires of her. This occurs with all the numinosity of a Pentecostal visitation, for the god speaks with fiery tongues (ll. 23, 43), though the *pneuma* does not *descend* upon her, but rather *rises* up (l. 20) to her from below.

Preciosa's unconscious reveals to her a telluric Christ-bearer, an "inspiring" *pneuma* that would fill her with new life. It is projected as a lascivious attack upon her person, but it cannot be dissociated from the idea of Christ. Why this is so is related to Lorca's strange concept of the *chthonic Christ figure* (if the reader can envision such an entity), described in the analysis of the poem *Cicada!* which follows. It can, however, be suggested here that the fructifying *inspiration* resulting in the conception and bringing-forth of a (Christ) child is connected symbologically to the power of the child-archetype evident throughout Lorca's work. In a sense, Preciosa, as the individual pursued by a numinous, fertilizing wind force, is a kind of self-image of Lorca; but a more detailed consideration of the matter must be deferred to our discussion of the child-archetype as this appears generally in his poetry.

CHAPTER TWO

The Mythic Perspective of the Macrocosm

Cicada!

Cicada!
Your lot is blest!
For upon the earthen bed
you die, drunk with light.

5   You know the secret of life
of the fertile fields,
and the story told by the ancient fairy
(who could hear the grass growing)
was vouchsafed to you.

10   Cicada!
Your lot is blest!
For you die beneath the blood
of a deep blue heart.
The light is God who descends,
15   and the sun
is a breach through which He flows.

Cicada!
Your lot is blest!
For in your agony of death
20   you feel the whole weight of the blue.

Every living thing that passes
through the gates of death
goes with head bowed
and the blank mien of the sleepwalker
25   talking to himself.
Silently . . .
Sadly,
covered with the silence
which is the mantle of death.

30   But you, enchanted cicada,

spilling forth sound, you die
and are transfigured
into heavenly sound and light.

Cicada!
35 Your lot is blest!
For you are enfolded in the very mantle
of the Holy Ghost,
which is light.

Cicada!
40 Sonorous star
above the sleeping fields,
old friend of the frogs
and of the crickets (dwellers in darkness),
yours are the sepulchres of gold
45 in the throbbing beams
of the sun that strikes you sweetly
in the full beat of summer,
and the sun carries your soul away
to transform it into light.

50 Let my heart be a cicada
upon the divine fields.
Let it die, singing slowly,
wounded by the blue sky;
and when it is about to expire
55 let a woman whom I divine
scatter it about the dust
with her hands.

And my blood upon the field:
let it be a soft, red clay
60 rent by the hoes
of the weary peasants.

Cicada!
Your lot is blest!
For you are struck by the invisible swords
65 of the blue.

¡Cigarra!

¡Cigarra!
¡Dichosa tú!,
que sobre el lecho de tierra
mueres borracha de luz.

5   Tú sabes de las campiñas
el secreto de la vida,
y el cuento del hada vieja
que nacer hierba sentía
en ti quedóse guardado.

10   ¡Cigarra!
¡Dichosa tú!
pues mueres bajo la sangre
de un corazón todo azul.
La luz es Dios que desciende,
15   y el sol
brecha por donde se filtra.

¡Cigarra!
¡Dichosa tú!,
pues sientes en la agonía
20   todo el peso del azul.

Todo lo vivo que pasa
por las puertas de la muerte
va con la cabeza baja
y un aire blanco durmiente.
25   Con habla de pensamiento.
Sin sonidos . . .
Tristemente,
cubierto con el silencio
que es el manto de la muerte.

30   Mas tú, cigarra encantada,
derramando son, te mueres

y quedas transfigurada
en sonido y luz celeste.

    ¡Cigarra!
35 ¡Dichosa tú!,
pues te envuelve con su manto
el propio Espíritu Santo,
que es la luz.

    ¡Cigarra!
40 Estrella sonora
sobre los campos dormidos,
vieja amiga de las ranas
y de los oscuros grillos,
tienes sepulcros de oro
45 en los rayos tremolinos
del sol que dulce te hiere
en la fuerza del Estío,
y el sol se lleva tu alma
para hacerla luz.

50   Sea mi corazón cigarra
sobre los campos divinos.
Que muera cantando lento
por el cielo azul herido
y cuando esté ya expirando
55 una mujer que adivino
lo derrame con sus manos
por el polvo.

    Y mi sangre sobre el campo
sea rosado y dulce limo
60 donde claven sus azadas
los cansados campesinos.

    ¡Cigarra!
¡Dichosa tú!,
pues te hieren las espadas invisibles
65 del azul.

The transformation of the virgin into mother means the creation of at least two new beings: a child, and—a mother. Because for her it means the unfolding of a new and unsuspected self that could not have been born except by submitting her reserved virginity to the libidinal forces which keep this planet alive. It is a self-renewal, biologically induced.

In an analogous way the man's capacity for self-renewal (while it cannot be the gift of biology) depends upon his ability to conceive and bring forth a new man out of union with those very forces that first brought humanity into being upon the face of the earth. Onto-genetically he must recapitulate in his spirit the history of the species. Spiritual fulfillment cannot be the result of denying unconscious strivings, but comes, rather, from recognizing their presence, and from attempting to assimilate them into conscious life.

Lorca's recognition of the creative powers of the unconscious (at a time when there was much talk of the destructive Freudian subconscious) reaches its conclusion in the belief that man's salvation must be realized tellurically. Salvation means a new and transfigured self, a transformation wrought by symbolic union with the primal energy of Dionysus. *This* is the force that is man's Saviour—the Saviour of the quick, not of the dead.

It is the primal quality of this energy that brings about Lorca's symbolization of it in the form of an insect creature—an unseen one, at that—in an early poem entitled *Cicada!*

It is its "invisibility," indeed, that makes the cicada an apposite libido-symbol, for it is not a creature that one typically *sees*. Rather, we become aware of it as a hidden presence because we hear its pervasive singing. It produces a steady, shrill, "electric" sound, and its magnitude on a hot summer afternoon charges the whole atmosphere with a frantic intensity. It is as though the entire being of the small creature were concentrated upon the one activity, as if all its vitality were being expended upon one gigantic effort which must leave it drained and lifeless. The summer sun pours down in hot waves, and the cicada reaches its greatest pitch of intensity, stimulated to a point of electrifying frenzy.

Under these circumstances, it is hardly possible not to gain a powerful impression of the sun as an *energic source*. The vital impulse with which the biosphere is endowed is ultimately solar energy, which living forms capture in quanta and transmute finally into libidinal energy. Plant forms bridge the gap between solar energy and libidinal energy, but they are still condemned to a life of inertia. When the energy crosses the threshold into the kingdom of mobile creatures with organized bodies, it becomes a concentrated reservoir of *potential* impetus: it becomes dynamic.

The extraordinary power of this nervous energy can be appreciated by anyone who will go to the cicada, for its frantic buzzing produces a very convincing impression of raw libido in a powerful, concentrated form. Unlike human beings, the hapless cicada cannot release this charge little by little, cannot channel it off in given quanta—or so it would seem. The solar energy seems to be pouring directly into him, seems to be overwhelming his minute structure, which absorbs lethal amounts that are converted instantly into raw power. The cicada, seemingly not built to take a power load of this kind, sizzles to death like a drop of fat in a holocaust.

Man's ego-consciousness normally serves as a kind of psychic circuit breaker, but it can be torn to pieces, even deliberately, as we know. The drunkard does it; and, having accomplished this, is overwhelmed by unconscious charges which erupt destructively—and herein lies the analogy with Lorca's cicada as described in the opening stanza of the poem:

Cicada!
Your lot is blest!
For upon the earthen bed
you die, drunk with light.

This light is the source of the destruction, and in ll. 14-16 Lorca explicitly identifies it with God:

The light is God who descends,
and the sun
is a breach through which He flows.

Now the identification of God with the sun is, of course, universal to man, and so this passage, by itself, tells nothing in particular as to what kind of god is meant. God as Light can be taken as a logos-symbol (light = understanding, orientation in the world), but this light of which Lorca speaks clearly functions as a source of energy, and so is closer to the god of phallic worship: the sun as the source of all instinctual energy. It is the Sun God seen under the aspect of heat.

In the seventh stanza Lorca says that the cicada is "blest" because it is enveloped by the cloak of the Holy Ghost—which is the light of the sun. The Biblical reference is clear enough here, since John writes that the Holy Ghost descended upon Christ from Heaven "and abode upon him" (1:32), but we have, obviously, to do with an idiosyncratic variant of the Christian idea. John himself heralds the coming of the sun (1:8-9) which is Christ—Christ who died upon the earth enfolded in the mantle of the Holy Ghost. Lorca has postulated a strange analogy between Christ and the cicada, and the more we examine this poem, the more we are driven to interpret the cicada as a *chthonic Christ figure*, absurd as the notion may seem at first glance.

This symbolic bond is established in a general way by the fact that the cicada is represented as being unique among all living forms, for its lot is "blest" in a special way: it is the very embodiment of the energy flowing from the Sun God. Here the analogy with Christ is not very difficult, since Christ Himself was unique in His possession of a dual nature as the son of man and the Son of God.

The cicada in its agony feels "the whole weight of the blue" (l. 20) upon it, for its agony is a fulfillment on earth of its creation by the Sun God. And ultimately, the cicada is "blest" because its death is followed by a transfiguration:

> But you, enchanted cicada,
> spilling forth sound, you die
> and are transfigured
> into heavenly sound and light. (ll. 30-33)

Similarly, Matthew describes the Transfiguration as a foretoken of the Resurrection: Christ led three disciples "up into an high mountain apart, and was transfigured before them: and his face did shine as the sun, and his raiment was white as the light" (17:1-2).

The symbolic bond uniting the Christ figure with the cicada, then, is clearly established in the poem, and it is not so outlandish as it might seem if we bear in mind the fact that we are dealing with a symbol within a chthonic context. That is to say, the cicada, as such, is clearly not assimilable to the Christ figure, *but libido is*.

The cicada, as a living species, has its own life cycle. Prior to summer (says Lorca) it was the friend of the frogs and crickets (ll. 42-43), for it dwells long within the earth before its dramatic entry into the fire of summer. But with the coming of summer, the passion approaches wherein will be fulfilled the significance of its life. For a while it lives among the offspring of Mother Earth, but a glorious transformation awaits it. All other living creatures die sadly, for they are mortal:

> Every living thing that passes
> through the gates of death
> goes with head bowed. . . . (ll. 21-23)

We will all of us one day be "covered with the silence which is the mantle of death" (ll. 28-29), but awaiting the cicada are "sepulchres of gold" (l. 44), the shining rays of the Sun God. It will die in the fullness of libidinal discharge—*because* of it—and will be transfigured into the naked form of that which made it to live, just as Christ was sent by the Father to die, and was then transfigured so that "his face did shine as the sun, and his raiment was white as the light," and so was gathered back into the bosom of God.

After the Transfiguration, man's salvation was accomplished; forever afterwards the Holy Trinity will pour down upon a mankind saved from death. It is here that the connection between libido and the Christ figure becomes apparent; for when the evolutionary "explosion" has reached the point where the solar chemistry of the plant world crosses the first great threshold, instinct is born into the earth, and libido becomes possible. Light, solar energy: this can ultimately be traced back to a Creator. But the Creator reaches all men in the form of libido (as He reaches Christians in the form of Christ). Christ saves Christians from death, but libido, the chthonic Christ, "saves" all men for life. Though I am mortal, it dwells within me for a while, and it is the part of me wherein I will find my highest fulfillment as long as I inhabit this illusory form.

The last three stanzas of the poem involve an explicit analogy which the poet draws between himself and the cicada. Lorca has already established for us the anthropomorphic macrocosm: the vault of heaven is a great living heart, and it is filled with the blood of the sun—libido in the form of solar energy (ll. 12-13). The pulsating rhythm of this heart determines the metabolism of Nature; hence it is transmitted into the diminutive body of the cicada, which in its death agony, feels "the whole weight of the blue" (ll. 19-20).

Now, in line 50, the poet speaks of the microcosmic heart: "Let my heart be a cicada upon the divine fields." All that we have said about the symbolic meaning of the cicada singing with the "deep blue heart" of the firmament applies with equal force to the living— the chthonic—center of the heart of the speaker: a *microcosmic firmament* vitalized by the same solar energy which inflames the cicada. The speaker too must be transfigured, reborn out of the return to the source of natural energy, reborn out of a "death" in the chthonic unconscious, the Earth Mother whom he intuits as the feminine principle ("a woman whom I divine," l. 55). Self-fulfillment must be realized in terms of a tellurically oriented consciousness, and must find its ultimate meaning in terms of the feminine element, the very matrix of fertility. Hence he envisions his lifeblood as belonging to the world of the peasant:

> And my blood upon the field:
> let it be a soft, red clay
> rent by the hoes
> of the weary peasants. (ll. 58-61)

This, because the peasants are a primal example of human beings whose whole life is a commitment of libido to the Earth Mother: devoted to her entirely, they grow weary in her service, making her to yield by the strength of their labor.

Such, then, is the anthropomorphic significance which Lorca attached to the cicada—and consciously so, it would seem; for in his lecture on that form of flamenco singing known as *cante jondo* ("deep song"), delivered in 1922—i.e., about the time of the poem *Cicada!*—he characterizes the best of the flamenco singers as remarkable human beings who burned themselves out in a total commitment to libidinal fulfillment. Each of them, in seeking the creative sources of his art, sacrificed his Apollonian individuality in the process:

> They were immense interpreters of the popular heart, who destroyed their own heart, among the storms of feeling. Almost all of them died a death of the heart; that is to say, *they exploded like enormous cicadas,* after having filled our atmosphere with ideal rhythms.[1]

These human beings are remarkable because they lived out in their own lives a commitment to the world of eros in a measure far exceeding the capacity of you and me to submit. The singers recalled by Lorca are his heroes and heroines, for in them he saw a material reflection of the world view which shaped his own existence.

This vision of human fulfillment is surely as old as man, and it may very well be the nonego way of sensing fulfillment; the way belonging to that repressed part of us which would speak if only it could be liberated from its enthrallment to ego-consciousness. An enlightening analogue to *Cicada!* appears, for example, in a little known but valuable book, published in 1857, by Fitz Hugh Ludlow, an American author. Entitled *The Hasheesh Eater,* it is a record of Ludlow's visionary experiences in the world of nonego; and out of them he comes to realize that the symbol embodies what he calls the "unpreconceived spiritual verities,"[2] i.e., truths appearing as such prior to all intellectual conceptualization. An example which he "cannot refrain" from giving is as follows:

> Hanging in a sky of spotless azure, within the walls of my own heart, appeared my soul as a coin flaming with glories, which radiated from the impress of God's face stamped upon it. This told me an unutterable truth of my being.[3]

Here we see a symbolic compression of the central notion which, in *Cicada!,* is worked out in greater detail. Ludlow intuits his own heart as a microcosmic firmament, a "sky of spotless azure," what Lorca himself calls *"un corazón todo azul,"* literally, "a heart all blue." In Ludlow's vision the energizing force, the "soul," appears as the sun in the form of a golden coin—not as a ball of flaming gases, but as a disk made of shining gold, gold which, after all, must be mined from the bowels of the Earth Mother. It is a "chthonic Sun," corresponding to the "chthonic Christ" of Lorca's poem, for Ludlow goes on to say: "Again the soul appeared as a vast store of the same coin shed prodigally upon the earth."[4] And after this, the hasheesh eater sees fiendish claws reach out of clefts in a rocky wall and draw the coins back into the depths of the earth, "while I," he recounts, "stood helpless, shrieking in the desert loneliness."[5]

This is substantially the same symbolic vision of the chthonic condition of man which pervades the work of Lorca: for sun and earth are not allegorical images of spirit and body as entities with separate destinies, but rather two aspects of an indivisible unity. The Sun God penetrates the Earth to generate life in her womb, and he is accessible only to the man who will descend into the telluric substratum to dig it out in the form of gold.

Only briefly does Ludlow glimpse his gold as a coin hanging in the firmament of his heart—and then it falls back into the recesses of the earth, and he is left shrieking in loneliness and grief. In the essay that follows, we will see this same calamity as it befell Lorca, not in the form of a frightful vision, but as an event in his own life, when he attempted to live, like a *déraciné*, in New York City. It left him "shrieking in the desert loneliness" of the megalopolis, for it is then that his spiritual gold appears to him in the awful guise of a girl drowned in a well—specifically a symbol for the loss of the poetry-making capacity, his primary faculty for mining the gold within.

CHAPTER THREE

The Esthetic Perspective

Girl Drowned in the Well
(*Granada and Newburg*)

Statues suffer through their eyes with the darkness of coffins,
but they suffer much more because of the water which has no outlet.
Which has no outlet.

The townspeople were running along the battlements breaking the fishermen's poles.

5   Quick! The ramparts! Hurry! And the tender stars were croaking like frogs.

. . . which has no outlet.

Tranquil in my memory, star, circle, goal,
you weep at the edge of a horse's eye.
. . . which has no outlet.

10   But no one in the darkness will be able to establish distances for you,
without sharply-cut limits, the future of the diamond.
. . . which has no outlet.

While people seek silences of the pillow
you throb forever defined within your ring.
15   . . . which has no outlet.

Eternal in the final fling of waves which accept
the struggle of roots and solitude foreseen.
. . . which has no outlet.

Here they come along the ramparts! Rise up from the water!
20   Each point of light will be as a chain to you!
. . . which has no outlet.

But the well holds out to you little hands of moss,
unsuspected undine of its chaste ignorance.
. . . which has no outlet.

25   No, which has no outlet. Water fixed at one point,
breathing with all its violins without strings
on the scale of wounds and uninhabited buildings.

Water which has no outlet!

Niña ahogada en el pozo
(*Granada y Newburg*)

Las estatuas sufren por los ojos con la oscuridad de los
ataúdes,
pero sufren mucho más por el agua que no desemboca.
Que no desemboca.

El pueblo corría por las almenas rompiendo las cañas de los
pescadores.
5   ¡Pronto! ¡Los bordes! ¡De prisa! Y croaban las estrellas
tiernas.
. . . que no desemboca.

Tranquila en mi recuerdo, astro, círculo, meta,
lloras por las orillas de un ojo de caballo.
. . . que no desemboca.

10   Pero nadie en lo oscuro podrá darte distancias,
sin afilado límite, porvenir de diamante.
. . . que no desemboca.

Mientras la gente busca silencios de almohada
tú lates para siempre definida en tu anillo.
15   . . . que no desemboca.

Eterna en los finales de unas ondas que aceptan
combate de raíces y soledad prevista.
. . . que no desemboca.

¡Ya vienen por las rampas! ¡Levántate del agua!
20   ¡Cada punto de luz te dará una cadena!
. . . que no desemboca.

Pero el pozo te alarga manecitas de musgo,
insospechada ondina de su casta ignorancia.
. . . que no desemboca.

25   No, que no desemboca. Agua fija en un punto,
respirando con todos sus violines sin cuerdas
en la escala de las heridas y los edificios deshabitados.

¡Agua que no desemboca!

Girl Drowned in the Well is a notable example of Lorca's preoccupation with the creative process itself as a subject matter of poetry. It belongs to the series of poems written during the sojourn in New York in 1929-30, at a time when he suffered a severe disorientation that represented to him the worst kind of spiritual damage possible: the apparent amputation of his creative powers in what he must have come to think of as their "normal" form. They were replaced by a chaotic eruption of unconscious material indicative of inner destruction. Indeed, the flow of imagery throughout *Poet in New York* is marked by a similarity to "automatic writing,"[1] accompanied by a sense of doom, or apocalypse, and the lurking fear that the habitual psychic organization has been permanently destroyed.

There is little doubt that the "girl" who has been drowned is an element of the speaker's own psyche. Everything points to her as a symbol for the creativity which proceeds out of contact with the feminine unconscious, and which frequently appears in the form of a helpful girl or woman. We are speaking here, of course, of what is known in analytical psychology as the *anima,* the feminine half of the man's psyche, that half which the male child is taught to repress in the process of developing a monosexual personality.

The creative person seems to be productive to the extent that he has resolved the problems raised by his monosexuality, since monosexuality represents a limitation within the bounds of behavior prescribed by one's culture. The "he-man" is one who has learned to repress elements of his feminine unconscious, and so lives out a "successfully" limited conscious life. For Lorca, loss of the creative flow appears in the present poem as the drowning (repressing) of a girl-image in the depths of his psyche—an enclosed circle extending, like a well, deep into the soil of the Earth Mother.

The use of the *well* as representative of the unconscious is certainly not farfetched, and Lorca's poem finds an explicit analogy in the Greek cycle, *The Twelve Lays of the Gipsy* (1907), by the Peloponnesian poet, Kostís Palamás:

> I bent down to my soul as at the edge of a well
> And cried out to it with the mind's cry;
> And from the deep, as from a voyage, a stranger,
> Ascending towards me my voice returned.[2]

The "psychic well" of Lorca's poem is a negative symbol, for the speaker suffers from a claustrophobic sensation of constriction. As we shall see, Lorca entertained negative ideas about wells in general; as a source of water, they are only a substitute for the never-ending supply of living water furnished by brooks and rivers. When the stream of libido becomes dammed up, when it no longer has an outlet, it is transformed into the standing water of a dark well. Hence the loss of outlet becomes the dominant theme of the poem, which begins:

> Statues suffer through their eyes with the darkness of coffins,
> but they suffer much more because of the water which has no outlet.
> Which has no outlet.

The well is to the river as statues are to people, since, when the libidinal stream stagnates, the system is immobilized. Sightless eyes are an affliction, but stagnant water is a far greater one.

And now the speaker appears to recall a dramatic vision:

> The townspeople were running along the battlements breaking the fishermen's poles.
> Quick! The ramparts! Hurry! And the tender stars were croaking like frogs.
> . . . which has no outlet.

We are evidently dealing with a mob scene of some sort, accompanied by a great hubbub, and one hears excited shouts ("Quick! The ramparts! Hurry!"), as if the emergency required some kind of defensive action.

The original Spanish says that the townspeople were running along the *almenas* ("merlons"), shouting *"¡Pronto! ¡Los bordes!"* What we have translated as "ramparts" (*bordes*), then, is literally "edges," which, because it is plural and in context with *almenas*, I have taken as referring to the outer rim, or wall, of a castle. The fact that the cries indicate a state of emergency suggests that the castle is under attack, since in a castle this is the emergency par excellence.

Lorca's use of the *almenas* proper to the defense of a feudal castle establishes a symbolic link between the castle and the general idea of the edifice as representative of the psyche. In his poem *Paper Bird*, for example, Lorca observes children playing with a toy bird fashioned out of a sheet of folded paper. They construct for it a "castle" of playing cards which, for Lorca, becomes a symbol for the fantasy world inhabited by the children. The "fragile castle" is doomed to collapse, but hopefully the children's joy will not be vitiated by any such foreknowledge; or, as Lorca puts it, addressing the paper bird, ". . . let not the children discover that . . . there is shadow in your castle."[3] The inner world of the child—his "castle"—is not, as he thinks, filled with "real" light and "real" festivities. If it were so, then it would not have to happen, as it always does, that one day we turn to look upon it and find that all the guests have departed: our playing-card castle, the dwelling place of our ingenuous young spirit, stands abandoned and full of shadows.

In similar fashion the image of the "psychic castle" appears in another early poem, the *Interior* [i.e., subjective] *Ballad*, as the symbol for the circumstances in which the speaker is currently living. The aimless love feelings which he is attempting to situate and to render operative in his life are like an uninhabited castle: "My aimless love, an unstable castle moldy with shadows. . . ."[4]

Given these explicit examples, then, it is reasonable to see a psychological allusion in the present reference to a castle in confusion.

The picture presented by the second stanza of *Girl Drowned in the Well* mingles battlements with fishermen, as if it were possible to fish from the castle wall, all of which appears to be a functional symbol[5] representing the division of the psyche into its "upper"and "lower" parts. The castle is built over water, or elevated above foundations supported by the ground of the transpersonal unconscious lying deep down.[6] Castles so situated are well known, of course, as, for example, the great sixteenth-century château at Chenonceaux, reared on stone piles and spanning the river Cher, not far from the city of Tours.

The battlement scene, filled with shouting, scurrying townspeople, takes place at night, for the poem goes on to say that "the tender stars were croaking like frogs." To liken the stars to frogs is to see them as Lorcan "low stars," or chthonic lights.[7] It is as if we were to say that the black heaven was a great marshy area filled with living creatures: the vast, sunless region of the preconscious world.

At the end of each stanza is repeated the refrain ". . . which has no outlet," the clause ending the opening sentence: ". . . but they suffer much more because of the water which has no outlet." The regular recurrence of this refrain—ending, finally, in the form of an exclamation—leaves no doubt that this constitutes the controlling idea of the entire poem. It is the speaker's obsession: "what worse fate than to suffer from water that has no outlet!" Since (according to the title) the trapped water is the water in a well, and since there seems to be an implied relationship between the well and the water in which the fishermen are fishing, it is appropriate here to discuss in brief detail Lorca's notion of wells and well water as it appears in his works.

In the Biblical poem *Tamar and Amnon,* the brother, erotically aroused, cannot tolerate the frustration occasioned by the incest taboo; and as he tosses restlessly in his bed one hot, oppressive summer afternoon, we are suddenly aware of the jars of drinking water standing at hand:

> At half-past three Amnon
> stretched out on the bed.
> The whole room was suffering
> with his wing-filled eyes.
>
> . . . .
>
> Constricted well-water
> makes silence in the jars.[8]

This is symbolic of his state of mind, of course, as he glances fitfully about the room; and what interests us here especially is the fact that his libidinal frustration is associated with *well water confined* (literally "oppressed") within jars. It is well water which has been transferred from its source to individual "ceramic wells" standing still: water . . . which has no outlet.

In the *Casida* [love poem] *of the Water-wounded One,* the speaker begins by announcing his intention to "go down into the well," and then describes to us an injured child, groaning with pain, and "crowned with a crown of frost":[9] a psychological image in accord with the immobilization of the well water in *Girl Drowned,* and with the libidinal frustration of the constricted Amnon.

In the play *As Soon As Five Years Pass,* death is described as "a well into which we will all fall,"[10] a clear enough association of the well with the permanent stagnation of the libidinal flow.

Yerma, the frustrated childless wife of the play which bears her name, states that she has found the well water of her region detestable;[11] and she characterizes her mounting frustration and despair by saying that she has the sensation of falling into a well, and that now she is reaching the darkest part of it.[12] And later yet, when an old lady suggests that her own son would make a more satisfactory husband for Yerma, the latter indignantly rejects the offer by saying, "I am like a vast, dry field—and what you give me is a little glass of well water."[13]

In the tragedy *The House of Bernarda Alba*, the protagonist curses her village because it has no river, and scornfully calls it a "well-town," where the water is as likely to be poisoned as not.[14]

Finally, we might quote from a personal letter of Lorca's to his friend, the poet Jorge Guillén, in which the writer says he is staying in the country; the weather is blistering, and he is living on a diet of well water and apples. How he longs for the luxury of a cup of delicious Puerto Rican coffee![15]—suggesting that well water is one of the hardships of life.[16]

All the above passages, taken together, present a clear picture of the connotations which well water and wells had for Lorca. In the poem *Girl Drowned* he is trying to describe the worst fate of all—psychic impasse, loss of contact with the creative unconscious—and he can find no better symbol for it than the well: water that does not run, that stands in one place, with nowhere to go.

By contrast, he recalls in the second stanza an episode which involved men fishing with poles, implying, of course, their contact with living waters. And now, in the third stanza, he addresses the girl herself:

> Tranquil in my memory, star, circle, goal,
> you weep at the edges of a horse's eye.
> . . . which has no outlet.

The "girl" of this poem is, as we learn in line 23, an "undine," or water nymph, and as such should probably be envisioned as a beautiful maiden, rather than as a "little girl" (since *niña* can have either meaning). Nevertheless, symbolic allusions cannot be interpreted rigidly. For Lorca this nymph is a beneficent symbol (by contrast to the "dangerous" water spirits) of that kind of self-fulfilling poetic creativity which can occur only when there is some kind of harmonious interaction between consciousness and the unconscious. As such, she is cognate with the "psychic child," or child-archetype, an image of completion, "born" into the light of consciousness after a period of gestation within the womb of the unconscious. The child-archetype is a symbol familiar to Lorca, and in a later essay we will give it the detailed consideration that it merits. Nevertheless, it is necessary to point out here that symbols of spiritual completion, of which the "psychic child" is probably the most impressive, occur in a variety of recognizable forms; and in this third stanza Lorca has made a deliberate allusion to this polymorphous phenomenon: "Tranquil in my memory, star, circle, goal. . . ." As such, the line is an independent corroboration of Jung's observation that the child-motif "can be expressed by roundness, the circle or sphere. . . ."[17]

Line 8 states that the girl is weeping "at the edges of a horse's eye"; and while the fuller significance of this image will be discussed elsewhere,[18] we can at present recall the fact, everywhere obvious, that Lorca had the surrealist's working awareness of the meaning inherent in symbolic transformations. We are all of us perfectly familiar with the phenomenon as it takes place in our dreams (". . . I dreamed I was playing the piano, when all of a sudden I realized that it wasn't a piano at all; it was some kind of animal that began to move around . . ."). Now for Lorca, the "psychic child," having been born into consciousness, could symbolize the beginning of a spiritual trajectory, a spiritual value growing and waxing, suffused with energy— and so could metamorphose into the well-known symbol of libido: the horse. The Lorcan *horse's head* can take on strange appearances indeed, for like something out of a Picasso fantasy, the position of the eye is not fixed at all, but (like a shifting value) moves about. Only when the value has been fully assimilated by the daylight of ego-consciousness can the eye take its proper place in the horse's head, after traveling upward along the neck. Thus, in the poem *1910* (*Poet in New York*), Lorca depicts the spiritual Gestalt of his pre-adolescent years by saying that those youthful eyes of his were "in the neck of the pony";[19] and elsewhere in *Poet in New York* the same symbol crops up in a delirious sequence of images: "The horse had an eye in his neck."[20]

In the present poem the girl, as an inaccessible image of completion, lies depotentiated on the periphery of the life of the psyche, and her loss causes the speaker an inexpressible sadness which is conveyed through the weeping of the girl—the silent, inward sorrow of exile.

The poet goes on to observe:

> But no one in the darkness will be able to establish distances for you, without sharply-cut limit, the future of the diamond.
> . . . which has no outlet.

The future in store[21] for a diamond is that of being cut and polished: given a "sharply-cut limit," or being faceted. This allusion to crafted finishing suggests very strongly the place which this inaccessible girl ought to occupy in the life of the poet: for like a muse, it is she who could establish the creative direction of his own life, who could lead him, indeed, to be not a "lost," not a "confused," but a "finished" poet; because the "finished" poet is one with a vision to be crafted, to be given a "sharply-cut limit," so that it reflects with increased brilliance the multiple lights that fall upon it. As an anima-image, the girl represents the poet's *attitude* toward his unconscious, his ability to achieve creative union with it, to raise unconscious contents into consciousness—so that they can be dealt with, or organized, as esthetic intuitions.[22] The drowned girl represents not so much a spiritual problem in the general sense (a "personality" problem), as she does a "vocational" one, the aspect described as follows by Baynes:

> As representative of the inherited psyche, the anima is the instigator of those ideas which lead a man to his life-work, his major achievement. She often personifies his best tendency before it comes to maturity. This beneficent character of the anima belongs only to her impersonal function; as a personal factor the anima is unreliable. . . . she is essentially the spirit of a man's vocation, albeit a possessive one.[23]

Beyond these considerations, an explication of the diamond-imagery in the fourth stanza requires us to review briefly the symbolism of the oriental mandala, in which are formalized the ideas with which we are at present concerned.

The mandala (Sans., "circle") is a painted design used as a mystical instrument of contemplation. As Jung puts it, "the mandala is meant to aid concentration by narrowing down the psychic field of vision and restricting it to the center."[24] It characteristically appears as a circular figure with symmetrical decorations which are dynamically concentrated around a center representing "the essential object or goal of contemplation."[25]

If the object of contemplation lies in the direction of nonego, then one must leave the world of the intellect, which is the world of categories and opposites. One's goal is to experience reality as whole and as *unified*, or *continuous*, as one must have experienced it as a young child, while the ego-structure was still a vague thing. We dimly seem to recall that reality was once a kind of numinous presence which freely yielded its vibrations—an unfaltering Becoming—to us; it was Lorca's "trembling" reality,[26] the magic reality which subsequently lost its magic, with ego's increasing insistence upon the importance of categories, opposites, and systems: the static ground of the world of ego-consciousness.

Hence the circle, rose, star, ring, crown, and so forth, all belong to the so-called mandala symbolism, since the mandala is properly a formalized version of the symbolism for wholeness—*wholeness as a limited phenomenon*, realized within the limitations of the individual psyche. Time and again Lorca falls into the mandala symbolism, as in his *Love Poem of the Reclining Woman* (*Casida de la mujer tendida*), where the beloved is told that "to see you naked is to recall the Earth . . . as pure form, closed to the future: a silver precinct."[27] This is a reality experience of unity which, because it is detached from the world of ego-consciousness and intellect, is also detached from the idea of sidereal time and of the future in store for "me." Within this magic precinct of the psyche, all points are equidistant from the center. There are no opposites or relative values.

If categories and opposites can disappear so utterly, it is because they have no existence beyond the world of the intellect—certainly not in the inward world of nonego. They are forms of thought whereby the intellect orients itself in the world; but when reality is experienced as a unified whole, as an irreducible One, then it typically reveals itself to the conscious mind as a *jewel*, viz., the "diamond body." The mandala of which Jung speaks in the foregoing, for example, contains at its center a "diamond thunderbolt."[28]

Girl Drowned is not, of course, concerned with a mystical transition to the world of nonego, but rather with raising to consciousness poetic material of which there exists only a premonition. This means "giving birth" to it, just as the mother expels the infant from the self-contained system of the womb into a world which the infant comes equipped to perceive as a world of time and space. Within the world of the womb the foetus is *coextensive* with its environment; there is no interval (so to speak) between where it leaves off and where its environment begins, and so consciousness must be allayed. As Bergson puts it (apropos of the sleepwalker acting out his dream):

> . . . unconsciousness may be absolute . . . because the [conscious] representation of the act is held in check by the performance of the act itself, which resembles it so perfectly, and fits it so exactly, that consciousness is unable to find room between them.[29]

When the infant is expelled from the womb, he finds himself in a world which is not coextensive with himself: a world of *distances*, precisely. The world within the amniotic fluid is an irreducible, self-enclosed system, self-contained like the uroboros, the circular snake biting its tail, which is a universal symbol for this kind of preconscious, nonego experience.

In the present poem, the psychic content is called a "girl," a "star," a "circle"—but not the diamond body which we have described as a symbol of unification:

> But no one in the darkness will be able to establish distances for you, without sharply-cut limit, the future of the diamond.

The diamond, after all, is extracted from the Earth Mother after much labor. It has in store for it a "future" of being cut and polished. The psychic content of which Lorca speaks is also to be "extracted from below"; but the integration into consciousness of this element means making it into a functional part of the consciously creative self. It is born into the world of distances (ego-consciousness), and functions creatively within a world of space and time. The girl down there in the well is weeping, and no one "down there" in the dark can "use" her, as it were, as part of a system of conscious discourse.

Concern with the integration process continues in the fifth stanza:

> While people seek silences of the pillow
> you throb forever defined within your ring.
> . . . which has no outlet.

Here the speaker contrasts his own introspective tendencies with the lack of them which he notes in the people among whom he lives. The contrast is not, however, the point of the statement, and Lorca does not emphasize it;[30] he simply observes that during the time in which others are seeking the amnesia of sleep, he remains awake, aware of the living-dead presence of an unconscious content "down there."

The sixth stanza characterizes well water:

Eternal in the final fling of waves which accept
the struggle of roots and solitude foreseen.
. . . which has no outlet.

The "struggle of roots" (*combate de raíces*) is the battle of the rhizosphere. It is literally a struggle for existence, for the roots growing in the ground must force their way through a compact mass of soil.

In the erotic poem of the *Reclining Woman*, from which we have already quoted, the speaker says to his beloved, "*tu vientre es una lucha de raíces*," which is to say, "Your belly (womb) is a struggle of roots."[31] Here we must understand that the sexual roots of the reclining woman represent a life-giving drive down into the earth, the soil of instinct. The reclining woman, i.e., the sexually approachable woman, is to human life what the rhizosphere is to plant life. The roots represent that part of the plant which is absolutely essential to continued survival (hence our symbolic use of the word *extirpate*); but in *Girl Drowned* the opposition is evidently another. There, roots represent nothing more than the area in which one finds well water. The opposition lies between well water and the easy fluidity of the tidal wave, an impulse that flows along without encountering resistance. Some waves have separated themselves out, have gone their separate ways within the ecological cycle, and have accepted the solitude of the rhizosphere, and so become water with no outlet.

The girl, then, is not only *in* the well; she shares the attributes of well water. She and it once functioned on the surface of the earth and have subsequently gone underground. Well water is actually an exhausted wave that has been trapped below, and the girl is a psychic element that was once part of the surging libidinal tide. She was once a functioning part of the speaker's conscious life, but she too has been trapped underground; and with her repression, communication has been broken with the instinctual region.

The seventh stanza reverts to the image of the castle, for the speaker cries out suddenly to the drowned girl:

Here they come along the ramparts! Rise up from the water!
Each point of light will be as a chain to you!
. . . which has no outlet.

This is not the only poem in which the *chain* is used by Lorca as a psychic symbol. In *Weather Vane*, we read:

> My memory
> possesses strong chains,
> and the bird is captive
> that with its trills
> sketches the afternoon.[32]

The meaning here is clear enough: the speaker finds himself in a state of high receptivity, and his impressions have an unusually strong impact. They are unforgettable—"chained" to consciousness—and will remain forever accessible to recall.

The early poem *Diamond* depicts a falling star:

> The diamond of a star
> has crossed the deep sky:
> a bird of light that would
> escape from the universe;
> and it flees from the enormous nest
> where it was prisoner,
> without knowing that it carries
> a chain about the neck.[33]

We have already made mention of the ecological network of life which makes it impossible to escape from the great sphere that we inhabit. We have also suggested that for Lorca those star-frogs of the night firmament represent points of consciousness against the black marshes of the unconscious. Combining these two notions, one sees the falling star as an indestructible psychic unit which has been raised to consciousness—and its *chain* means that it is indissolubly a part of the system. It is an epiphenomenon which can never escape from the microcosmic universe.

Elsewhere[34] *chain* appears as the commonplace symbol for slavery or oppression. But the above examples indicate that we need not impute to it this more-or-less allegorical meaning. On the contrary, it is apparent that Lorca has used *chain* in a way that is distinctly applicable to the psychological point of view developed in *Girl Drowned:* the phenomenon of integration—here frustrated. If creative material has been formed into a functioning part of the conscious psyche, then we may say that it has been linked indissolubly with it—"chained" to it.

The speaker cries out to the girl to rise up out of the well, and assures her that her liberation will be aided and secured by "chains" which "points of light" will provide. This stanza is a reminiscence of the second stanza (by virtue of the "ramparts"—merlons there, ramps [*rampas*] here), and I take the points of lights to be the stars seen there as frogs.

The whole context may be used to corroborate the psychological point of view according to which stars are points of consciousness; for if the "psychic child" can be raised out of the unconscious where she now languishes, she will assume a role dynamically related to the complex structure of the conscious mind—which is formed of numberless constellations shining out against the black night of the unconscious.

The reader will recall that the second stanza depicted a scene in which a castle seemed to be the object of an invasion; and men, fishing from the battlements, were being attacked by the townspeople who were breaking the fish poles.

It is easy to see why fishing is an appropriate symbol for mediation between the conscious and the unconscious. Another Spanish poet, Antonio Machado (1875-1939) describes it clearly (though he is not specifically concerned with the problem of psychological integration) in a poem which begins, "There are two modes of consciousness."[35] The two modes are, of course, intellect and intuition; the intuitive man is (says Machado) a "visionary who looks into the deep aquarium and sees living fish," while the intellectual man is a fisherman who always ends up "throwing the dead fish on the sand."[36] Fish in the ocean, like shimmering stars in the night sky, are strongly suggestive of individual psychic units.

Since *Girl Drowned* belongs to *Poet in New York*, it forms part of the general pattern of anxiety which we have already noted. The poet senses that his confrontation with the American megalopolis has unbalanced him, i.e., has produced a psychic impasse by disrupting the integration process which, after all, proceeds according to its own inner rhythms. His conscious mind finds itself invaded by vast amounts of repellent material that have destroyed a relationship between the conscious and the unconscious gradually established and fostered over the years. In this sense, he himself is the "vomiting crowd" of which he writes in *Poet in New York*.[37]

Getting the girl out of the well and catching fish from the river are both assimilable to the integration process; they are symbolically analogous. But certainly they are not qualitatively equivalent, for the very good reason that human beings and fishes are not. We should not forget that the poem is subtitled "Granada and Newburg," which is to say, "Spain and America"; more accurately, Lorca's spiritual outlook at some time in the past, as contrasted with his spiritual outlook at the present time. All his adult life he has been accustomed to "fishing from the battlements" of his castle precinct, and the violent disruption of this spiritual activity habitual to him produces a frightful anxiety. But the drowning of the girl is a far more sinister symbol.

We understand that she is not dead, since it is taken for granted in the text that she can be restored to her original position. This is true of necessity, since psychic material cannot be destroyed—but repression can be so severe as to constitute a kind of *de facto* destruction. The fact that the poem is addressed to a girl, and that it is subtitled "Granada and Newburg," signifies something far more serious than the temporary disruption of the speaker's spiritual organization (which could presumably be reinstated by a return to Granada); it signifies destruction of self, or the fear that self may have been destroyed.

In the final stanzas of the poem Lorca suggests this, for it appears that the girl will remain below, to be covered with moss—a symbol of libidinal stagnation recalling the lines of Antonio Machado, written while contemplating the mystery of soul and body in the form of water playing in a marble fountain; he would fain rest there in meditation, he says, "until I might feel . . . my head covered with moss."[38]

The stagnant depths of the well are like "violins without strings," bereft of the vital tension that sings. The poetic "singing" in *Poet in New York* is an agony which has only one musical scale available to it—the "scale of wounds and uninhabited buildings." And so the poem ends with an allusion to the symbolic edifice which we have seen earlier in the form of a castle under attack.

Lorca's poetry attests to the fact that from childhood on he retained the ability to experience reality as children do: as a magic and numinous presence vitalizing all natural forms. It is an ability which most of us lose, the price we pay for "maturing" according to the canons laid down for us by society. No reader of Lorca can fail to realize that this was his most precious possession. His entire life revolved around it; it was the nucleus, as it were, of his conscious psyche, the central point—the *glorieta*—at which all paths converged. He lived bathed in a feeling that his own inner rhythms were in harmony with the rhythms of the biosphere. He always seemed to know that "maturing" had a spiritual meaning involved with the creation of a *self* (rather than an ego) at the center of psychic life. The development of this self required not a repression of unconscious materials, but rather a liberation of them in assimilable form. This is a fusion of the logos and eros functions, a marriage of the masculine consciousness and the feminine unconscious; hence the appearance of the feminine symbol, the anima-image hinting at the fact that contact with the feminine unconscious is essential to any kind of inner creativity. For the young Lorca, the self-fulfilling spiritual harmony manifested itself specifically in the form of esthetic achievement. He was living out a creative equilibrium and his cup overflowed—when his immersion in the life of the foreign metropolis brought to light psychic conflicts hitherto latent, and he felt his creative powers as a poet falling away into the blackness of a deep and stagnant well.

CHAPTER FOUR

The Psychological Perspective

As Soon As Five Years Pass

1. INTRODUCTORY NOTE

Así que pasen cinco años (*As Soon As Five Years Pass*), dated 1931, is undoubtedly Lorca's most difficult work, for it makes minimal concessions to logic or to rational thought processes. It is a psychological drama in the truest sense of the term, since it concerns the psychological transformation of a young man. Not only are various psychic functions embodied in the form of dramatic characters, but the libidinal transmutations experienced by the protagonist also find their way into the *dramatis personae*. These transmutations are all implicit, of course, since the play lacks a narrator to describe them as they occur. It is perhaps this lack of explicitness that makes the play seem doubly difficult, and which produces the temptation to interpret it allegorically—which is to say statically.

Nevertheless, the phenomenon of psychic transformation is a major aspect of the play, and it must be dealt with dynamically. Comparison with a like phenomenon in the fairy tale may help to familiarize us with Lorca's seemingly elusive technique, especially if we consider a story like the Grimm tale entitled "The Poor Miller's Boy and the Cat,"[1] which bears some striking resemblances to the material dealt with by Lorca in *Five Years*.

"The Poor Miller's Boy and the Cat" concerns a quest. An old miller sends forth his three apprentices to see which can bring back the finest horse and so inherit the mill. Hans, the youngest of the three, is thought by the other two to be a simpleton, and the first night out they abandon him in a cavern. The following morning he climbs out and finds himself in a forest, where he meets a friendly tabby cat who promises to help the boy if he will serve her faithfully for seven years. One of the tasks assigned him is the construction of a small house for his feline mistress. At the end of seven years the tabby cat sends him home, with the assurance that the promised horse will follow him shortly. Three days later a fine carriage stops in front of the mill: "A magnificent Princess alighted from the coach and went into the mill, and this princess was the little tabby-cat whom poor Hans had served

61

for seven years."[2] She presents the horse, takes Hans, and drives away with him to the little house which he had built—which is now a great castle of silver and gold. They marry and live happily ever after.

Hans's growth into a successful young man is clearly depicted as a *transformation process*. His "success" is undoubtedly a *spiritual* success: the realization of his inner potential. Characteristically the fairy-tale quest tells how a young person develops successfully into an adult, how he detaches himself from dependency upon the home circle by learning to depend upon himself through development of his own resources. It is these resources which constitute the object of the quest, for they are the "treasure hard to find."

Hans's success is envisioned in terms of three symbols: the horse, the cat, and the princess. Ostensibly the boy needs the horse in order to inherit the mill—but by the end of the story the mill no longer retains any importance. What matters is Hans's successful confrontation with the three symbols—three different aspects of the same thing—which signifies lifelong success.

This is perhaps the single great issue of the fairy-tale quest: how to acquire a treasure which will successfully resolve the problem of life; and this treasure may be described as the development of inner potential which allows the hero to establish himself as a sound adult, safely beyond the threat of regressive tendencies. The passage through adolescence is successful only if the youngster's own inner forces are mobilized and integrated into a viable adult personality. If this can be accomplished, then his chances are very good for meeting and dealing with the accidents and crises of everyday living which await him as an adult—and it is in this sense that we can speak of living "happily ever after."

It is clear that Hans cannot acquire the fine horse except by living cooperatively for seven years with the cat. It is equally clear that at the end of this test the cat is transformed into a princess who becomes the bride of the young man who has earned the horse. Now from a psychological point of view the three symbols of the horse, the cat, and the princess must be seen not as three distinct objects, but rather as three different forms of the same thing: the activation of unconscious, instinctual attitudes. Seven years of living on friendly terms with the cat assures that Hans, as an adult, will never fall into the error of ignoring the demands of instinct, of thinking that his instinctive side is somehow inferior to his rational side. He has learned, in growing up, how to cooperate with his instincts; he has made them a living part of his character, and so they are at length differentiated as a specifically human form. The feminine unconscious ("helpful animal") is born into consciousness as a princess who will become his wife—his "other half." At the same time his efforts are crowned by the public presentation of a fine horse, which is the "official" recognition of Hans's libidinal worthiness. The little house which he made for the helpful animal turns out to be a lifelong accommodation for the hero.

The psychological basis of this story is to be found in what has come to be called (after Lévy-Bruhl)[3] a *participation mystique:* fusion of the conscious mind and the unconscious. Primitive man experiences this as "an *a priori* feeling of union . . . with the persons and objects of the environment," which "precludes the sense of individual distinctiveness."[4] This state of "mystic participation" means that ego-consciousness and instinctual forces do not exist in a subject-object relationship. The subject-object relationship, when it arises, heralds the birth of "civilized" man, who lives under threat of being cut off entirely from the helpful counsels of his unconscious, and who may even identify himself so closely with his waking life that his dream life is nothing more to him than a mildly amusing object of contemplation.

In the fairy tale the youngest brother or sister is typically considered by his elders to be stupid, which is to say that by reason of his tender years he is less hedged in by a rigidly developed and practical ego-consciousness, and therefore still in possession of intuitive and instinctual knowledge. Hence it is characteristically he who enjoys the advantage of counsel from entities who appear to him in dreams, and from all manner of helpful animals. A sense of unity with natural forces, before ego has set itself apart from nature, appears in the fairy tale as a friendship with those forces. The story of the miller's boy tells us that a period of apprenticeship with instinct is a necessary prerequisite to the integration into consciousness of instinctive knowledge possessed only by the feminine unconscious— which is nothing less than Mother Earth herself in psychic form.

She must, however, be assimilated not as a mother, but as a helpmate—a "peer." Devoted service to and sympathy with instinct will be rewarded: for eventually that intimate and sympathetic knowledge of instinctual forces will enable one to make them a functioning part of one's personality. They are liberated in order to unite with ego-consciousness, and for that reason may appear symbolically as a bride. The tabby cat, transformed into the hero's helpmate, becomes a permanent addition to his life; and at the same time the hero's triumphal entry into manhood is marked by his ability to produce on demand a superlative horse.

These ideas find analogous expression (though in a much more complex form) in the play *Five Years;* for here we are again concerned with a young man's attempts to come to terms with unconscious potential. The reader will note throughout the play an explicit concern with the "treasure hard to find," and he will note also that this treasure undergoes a series of transformations, as the young man seeks to acquire it in the form that will best serve his vital interests in the future.

It would appear that the young man suffers a schizophrenic crisis terminating in catatonia—though a psychiatrist would undoubtedly find it impossible to give us a meaningful diagnosis, since we are dealing not with a clinical record, but with imaginative writing. In any case, it is helpful, in characterizing the general direction which the play takes, to point out that the protagonist's condition accumulates psychotic proportions, and the following description of schizophrenic crises undergone by disturbed persons seems to apply with reasonable accuracy to the protagonist of *Five Years:*

> Their ties to their intimates had become tenuous and fraught with intense, disturbing emotions and fantasies. They were very withdrawn—in most instances confused and delusional, in some instances suffering from terrifying hallucinations. The immediate past and present were frightening, painful, confused, and unreal, and no predictable and tolerable future could be convincingly envisioned. Their everyday world and their customary, implicit scheme of living had shattered.[5]

The patients dealt with in the preceding quotation are adults whose adolescent development was unusually desultory, as it were. They attained young adulthood with no working spiritual organization, no deeply rooted sense of *who they were.* In subsequent years they were unable to mobilize any meaningful reaction to crucial events in their lives, and so retreated in terror and confusion from the whole problem of ego-consciousness. The principal reality of their lives was the reality of their own inner chaos—and so it is with the young man of Lorca's play.

2. RÉSUMÉ OF THE DRAMA

Act I

The opening scene is in the library of the Young Man's home. Attired in blue pajamas, he sits chatting amicably with a bearded and be-spectacled Old Man, who wears a gray cutaway coat.

"I've always been like that," says the Young Man. "I recall that I always used to save my candy for later." The Old Man agrees that this makes it taste better; and as the Young Man continues to reminisce, the Old Man interrupts: "I always liked the word 'remember.' It's a green, juicy word."

The Young Man seems particularly happy to hear someone else say this, for he is not entirely convinced that the importance he attaches to reminiscences is justified. To him, *forgetting* is a form of decay—and one must keep one's memories well ordered and clearly in focus.

The Old Man again agrees, but with a peculiar qualification: to reminisce is fine, he believes, as long as one remembers *before the event*. "One must remember, yes—but previously."

The clock strikes six. A storm is brewing outside, and as the Young Man complains of the humidity, a young lady, the Typist, walks across stage, weeping silently.

The desultory conversation turns on the subject of the Young Man's *Novia*—his fiancée—who is absent on a long trip with her father. The Old Man asks if the latter has been to the house (presumably to formalize the marriage contract). The Young Man replies that this can happen only after five years have passed.

> Old Man: [joyfully] Very good!
> Young Man: [seriously] Why do you say "very good"?
> Old Man: Well, because . . . [indicating the room] Is this nice?
> Young Man: No.
> Old Man: Aren't you distressed when the moment of departure arrives? Aren't you distressed by events, by what is about to happen?
> Young Man: Yes, yes. Don't speak to me of that.

The Young Man declares his antipathy to activity outside his house—the constant noise, dust, heat, and offensive odors of the street.

Suddenly a long moan is heard, and the Young Man calls to his valet, John, to close the window. (John is an unusually discreet servant who moves about silently, always walking on tiptoe.)

The Young Man says that his fiancée is fifteen years old, whereupon the Old Man suggests that the word "year" is too abstract. People don't live simply in *years:* they live the fullness of *seasons.* "Why not say that she is fifteen snows old, fifteen breezes, fifteen twilights?" Time is full of real things which never cease to change, and life is an incessant transformation—a *Becoming.*

The Young Man is upset by these remonstrances, and complains:

> You want to separate me from her. But *I* know how you operate. One has only to observe a live insect on the palm of the hand, or watch the afternoon sea, paying close attention to the shape of each wave, in order for the face or sore in our breast to dissolve in bubbles.

He, however, is bent on retaining an unchanging vision of his *Novia.* Having glimpsed her once, he will not admit the possibility that his "girl" might have changed during her protracted absence. Here the Old Man asks why he refers to her as his "girl": why not call her his fiancée? But the Young Man takes this to be only another attempt to change her original image. He recalls that in similar fashion her physical proximity disconcerted him from his need to "focus":

> The last time I saw her I couldn't look closely at her, because she had two little wrinkles in her forehead, and at the slightest carelessness on my part they would cover her whole face and make her look withered and old, as if she had known great suffering. I had to separate myself in order to *focus* her—that's the word—in my heart.

The Old Man points out that this impression is the natural result of feeling that the *Novia* was indisputably his—that she "belonged" to him, as it were:

> I'll bet that if at that precise moment she had confessed that she had deceived you, that she didn't love you, her wrinkles would have changed into the loveliest rose in the world.

The Old Man sums up the conversation by agreeing with the protagonist that since reality is a Becoming, a flux, it can bring only death
and a sense of loss. Hence anticipation is better than experience:

> That's why we will . . . remain here . . . and wait. Because any-
> thing else is to die on the spot, and it's more beautiful to think that
> tomorrow we will still see the hundred horns of gold with which
> the sun raises the clouds.

The Young Man is evidently much encouraged to hear the Old
Man say this, and he thanks him effusively. At this point the weeping
Typist makes another appearance, and the Young Man asks her if
she has "finished the letters." The conversation which follows makes
it clear that for years she has been desperately in love with him, and
it is this which keeps her in his employ. Unfortunately, however, he
does not reciprocate, and he tells her that if her continued presence
in the house makes her unhappy, she is perfectly free to depart at any
time. She exits, more miserable than ever at this obvious display of
indifference. The Old Man warns the protagonist that the Typist is
"dangerous." The Young Man protests that he would like to return
her affection, but that it is impossible.

Enter the First Friend noisily. He is a sensualist who lives life as
an orgy. The Old Man finds his presence repugnant and departs
without a word. The First Friend tries to put the Young Man into a
festive mood and goes on at length about his latest conquests. The
Young Man remains indifferent, until the irrepressible First Friend
begins to tickle him, whereupon he laughs in spite of himself, and the
two of them begin to wrestle playfully. The Old Man suddenly reappears—"gravely"—explaining that he "will forget his hat." The
First Friend looks at him quizzically, and the Old Man falls into a
rage: "I mean, I *forgot* my hat!" Here there is a great crash of
breaking glass offstage. The Young Man calls to John to close the
windows.

The storm outside grows more threatening. Though the First
Friend looks forward to it, the Young Man does not want to hear any
thunder. "I don't care about what happens outside. This house is
mine, and nobody is going to come in." The Old Man supports this
statement, but the First Friend counters with the observation that
anybody who so desires will come in—"not here, but under your
bed." The Young Man's violent resistance to this idea is applauded
by the Old Man ("Bravo!").

Again the thunder rolls. The stage is suffused by the "bluish luminosity" of the storm. The three characters suddenly step behind a black screen bordered by stars—whereupon the Dead Child enters, dressed for burial in his First Communion suit and accompanied by the Blue Cat (*Gato*), who shows great spots of blood on his chest and head—made, he says, by children cruelly throwing stones at him. The Child describes how he was laid out for burial in a small coffin, and as he addresses the cat in the masculine (*gato*) the cat informs him that she is female (*gata*). The two of them reminisce about their happy days on earth, and are terrified by the thought of lying buried within the sunless bowels of the soil. A hand reaches out and snatches first the Cat and then the Child, who faints upon feeling himself being "spirited away" from this life on earth.

The original lighting is restored and the Old Man, the First Friend, and the protagonist come out from behind the screen. They are suffering from the heat, and are all exceedingly agitated. They fan themselves, the Old Man with a black fan, the First Friend with an "aggressively red" fan, and the Young Man with a blue fan.

From offstage comes a scream of anguish: "My son! My son!" John, the valet, tells the Young Man that it is the *portera*, or concierge, mourning the death of her child. He then asks for the upstairs key, for it seems that some children have killed a cat and thrown its corpse upon the roof over the garden—which is evidently accessible from the window of the Young Man's bedroom.

Meanwhile the Old Man and the First Friend have been arguing, and the latter declares with some pride that he at least knows for certain that snow is cold and that fire will burn. The Old Man replies ironically, "That all depends." The First Friend assures the protagonist that the Old Man is deceptive, but the Young Man rejects this assurance as needless, since the Old Man

> . . . hasn't the least influence over me. I am who I am. But *you* can't understand that a person might wait five years for a woman, overflowing with and burned by a love that grows every day.

The First Friend believes such waiting to be wrong, for it subordinates one's own desires unselfishly—"and you," he says, "*you* come before anybody else." The protagonist defends "waiting" as ultimately valuable, for it is an anticipation of ripe enjoyment—the enjoyment of mature fruit.

The First Friend, however, has no interest in ripe fruit. "I would rather eat it green—or better yet, cut the flower to wear in my lapel." This initiates a new argument with the Old Man, who says that all his life he has defended the dove from those who would have killed it; it was he who stayed the hostile hand. "And naturally," rejoins the First Friend, "the hunter has died of hunger!"

"Then long live hunger!" exclaims the Young Man—which occasions the appearance of a new character, the Second Friend—an effeminate adolescent extravagantly dressed in a white woolen suit with enormous blue buttons, and with a good deal of lacy ruffling at his throat and chest. He enters praising both hunger and the satisfaction thereof. He explains that he entered via the window, thanks to the help of two children with whom he is good friends. The imminence of rain reminds him of the "lovely downpour" of last year, when "there was so little light" that his hands turned yellow.

Rain, as a matter of fact, seems to constitute the Second Friend's special interest. He tells of how, at the age of one year, he captured one of the little "rain-women" who fall to earth in drops of water whenever it rains. He kept her in a fishbowl, he recalls, but she gradually shrank to nothing, singing all the while a song about wanting to "go back": "I'm going back for my wings . . . , I want to die at dawn yesterday as a spring, outside the sea." Since then, he says, he has taken that rain song as his own, for he too would like to die and be buried in a little coffin similar to the one he noticed in a funeral procession which happened to be passing the house just as he entered.

The Old Man can no longer tolerate the presence of these two friends, and he leaves precipitately, followed shortly by the First Friend. The Typist enters carrying a suitcase and asks the protagonist, "Did you call me? Do you need me?" He sends her away; and while the Second Friend continues to sing his rain song, we learn that it is still six o'clock. The curtain falls as the Young Man sits drumming the table with his fingers.

Act II

Act Two takes place in the boudoir of the *Novia*, the Young Man's voluptuous fiancée. As the curtain goes up she leaps from her bed at the sound of an auto horn announcing the arrival of her illicit lover— a silent, virile figure called the Rugby Player, and dressed accordingly.

He carries a bag of cigars which furnishes him with a noteworthy bit of stage business, for he is constantly half-occupied with lighting up and crushing out cigars.

This entire scene is erotically charged as the *Novia* reveals the irresistible attraction which she feels for her lover's sexuality, and keeps up an enthusiastic litany in praise of his libido, which she likens to the raging torrent of a river. He is more beautiful than his stallion; he is a dragon; he must take her away with him, for she cannot bear the thought of marrying the colorless creature to whom she is engaged.

Their meeting is interrupted by the servant girl announcing the arrival of the Young Man, at which point the blue lighting again suffuses the stage. The Rugby Player departs.

Both the servant girl and the *Novia's* father press her to honor her commitment to the Young Man, but she is adamant: the engagement must be broken.

The Young Man arrives, telling how he has punished some children whom he caught stoning a cat to death. The *Novia* is not interested in anything he has to say, for she finds him cold and passionless. He seems much changed to her since she last saw him, for she recalls that his appearance was formerly quite different; as a matter of fact, she remembers him as looking precisely like the Rugby Player. His present lackluster appearance profoundly disappoints her, and she tells him that the union cannot possibly take place. The Young Man refuses to accept this, not because he would lose *her*, specifically, but because loss of her would leave his love without an object:

> What hurts me is not your deception. You're not *bad*. You are of no importance. [What matters] is my lost treasure, my aimless love. But you will come!

The *Novia* steadfastly refuses to change her mind, and tells her father that they must return the Young Man's presents—all except the two fans, which were broken anyway, and which are now missing. The Young Man fondly recalls these two fans—a blue one decorated with a picture of "three sunken gondolas," and a white one displaying the head of a tiger. He says that their loss is unimportant, since he can still fancy that his skin is being burned by the breeze which they made.

The scene ends with the termination of the engagement. The *Novia* runs away with the Rugby Player, and as the Young Man stands alone and disoriented, we hear a moan—whereupon the spectacular figure of the Mannequin appears. She is a window dresser's dummy wearing the *Novia's* bridal gown, and her face is painted gold. She sings a mournful song, asking, "Who will wear my gown? The estuary, in order to marry the sea." And she adds, "The train of my gown is lost in the sea." She blames the Young Man for the loss: "You could have been like a colt . . . and you are a sleeping lagoon. . . ." The golden wedding ring is lost; the Young Man should have come earlier, when the *Novia* "was waiting naked like a serpent of wind."

The Mannequin shows the Young Man a boy's suit, rose-colored, which she has appropriated, she says, from the *Novia:* for now the Mannequin plans to have a child by the Young Man.

He responds enthusiastically—not to the Mannequin herself, but rather to her intense assurance that he will surely father a child. She joins in with his enthusiasm and says that his bride awaits him; let him bring her to the Mannequin so that

> my silks may,
> thread by thread, and one by one,
> open the rose beneath
> her belly of golden flesh.

The Young Man is filled with confidence that a fertile union will take place. He snatches the boy's suit; and as the stage lighting becomes an intense blue, a maid enters with a candelabrum. The lighting returns to normal, and as the maid looks remorsefully at the Young Man, the Old Man reappears.

He is greatly upset; the Young Man tells him that his presence is not needed. The Old Man replies that his presence is now required more than ever. "You have injured me! Why did you come up? I knew what would happen." But the Young Man happily informs him that he is going to seek the Typist—whom the Old Man does not seem to recall.

We hear the automobile horn, and as the household scurries about frantically searching for the missing *Novia,* the Young Man runs off, determined to find the Typist. The Old Man follows, beseeching him not to leave him behind, injured as he is. The Maid runs in long enough to take the candelabrum; the Mannequin sings her mournful song about the lost wedding ring and the bridal gown: "the estuary

71

will wear it in order to marry the sea." She suddenly collapses in a faint, and a rapid curtain ends the act as we hear a voice offstage screaming, "Waaaaait!"

Act III (Part I)

The curtain goes up on an unexpected set, in the midst of a deep, dark, archaic forest. Center stage is a miniature (but practicable) baroque theater, with curtains drawn. Steps make it accessible from the main stage.

We hear distant music and can make out, moving among the immense tree trunks, two figures in black with white masks and white hands. Enter Harlequin, dressed in black and green. He carries two masks, one smiling and the other sleeping. He moves about like a dancer and says:

> Sleep moves over time,
> floating like a sailboat.
> No one can open seeds
> in the heart of sleep.

With the smiling mask he says:

> Ah, how the dawn sings!
> What blue icebergs does it raise up!

Without the mask he says:

> Time moves over sleep,
> immersed up to its locks of hair.
> Yesterday and tomorrow eat
> dark flowers of mourning.

With the sleeping mask he says:

> Ah, how the night sings!
> What thickets of anemones does it raise up!

Without the mask he says:

> While sleep and time
> are locked in embrace,
> the moan of the child
> and the broken tongue of the old man
> cross upon the same column.

From this opening scene onward we will hear faintly at intervals the sound of hunting horns. Enter a Girl in a black toga. She dances about with a garland, singing that her lover awaits her at the bottom of the sea. Her entire interest is centered upon her "lost treasure": "I lost my desire, I lost my thimble, and among the great trunks I found them again." And then again:

> I lost my crown,
> I lost my thimble,
> and just behind me
> I found them again.

Here Harlequin tells her:

> Right now. . . .
> You will see your lover
> right behind the wind and the sea. . . .
> I will give him to you.

The Girl is frightened by this, and denies what Harlequin says:

> You shall not give him to me.
> One can never reach the bottom of the sea.

At Harlequin's bidding a splendidly costumed Clown appears, guffawing. His whitened face "suggests a skull." It is evident that Harlequin and the Clown are willing to lend a hand in recovering the lost treasure, but their generally festive behavior and the irony with which they speak suggests that they do not seriously intend to be helpful; rather, they are pranksters mocking the attempt to undertake an impossible quest. Or (to put it another way) their knowledge that the Girl lacks the necessary fortitude to prosecute the quest leads them to deride her by insisting that she accompany them forthwith. She in turn is "frightened by the reality"—i.e., the substantial realness—of their attempt to make her undertake the quest, and she shrinks back, refusing to go. "Later," she says, after she has "leapt about in the tall grasses"; then it will be time for the three of them to descend into the sea.

The Girl exits weeping, and Harlequin and the Clown put on a short performance. The Clown says, "Let's do a small boy who wants to change his piece of bread into steel flowers." Hereupon they sing a variant of the Girl's song, as the following comparison shows:

Girl's song	*Variant*
I lost my desire,	I lost rose and curve,
I lost my thimble,	I lost my necklace,
and among the great trunks	and in new ivory
I found them again.	I found them again . . . ,
	in ivory of clouds
	I found them again.

As the two of them make their exit Harlequin sings the phrase "the turning wheel of the wind and the sea."

Lorca's stage directions for the following extraordinary scene read as follows:

> The hunting horns sound. Enter Typist. She is wearing a tennis outfit, with a brightly colored beret. Over her outfit, a long cape. She is accompanied by the *First Mask,* who wears a turn-of-the-century gown with a long train of vivid yellow, hair of yellow silk which falls about her like a mantle, and a chalk-white mask; elbow-length gloves of the same color. She wears a yellow hat, and her bosom is covered by gold sequins. This character should give the effect of a burst of flame against the background of mottled blue and nocturnal tree trunks. She speaks with a slight Italian accent.

The Typist and the First Mask are engaged in amiable conversation, and as they make their entrance the Mask says laughingly, "How very charming!" It seems that the Typist is recounting the episode which we witnessed in the first act:

> I left his house. I recall that on the afternoon of my departure there was a great summer storm, and that the concierge's little boy had died.

This is familiar enough; but then she distorts:

> He said to me, "Did you call me?", to which I replied, closing my eyes, "No." And then, when I was already at the door, he said, "Do you need me?"; and I told him, "No, I don't need you."

The First Mask is struck by this anecdote, for it is quite like a recent episode in her own life. The Young Man who allegedly loved the Typist was "just like" a man who was desperately in love with her —one Count Arturo of Italy. She goes on to make the following bizarre statement:

In the foyer of the Paris Opera House there are enormous balustrades which give onto the sea. Count Arturo, with a camellia between his lips, would approach in a little boat, accompanied by his son (the two of them deserted by me). But I would close the curtains and throw them a diamond. Oh, what sweet anguish, my friend, *¡qué dulcísimo tormento!* [She weeps.] The Count and his little boy would go hungry and sleep in the shrubbery, with a whippet which a Russian gentleman had made me a present of. [Forcefully and supplicatingly.] Haven't you a crust of bread for me? For the child whom Count Arturo let die in the frost? [Upset.] And afterward I went to the hospital, and there I learned that the Count had married a great Roman lady . . . ; and since then I have begged, and shared my bed with the men who unload coal at the docks.

The Typist is surprised by this speech, not because she fails to understand it, apparently, but rather because the Mask is speaking at all; for she replies, "What are you saying? Why do you speak?" But the Mask goes on:

I'm saying that Count Arturo so loved me that he would weep behind the curtains with his little boy, while I, on the other hand, was like a silvery half-moon among the opera glasses and the gaslights which shone beneath the dome of the great Opera House of Paris.

She says that Count Arturo carries on his right hand the scar left by a dagger—all because of her, "naturally." *Then she holds out her hand and exhibits the scar:* "See it?" And, pointing to her neck, "And here's another one—see it?" "What would I do without wounds?" she asks rhetorically. "Of whom are my Count's wounds?" And the Typist replies:

Yours. It's true! He's waited five years for me, but . . . how lovely to await confidently the moment of being loved! . . . That's why we'll laugh! When I was small, I used to save my candy in order to eat it later.

The First Mask agrees that this makes it taste better. As she exits, we hear the hunting horns, and the Young Man enters, wearing knickers and blue-checkered stockings. He is seeking the way home, and Harlequin suddenly reappears, telling him that he cannot continue in the direction in which he is going because the way is blocked by "the circus," "full of spectators who are definitely quiet. Doesn't the gentleman wish to enter?"

75

The poet Virgil made a golden fly, and all the flies died which were poisoning the air of Naples. In there, in the circus, there is some soft gold, enough to make a statue the same size . . . as yourself.

The Young Man wishes only one thing—to return home—but he finds insurmountable obstacles no matter where he turns.

Young Man: Is Poplar Street blocked also?
Harlequin: That's where they keep the wagons and serpent-cages.
Young Man: Then I'll go back the way I came. [He starts to leave. Enter Clown.]
Clown: But where is he going? Ha, ha, ha!
Harlequin: He says he's going home.

The two of them engage in some slapstick business, at which the Young Man demands impatiently: "But would you please tell me what kind of joke this is? I was going to my house—I mean, not *my* house; to another house, to . . ."

Clown: [Interrupting.] To seek.
Young Man: Yes; because I have to. To seek.
Clown: [Happily.] Seek! Just turn around and you'll find it.

Now we hear the Typist singing offstage:

Where are you going, my love,
with the air in a glass
and the sea in a windowpane?

The Young Man stands with his back turned as Harlequin and the Clown creep away. There follows a love scene with the Typist, and her union with the Young Man seems assured.

At this point the curtains are opened on the miniature baroque theater midstage, and to our surprise we see the library setting of the first act, reproduced on a reduced scale. On it appears the First Mask, hysterically upset, who continually sniffs smelling salts to keep from fainting. She announces:

I have just abandoned the Count for good. He stayed behind with his son. [She descends the steps.] I am sure that he will die. But he loved me so! [She weeps. Speaking to the Typist:] Didn't you know? His child will die in the frost. I have abandoned him. Can't you see how happy I am? Can't you see how I laugh? [She weeps.] Now he will seek me everywhere. [On the floor.] I am going to hide in the blackberry bushes. [Loudly.] *In the blackberry bushes*. I talk like that because I don't want Arturo to hear me. [Loudly.] *I don't! I've already told you that I don't love you!* [Exit weeping.] You love me; but I don't love you.

Two servants dressed in blue livery bring out a pair of stools. Their faces are "exceedingly pale." Simultaneously John tiptoes across the stage of the miniature theater. The Typist ascends the steps connecting the small stage with the main stage, and it is apparent that she is now in control of the house, for she begins to order John about; and when the Young Man addresses her she demands of him (as he had of her in the first act), "Have you written the letters?" As they begin anew to make love, the Old Man reappears, this time dressed in blue and carrying a blood-soaked handkerchief. He is upset and observes closely the action on the miniature stage—which, at this point, is crossed by the Dead Child, as we hear a voice offstage screaming, "My son! My son!"

"Yes," says the Young Man, "my son. He is alive within me, like an ant alone in a closed box." Turning to the Typist, he pleads: "A little light for my son. Please. He is so small. . . . He flattens his little nose against the window of my heart, and yet he cannot breathe."

The First Mask appears onstage to cry, "My son!" Here the stage direction calls for "two more Masks" without, however, describing them; presumably they would form a trio with the First Mask. The three of them stand (like the Old Man) observing the action on the miniature stage.

The Typist suddenly remonstrates with the Young Man in an "authoritarian and harsh" manner: "Have you written the letters? It's not your son, it is I." She reproaches him for his past behavior toward her, and then says "passionately":

> I love you—but at a greater distance from you. I have fled so long now that I must contemplate the sea in order to evoke the tremor of your mouth. . . . You [however] have not the eyes to look upon me naked, nor the mouth to kiss my inexhaustible body. Leave me! I love you too much to be able to look upon you.

He takes the initiative, and as she yields to him the Clown and Harlequin, seated on the stools furnished them, make violin music— "a music of years, of unopened moons and oceans." ("Unopened" is here used in the same way that it would be applied to flowers which have not yet bloomed.) It seems that the lovers are on the verge of consummating their love, when the entire episode is undone in a moment by a simple—and quite unexpected—remark of the Typist. As she seems to have yielded herself totally, he says, "My love! I am yours!"—and she replies ("timidly"), "As soon as five years have passed!"

This is evidently a crucial remark, for the Young Man, stunned, accepts its finality, claps a hand to his brow and murmurs, "Ah!" The Old Man approves with a quiet "Bravo." The Clown and Harlequin repeat their "music of the years," of "unopened moons and seas"; "the shroud of the air" is "left behind." As John tiptoes out and covers the Typist with a large white cape, we hear the following:

> First Mask: The Count kisses the picture of me in my riding habit.
> Old Man: We'll not arrive, but we will go.
> Young Man: [Desperately, to the Clown:] The exit—whereabouts is it?
> Typist: [On the miniature stage, and as if in a dream.] My love, my love.
> Young Man: [Shuddering.] Show me the door.
> Clown: [Ironically, pointing left.] That way.
> Harlequin: [Pointing right.] That way.
> Typist: I'll wait for you, love! I'll wait for you! Come back soon!
> Harlequin: [Ironically.] That way.
> Young man: I'll sunder your cages and bindings. I can leap over the wall.
> Old Man: [Distressed.] This way.
> Young Man: I want to go back. Unhand me everyone!
> Harlequin: The wind remains.
> Clown: And the music of your violin.

This ends the first half of the last act, and the curtain falls as the Young Man desperately seeks the way back to his house.

Act III (Part 2)

When the curtain is rung up on the second half of the act, we are back in the library of the first act. The situation would seem to be reversed, however; for whereas in the beginning of the play the Young Man was waiting for the *Novia* to return from a long trip, now it is the Young Man who has been traveling. The stage directions call for open luggage to be scattered about the library, while to one side

we see the famous bridal gown on a headless and handless mannequin.
Enter the Valet and a Maid, talking about the Concierge:

> She's a concierge now, but she used to be a great lady. For a long
> time she lived with a wealthy Italian count, the father of the boy who
> was just buried. . . . That's where she gets her mania for living
> on a grand scale. That's why she spent everything she had on the
> child's burial suit and coffin.

At this point the Young Man enters, showing signs that he is about
to faint. He remarks that everything seems much smaller than he
remembered—the impression familiar to anyone who has revisited a
childhood scene. The Valet inquires solicitously if the master is feeling all right, and the Young Man replies rhetorically: "Does a
fountain feel all right spouting water? Answer."

> Valet: I don't know.
> Young Man: Does a weather vane feel all right turning with the
> wind?
> Valet: The master gives such strange examples . . . But I would
> ask (if master permits me) : Does the wind feel all right?
> Young Man: [Drily.] I am fine.

It appears that the Young Man must change into formal dress, and
the Valet informs him that the tail coat is laid out on the bed. The
Young Man reacts to this mention of his bed, for it is "so big" and
"so empty." He fondly recalls the little bed he slept in as a child:

> How comfortable it was. I remember that when I was a child, I saw
> an enormous moon rise behind the railing at the foot of the bed . . .
> or was it through the grille of the balcony? I don't know. Where is
> it?

The Valet tells him that he gave away the little bed—to his former
Typist. "The Young Man stands there lost in thought."

A moment later he is complaining that the air inside his house always seems rarified. The doorbell sounds, and as the Young Man
leaves to dress, the Valet lets in the three Card Players (or Gamblers).
They are dressed formally, and wear long, white satin capes. They
have come to "collect" the Young Man's life. Though the "collection"
takes the form of a card game which could presumably be either won
or lost by the Young Man, it appears to be a mere formality.

The three are telling anecdotes of persons who have managed to escape from them through trickery or under special circumstances. The First Player says that he once played cards with a young man in Venice who was on the point of having to play his Ace of Hearts—a Heart filled with blood:

> He played it, and when I went to pick it up. . . . He had an Ace of Cups overflowing, and he fled drinking from it, with two girls, down the Grand Canal.

The Third Player tells a similar anecdote concerning an old man with whom he played cards in India. Here again the opponent produced an unexpected supply of blood and managed to escape into the jungle at the last moment.

The Second Player recalls that a Swedish boy defeated them at the last moment by nearly blinding them with a great stream of blood. The three of them are agreed that they must be cautious at the present time, "even though neither the other woman nor the Typist will think to return for five years—*if they return at all*."

When the Young Man enters to play cards with his visitors, he is dressed so elegantly that they all compliment him on his appearance: he looks so fine "that he should never take those clothes off again."

> Third Player: There are times when our clothes look so well on us that we should never like to—
> Second Player: [Interrupting.]—that we can no longer tear them from our body.

The card game begins, and the Young Man, as he realizes that he is bound to lose, attempts to delay the final showdown; but his time has run out. He must play the last card—which is the Ace of Hearts. At the moment he puts it down, an illuminated Ace of Hearts appears reproduced on the bookshelves. The First Player draws a pistol and fires a silent "shot" at it (for the pistol is loaded with an arrow) at which point the Young Man begins to die. The Third Player brandishes a pair of scissors as if snipping a thread, and the three of them leave precipitately.

> Young Man: John. John. I must live.
> Echo: John. John.
> Young Man: I've lost everything.
> Echo: I've lost everything.
> Young Man: My love . . .
> Echo: Love.

Young Man: [On the sofa.] John.
Echo: John.
Young Man: Is there no . . .
Second Echo: [Farther away.] Is there no . . .
Young Man: No man here?
Echo: Here . . .
Second Echo: Here . . .

The Valet appears with a lighted candelabrum. The clock strikes twelve as the final curtain falls.

3. COMMENTARY

The first detail to be remarked is precisely the first one mentioned in the text: *biblioteca*. The library of the Young Man's house is the dominant setting of the play, but symbologically it would be unsatisfactory to attempt a simple, allegorical identification of this library with the Young Man's conscious mind, for an overly simple interpretation of this kind does an injustice to the subtleties of Lorca's intuitions about the human psyche—among which surely a primary one was his realization that not much was to be gained by talking about the psyche as if it consisted of two parts—a "conscious" and a "subconscious" mind.

We have seen that Lorca had a mythic grasp of reality, and this necessarily implies a belief in the transcendent reality of symbols. In his lecture on Góngora, he compares the creative act to a hunter's search within the depths of a deep, dark forest; here it is that one glimpses elements which (unlike elements of an "ordinary" dream) are dramatically unconnected with the facts of one's own personal life. Just as one has inherited a body, which means the capacity for a potential kind of physical behavior, so has one inherited a psyche, which means the capacity for a potential kind of symbolic behavior. Out of this is created a precinct, the circle of activity known as the personal psyche, consisting of one's ego-consciousness and one's personal unconscious—one's store of personal memories and repressed thoughts, all filed away and catalogued according to an intricate system of associative thought processes.

It is with such a precinct, then, that we can identify the symbol of the personal library; certainly care should be taken not to establish too strong a link between "library" and "reason." Libraries contain all sorts of books, and as the symbol for one's personal psyche the library is appropriate as the storehouse of all that was once conscious, and which has been stored away, theoretically accessible to reexamination.

The Young Man's attire (blue pajamas) is doubly significant. While we cannot conclude that he is asleep, we can minimally interpret "pajamas" as indicative of a lowered level of consciousness characterized by a free play of associative thought processes. It is the threshold where we saw the Gypsy girl, Preciosa.

Of greater significance, perhaps, is the color of the pajamas, since it is obvious that throughout the play a deliberate symbolic use is made of the color blue. It is the only color which achieves the status of motif, not only in the play *Five Years*, but perhaps throughout the poetry of Lorca.

Blue, as used by Lorca, is primarily the sky illuminated by the light of day. From this everything else flows: for blue means the vaulted ceiling of heaven energized by the presence of the sun which, as we have seen (in *Cicada!*), means both light and heat, both understanding and energy. The cicada, which we have discussed as a libido symbol for Lorca, fulfills itself and dies "beneath the blood of a heart entirely blue." It is really impossible to dissociate the blue sky from the warmth of the sun which illuminates it: blue sky and warm sun together make an indivisible unit—what Lorca's contemporary, Jorge Guillén, has called a *blue sun*.[6]

Shortly after the play begins, an electric storm breaks "outside" the house, and it is characterized by a suffused "bluish luminosity" and peals of thunder. Psychologically a storm is indicative of an inner commotion, since it signifies a violent displacement of energy, as H. G. Baynes has pointed out:

> The process of transition, in which a fundamental change of attitude is taking place, is frequently accompanied by dreams of storm and commotion. A reorientation of the vital attitude necessarily involves a great displacement of vital energy, and what is a storm of rain but a kinetic displacement of energy from a higher potential to a lower?[7]

This is precisely the manner in which the symbolic storm is used in the Grimm tale called "The Juniper Tree"; for there, when the wicked stepmother is about to be confronted by evidence of her crimes, she says, "I feel very low, just as if a great storm were coming." The "storm" is inward, and she is powerless to escape it: "And the mother stopped her ears and hid her eyes, and would neither see nor hear; nevertheless, the noise of a fearful storm was in her ears, and in her eyes a quivering burning as of lightning."[8]

In our play the Young Man of the blue pajamas senses that he is under attack from the blue storm liberated "outside" the house—i.e., beyond the threshold of the personal unconscious—and which ends by "invading" the scene, as Lorca describes it. This diffusion of blue lighting is a most ingenious way of representing symbolically the diffused chaos of libidinal energy. The conscious structure of the protagonist is temporarily abolished by the eruption of the blue storm, since the three characters onstage at this point (the Young Man, the Old Man, and the First Friend) abruptly hide themselves behind a black screen. This is to say that the conscious continuity of activity in the house is shattered by the stormy breakthrough of unconscious material; it is "blacked out" for the moment, whereupon the Dead Child and the Blue Cat dominate the scene. This indicates a fresh transformation, for the color blue has been "concentrated," or brought into perceptible focus by means of the cat form, while the violent displacement of the electrically charged libidinal storm represents the mechanism of the transformation.

The cat figure suggests a kind of archaic and relatively undifferentiated form of libido, comparable to the level symbolized by Hans's feline mistress in "The Poor Miller's Boy and the Cat." Lorca seems to emphasize this point by introducing an element of ambiguity concerning the sex of the Blue Cat. It is identified by the Child and in the stage directions as a male (*gato*), whereupon the animal calls attention to its "real" gender. The passage indicates not so much that the cat is "really" female, but rather that its gender is not self-evident.

The appearance of the Second Friend occasions the next metamorphosis of the color blue, for now we are confronted by an avowedly effeminate adolescent dressed in white, and wearing "enormous blue buttons" on his coat. The contradiction between his attire (basically masculine) and his behavior (grossly effeminate)[9] enables us to say at the very least that the development of the Young Man is characterized by a certain confusion concerning his psychological sexual differentiation, and possibly by a drive to avoid the spiritual limitations which adult monosexuality brings in its train.

Such is, in its main lines, the use of the blue motif in the first act of the play. Returning to the initial stage directions, we read that the Young Man is engaged in conversation with an Old Man who is dignified and serious, though not nearly so authoritative as his general appearance might lead us to expect. While the Young Man evidently respects him and believes him to be a trustworthy confidant, the elderly gentleman exercises little actual power over the lad's behavior. This would seem to establish the Old Man as a symbol of the protagonist's rational function and sense of reality *as defined by the society of which the Young Man is a part.*

Historically considered, "reason" and "reality" are notions which vary considerably from one society to the next. What the people of one culture and epoch think of as "real" and "reasonable" is by no means common to the generality of mankind; nonetheless, this does not prevent them from equating their collective consciousness with "reality." And the fact that this collective consciousness is culturally inherited and represents a world view of long standing is what is appropriate in embodying it in the figure of a serious and dignified Old Man.[10]

At the same time, one who is intensely aware of the inward existence of a transpersonal unconscious cannot grant much authority to the Old Man, and such is the situation of the protagonist here, who progressively detaches himself from the elder's sphere of influence, eventually to "wound" him and desert him entirely.

The opening conversation of the play deals with the idea of "saving candy for later." Because this is closely associated with the conversation to follow concerning the Young Man's attitude toward his fiancée, it behooves us to inquire into the meaning, or psychological stance, implied by the habit of saving one's candy for later.

In the child's world candy occupies a special place among eatables, for it is sheer enjoyment: it represents eating as an end in itself. Now if the Young Man had the habit of saving his candy for later—i.e., not eating it on the spot—it seems to me that his enjoyment of candy has been displaced from the actual eating of it to the *anticipation* of eating it. When he says, "I always used to save my candy for later," he is saying in effect, "I was in the habit of enjoying prolonged anticipation."

Having enjoyed a thing once—a thing which was expendable— the next time one possesses it, its expendability may give pause. If

I have eaten candy in the past, and have none now, my thoughts about it will appear as nostalgia, as a sense of loss; and if I am given another piece of candy, I may hesitate before devouring it on the spot: "If I eat it now, I will only renew my sense of loss; whereas if I save it till later, I can look forward to eating it anytime I choose." In a sense, I am having my candy and eating it. *I am its master*, i.e., master of my own enjoyment of life, because I now control the rationing of it. With my candy safely stored away, I need not be overcome with nostalgia by thinking of candy. I have deterred that threat, for now I am free to take out my cache and revel in my possession of it, remembering how good it tastes, and anticipate eating it . . . later.

All this suggests that anticipation has an important role to play in the value one attaches to experience. It wards off a sense of incompleteness and, at the same time, absolves one from the necessity of materially renewing the experience . . . till later. The hoarded "candy" thus becomes a kind of talismanic substitute for material experience.

The reference to candy is followed in our play by a discussion of *reminiscing*, of which the Old Man approves, as long as one "remembers previously," he says, which means remembering before the event. Now the trick of prolonging anticipation by "saving candy till later" is precisely that kind of experience-control of which the Old Man speaks; and if one believes, as he does, that one *ought* to remember in this way, one's attitude can have far-reaching effects on one's entire approach to the living of life.

At this point in the dialogue the clock strikes six and the weeping Typist make her first appearance. Since it is she who is in charge of the Young Man's correspondence, it seems reasonable to associate her with the persona-function—the social "mask," the "personality," the role player mediating between the psyche and the outside world. She is the only symbol in the play whose manifest content can be so rigorously identified: the typist (or stenographer) has as her job the preparation of communications to the world outside, in accordance with the formal standards developed and demanded by that world, and this is a tolerably accurate description of the function filled by the persona, which maintains conventional social relationships for better or for worse.

The Typist is in love with the protagonist and is eager to marry him—that is, to enjoy a principal role in the house of the psyche.

Psychologically this means that the Young Man ostensibly has a choice between two brides, the Fiancée and the Typist—a fact of general importance which will require detailed consideration.

The extent to which any man identifies with his persona-function is an exceedingly subtle question. The less I think that my persona represents the "real" me, the more I am apt to think of it as hollow, superficial, hypocritical, and the like. The Young Man is evidently hostile toward his Typist, and this can certainly be attributed in part to the unusual fact that she is a woman: that is to say, that even though a man may accommodate himself to playing the role of a woman in certain circles (the phenomenon is not at all uncommon), nevertheless, the possession of an effeminate social mask can create difficulties and disturbances which would render "her" existence a mixed blessing, at the very least. One's hostility toward the persona-function would *normally* indicate an antipathy to social role playing; but we are not now dealing with normal circumstances, and so the Young Man's apparent dislike of his Typist seems not to be directed toward her "sociability" as such, but rather toward her general social inacceptability. His inner attitude has been tempered and modified out of obedience to the demands of social decorum, so that his genuine "feminine" feelings have been twisted by society into "effeminate" feelings.

The first appearance of the Typist is marked by silence. The clock then strikes, the Young Man complains of the humidity (the gathering storm), and the conversation centers on the Fiancée, whom the protagonist seems to have met only briefly, after which she went on an extended journey. Her return is imminent, and is to be celebrated by the wedding.

Symbolically a marriage represents the initiation into a new world, and hopefully a consequent spiritual enrichment of some kind: a new whole is created out of the union of bride and groom. In the case of the Young Man, union with the Typist would lead him into a world of human relationships; "union with" the persona-function means adapting oneself to it as the vehicle of one's social "personality." In this sense it fulfills a mediating role by means of which the idiosyncrasies of the impersonal, multifarious world "out there" and the idiosyncrasies of one's own personal psyche find a common meeting ground. It is this mediative function which characterizes the role of the anima-figure also, who, in the present play would seem to be related to the character of the Fiancée.

We have already discussed in a general way some aspects of the theory of the anima-image apropos of *Girl Drowned in the Well*, where we recalled that it represented those tendencies of the psyche which the male has learned to repress in the process of developing a monosexual personality. At this point in our discussion a practical example of the anima-phenomenon might clarify its dynamics—and there is hardly any better example than the occurrence of what is usually called "love at first sight."

By lucky chance a young man encounters one day a woman the very sight of whom stirs him to his depths, and with blinding rapidity he falls desperately in love. Suddenly he finds himself experiencing what appears to be an entirely new facet of his psyche. He has new sensibilities, new emotional capacities, and different ambitions—all because of a chance encounter with the one young lady of the world (it seems) who has the mysterious and extraordinary power to work this transforming magic, and to thrust him into an entirely new world of profound experience.

If this "magic" can be at all accounted for, we must have recourse to the phenomenon of the psychological projection. The physical appearance of the beloved has captured the young man's attention because she is the material embodiment of a specific force operating unconsciously within his own psyche. Her looks and behavior have "reminded" him of something deep within himself which he had "forgotten." He was reared to act and think "like a man," which means that from a very early age he learned to inhibit modes of acting and thinking which in his culture were not held to be appropriate to men. The consequence was the development of a psychological uni-sexuality: "half" of his psychic potential was repressed—until he met by chance a woman (to him, "the" woman) whose individuality (like a long-forgotten word) suddenly "reminded" him of his re-pressed half.

But this is not a reflective phenomenon, of course. The woman does not simply "remind" him of himself; she symbolizes it. "He"—that is to say his ego-consciousness—is not aware of what she symbolizes. He cannot stand to her in a subject-object relationship, just as in the dream one's sense of reality is somehow blocked. There is an *apparent* subject-object relationship, of course, of the oneiric kind, just as in a dream we apprehend a specific force within ourselves in terms of a dream personage with whom we can converse. I, the dreamer, am the subject; he, the dream personage, is the object.

So it is with the beloved. She, as a person in her own right, is obviously not the object of the young man's love; indeed, how could she be? We are dealing with love at first sight, and so, by definition, he does not even know her. But as the individual embodiment of an unconscious force (cf. the Blue Cat), as a kind of epiphany, she is perceived as a symbol; which is to say, a specific image in whose urgent significance the beholder believes heart and soul. It is here that the profound *personal* importance of the symbol can be felt, as the image that enables an unconscious force to be mobilized into consciousness; that enables consciousness to enter into union with it; that makes it possible for a *wedding* to take place, precisely.

It is clear that ego-consciousness and rationality have little to say in the matter of love at first sight. What appears to be an alien power is suddenly upon us, promiscuously invading our ego-structure, as if by surprise attack. If we manage to keep our wits about us we can, of course, assimilate this new experience and eventually make it a permanent addition to our conscious life. In this sense, love at first sight is no different from what has come to be popularly known as a "psychedelic experience," whereby the conscious mind is expanded, or enriched, by the addition to it of new material raised from the unconscious.

This "mind-expansion," then, is accomplished by means of the symbol, whether this appears to us in the form of another person (or object) mysteriously endowed with power over us, or whether the symbol is raised directly into consciousness in the form of some kind of religious or artistic "inspiration." As a *psychological* (rather than esthetic or mythic) problem, the symbol may appear in adolescence as part of the search for a conscious identity, as it does in *Five Years;* for here we are confronted by a young protagonist whose precariously organized ego-system makes it impossible for him to have any dependable and continuous sense of reality. One's sense of what is "real" and what is "unreal" depends crucially upon where the line is drawn separating the conscious mind from the unconscious.

The protagonist of *Five Years* undoubtedly reflects Lorca's own habitual drive for contact with creative elements from the unconscious. Here Lorca has made it the issue of an entire drama; but as an issue, it already appears in résumé, in the form of a stark little poem written in the early twenties entitled *Suicide*.[11] There, Lorca tells of a young man who gradually forgot who he was,

> And when he took off his gloves,
> soft ashes fell from his hands.

His clock appeared to be stopped. He felt "rigid" and "geometrical"; and with an ax he smashed his mirror, whereupon a great stream of darkness flooded his room. Lorca appends an explanatory comment to the title: "Perhaps it was because you hadn't learned your Geometry." The young man felt *invaded* by "geometry," as it were, but could not assimilate it, could not identify his life with it. To be imprisoned within the repetitive and monotonous routine of an ego-consciousness effectively sealed off from the world of the unconscious was evidently something like a living death to Lorca, comparable to the desperate feelings engendered in the incorrigible schoolboy forced to apply himself to his lessons so that he can "learn his Geometry" and grow up to be like the adults who invented schools—the adults for whom living has been reduced to a series of demonstrable theorems.

Now in similar fashion, the Young Man of *Five Years* appears to be "forgetting who he is," and this is certainly related to the *absence* of the fiancée—a symbol of the creative unconscious which progressively disappears from our conscious life as we leave our childhood farther and farther behind. The fiancée has been away on a long trip —i.e., repressed—and the protagonist, in a search for a viable identity with which to embark on his adulthood, is not prepared to forsake the numinosity, the "magic" of unconscious realms, for the dubious values of a life structured and limited by a socially obedient ego-consciousness. The numinous reality of childhood is dimly remembered by him in the symbolic form of a *Novia* who has been missing these past five years. Surely she will return so that he can look forward to an adult future rich in spiritual promise! Surely the principal *mediator* in his life will be the one from the "other" world!

Whether or not one wishes to argue concerning the status of an unconscious world which is transpersonal, Lorca's belief in the existence of such a world can hardly be denied. For most of us "reality" consists of (1) the outside world, (2) our ego-consciousness, and (3) our personal unconscious (the "subconscious" mind); and it is for this reason, I think, that all attempts which have been made so far to deal psychologically with the poetry and drama of Lorca have been ineffectual—because they rest on a crude and inadequate distinction between a "conscious" mind and a "subconscious" mind.

Lorca's characteristic feeling for the reality lived by children suggests more than anything else his recognition of the great world lying beyond the personal psyche: a great world buried deep within us, as vast as the universe around us, and not easy to establish contact with, once one has passed into the world of civilized adults. In one of his lectures Lorca tells us that the creative act involves a journey to a forest "far, far away":

> The poet who is going to make a poem (I know from personal experience) has the vague feeling that he is going hunting at night in a very remote forest.[12]

Remote (*"lejanísimo"*) can only mean remote from the personal elements of the psyche. It is the realm of the *absent* in which the Gypsy girl, Preciosa, suddenly found herself. It is the extraordinary realm of the child, who lives

> . . . within an inaccessible poetic world closed off to rhetoric, imagination (*that* go-between!), and fantasy; with his nerve centers exposed, he inhabits a region of horror and profound beauty. . . .[13]

If that world is closed to imagination and fantasy, it is because it cannot be willed into existence, like a daydream. It is a numinous world: it seems to have an objectivity about it (like the world of nocturnal dreams) which is so impressive that the personal psyche is dwarfed by comparison, and reels back as before a *numen*.

To lose contact with this world, then, was (for Lorca) to lose the source of nourishment. The *need* to live the numinous life afforded by contact with the transpersonal unconscious can of itself constellate a symbol, which is the anima-image in the aspect of a man's *soul*, or his *soul-bearer*.[14] For apart from his social and professional ambitions and aims (characterized by the attitude of his persona), he has also a spirit: not a "soul" in the religious sense, but an inward attitude toward life which will determine what he wants to achieve for himself spiritually; what kind of inner self he would like to strive for—if, indeed, the persona does not make him forget entirely the possibility of such a quest. It may happen that one's soul-striving appears now as an individual vocation (cf. the girl drowned in the well), and again as a general human need not necessarily related to one's own special talents; for while one may, via the persona-function, be involved with a particular society or cultural framework, the striving toward contact with the transpersonal unconscious involves one with the entire human race—that is, with its whole history of living in the bosom of Mother Earth.

This collective unconscious that we carry within is, so to speak, a nonmaterial form of the Earth Mother herself.[15] We have already noted that, in order to establish a constructive communication with her, the personal psyche must work through a mediator, just as it communicates with the external world through the mediation of a differentiated social stance—the persona. At the unconscious level, however, the mediator must possess qualities denied to the modest and somewhat compliant persona-function; for while the latter is created by means of the repressive demands of social canons, the inward mediation has *liberation* as its goal: the liberation of repressed elements which the man experiences as a "soul," or helpful female. She is a *mediator* precisely because she possesses attributes of both parties to the undertaking: like the Mother idea, she is an instinctual guide; like the personal psyche, she is an *individual*. She is a soul mate, whether freely recognized as an inwardly liberating symbol, or whether naively and joyfully projected onto the person of a beloved woman.

The anima-figure is readily recognizable in the diaphanous symbolism of the fairy tale, where contact with deep levels of the unconscious is sometimes depicted in the motif of the secret chamber. In the Grimm version of "Faithful John," for example, the Old King gives his trustworthy servant instructions concerning the tutelage of the young Prince and makes the following remarkable statement:

> After my death, you must lead him through the whole castle, into all the chambers, halls, and vaults, and show him the treasures that in them lie; but the last chamber in the long gallery, in which lies hidden the picture of the Princess of the Golden Palace, you must not show him. If he were to see that picture, he would directly fall into so great a love for her, that he would faint with the strength of it, and afterwards for her sake run into great dangers. . . .[16]

It is in this concept of the personal soul-image, the anima (> Sp. *alma*, "soul") as a bridge across the chasm separating the personal psyche from the transpersonal unconscious wherein we can find a means of identifying the role played by the *Novia*—the betrothed, the fiancée, the sweetheart—in *Five Years*. In the opening conversation between the protagonist and the Old Man, we have seen how their talk (ostensibly about the *Novia*) actually centers on the psychological meaning of reality. The Young Man is concerned with the kind of reality that awaits him as an adult, and his aspirations are bound up with the figure of the *Novia*. Here we are not saying that the *Novia* is "only" a symbol; we are saying, rather, that she is *nothing less than a symbol*—the symbol of a future characterized by a constant spiritual Becoming.

In his discussion with the protagonist the Old Man recognizes change, or Becoming, as characteristic of external reality, which constantly produces within us a sense of loss. The Young Man adamantly rejects attempts to make him recognize the *Novia* as subject to change, and he seems determined to hang on to a kind of reality rooted in Being. He needs an unchanging reality upon which he can *focus* steadily: "that's the word," he says.

But is there such a reality? If this is understood to be a psychological question, then we must answer it in the affirmative—for there is indeed such a thing as a permanent spiritual acquisition, the permanent possession of a symbol. Realities which enter consciousness from the world outside are naturally subject to the mortal conditions of that world, whereas realities which enter consciousness from the transpersonal unconscious can become indestructible components of the personal psyche. The symbol, as a mediator between myself and the transpersonal unconscious, is my key to the world of spiritual expansion; but it functions by virtue of my ability to *focus* upon it, to prevent its loss in a welter of trivial Becoming, characteristic of external reality. The Young Man (like Lorca himself) seeks a soul mate—a literal soul mate, and not a substitute in the form of a psychological projection.

The spiritual reason for the quest and the discovery in the form of a symbolic woman who causes great anguish to the Young Man can easily be misunderstood by anyone who is tempted to account for Lorca's symbolism in terms of his biography. Since this tendency does exist, it is needful, I think, to point out that too much attention has been given to Lorca's own personal and ambiguous attitude toward sexuality. Critically relevant is the manner in which Lorca employed sexuality as a means of grasping and stating deeply subjective spiritual problems. If we think that *Five Years* is simply a play about a confused young man trying to find himself by facing the problem of love and marriage, we will shortly find ourselves equally confused.

It seems evident that the majority of men who raise their anima-function to consciousness do so by projecting it upon a "soul mate." We can say that it seems evident because long-term contact with the creative unconscious is a rare phenomenon. Most of us are not deeply introspective, and are very little inclined to mobilize the energy necessary to address ourselves to the inward search for a soul or to the task of expanding our consciousness through the integration of unconscious contents. Nevertheless, the fact that these contents are latent does not mean, of course, that they play no part in the economy of the psyche. The man who has a high disregard, or even scorn, for the feminine side of his psyche is not thereby free and independent of it, for then it may very well happen that he will seek a woman "not for an evolved relationship, but so that she may carry and live out his own unlived feminine side."[17]

The *Novia* of *Five Years* represents what is primarily an inward, not an outward, problem. The "outside" world, as such, does not really occupy a place in our play. Through the figure of the *Novia* we are aware of the confusion and anxiety of the Young Man seeking to construct a working relationship between his ego-consciousness and his soul. He has glimpsed the possibility of creating a self—an inner life based on contact with the creative unconscious; and (like all of us) as he passes through adolescence ("five years")[18] finds himself drifting farther and farther away from his source, the great feminine unconscious, the *Magna Mater* in whose bosom the little child experiences reality. Every man, as he matures, must escape from the grasp of the mother; he must learn a new way of relating to the female, and this is typically depicted in myth and fairy tale as a struggle with the dragon-serpent inhabiting a cave. The chthonic dragon guards a treasure, or holds captive a virgin. The hero struggles with the dragon and defeats it, thereby coming into possession of the treasure, or liberating the captive virgin—the anima-figure:

> The transformation which the male undergoes in the course of the dragon fight includes a change in his relation to the female, symbolically expressed in the liberation of the captive from the dragon's power. . . . the feminine image extricates itself from the

grip of the Terrible Mother, a process known in analytical psychology as the crystallization of the anima from the mother archetype.[19]

Once this has occurred, the hero "lives happily ever after," which is to say that his psychic development has attained to a new level safely beyond the threat of regression. He has a new spiritual constellation which is permanently his.

Now the Young Man of *Five Years* has glimpsed the possibility of union with the soul-image, the realization of which would mean the liberation of enormous spiritual potential. It would mean the possibility of a spiritual life as richly endowed as that of . . . a Federico García Lorca. But as the Young Man approaches his maturity, the chances for permanent union with the soul-image become more and more remote. The older we grow, the farther away from childhood we are, the more repressed we become. The unconscious ceases to be a shining and numinous world, and comes more and more to be overlaid with the ugly crust of the personal unconscious, laden with all kinds of material adjudged as unacceptable to our "socialized" and inhibited cultural self. The Young Man believes that he still loves that soul-image which he glimpsed long ago, and he also believes that he is looking forward to her joyous return, when they will be married.

One may say that he *believes* this, but the Old Man makes him face the issue more squarely by asking abruptly, "What's going on in the street?" It is here that the Young Man complains:

> Noise, always noise, dust, heat, offensive odors. It disturbs me that anything to do with the street should enter my house. [A long moan is heard. Pause.] John, close the window.

This passage is laden with significance if we keep in mind that the "outside," in the context of the play, does not refer to external reality, but rather to the unconscious. This will be demonstrated explicitly in the third act, where we see that the house is actually built in the middle of a huge forest—which contains, nevertheless, roads and streets. Thus, though the Young Man allegedly looks forward to a union with his soul-image, when the Old Man tests this attitude, a negative quality is revealed. We recall that the Old Man begins his probing by asking the Young Man about his habitation: "Is this nice?" The Young Man replies that it is not.

> Old Man: Aren't you distressed when the moment of departure
> arrives? Aren't you distressed by events, by what is about to
> happen?
> Young Man: Yes, yes. Don't speak to me of that.

And then the question which elicits complaints about the street "outside."

Psychologically this series of questions reveals the real state of affairs. The Young Man desires to be oriented inwardly—*but he expects his soul-image to come to him.* She is "away," on a long journey, and he rather naively expects her to return so that they can be united, whereas myths and fairy tales (authorities in these matters!) are in common agreement that the youth must himself go in quest of the virgin or the treasure. It would seem that the Old Man (hence the protagonist) suspects the truth of the matter: that the Young Man has not got a stable ego-consciousness adequate to the task of achieving his spiritual goal. Consequently this interrogation tells us that (1) the protagonist is dissatisfied with the present state of his psychic house, (2) change, transformation, and setting out upon the quest distress him, and (3) contact with unconscious material—passage through the personal unconscious—is disgusting to him.

This disgust felt by the Young Man is familiar enough to all of us. Any kind of inner spiritual achievement is bound to come about through descent into the turbid waters of the personal unconscious, since they stand between us and the shining realm beyond. We like to fancy that "spirituality" lies elsewhere—"up," perhaps, in the dazzling purity of the stratosphere—but this is a fantastic illusion.

> "Spirit" always seems to come from above, while from below comes
> everything that is sordid and worthless. For people who think in
> this way, spirit means highest freedom, a soaring over the depths,
> deliverance from the prison of the chthonic world, and hence a
> refuge for all those timorous souls who do not want to become
> anything different. . . . The unconscious is the psyche that reaches
> down from the daylight of mentally and morally lucid consciousness
> into the nervous system that for ages has been known as the
> "sympathetic."[20]

Since the Young Man thinks of the *Novia* by association with the childish habit of "saving candy till later," and since he believes that she will return to him of her own volition, the suspicion is raised that he has not gone beyond thinking of her as a wish-fulfilling fantasy. She is something to be possessed, held in abeyance, and not to be used purposively; something to be saved . . . for later.

If he came into possession of her he could "use" her in one of two ways, each of which is described by the Old Man, who asks, "Are you afraid to flee? To fly? To extend your love over all heaven?" That is to say, he could project her outwardly, find her embodiment in a real, live woman, and fall in love. But the Young Man cannot face this thought; he buries his face in his hands and cries, "I love her too much!" For then he would be forsaking the anima by projecting her upon another woman, who would then "live out his own unlived feminine side" for him—thus avoiding the issue of his own inward Becoming.

But then the Old Man states the alternative: "Are you afraid to concentrate your love, to make it cutting and tiny within your own breast?" This is the deep dedication to love of the anima-figure, which means concentrated devotion to her as the means to an end—to her mediation with unconscious forces which, as they are integrated into the personal psyche, create spiritual transformations which an untransformed consciousness (such as that of the Young Man) could only anticipate with terror, since to it, "transformation" means "destruction."

Hence the Young Man is aware of three spiritual possibilities: he can externalize his spiritual problem; he can pursue an inward transformation; or he can "save his candy for later": hold the anima figure in abeyance and deceive himself into thinking that he is comfortably in control of his anticipated joy. This last is his preference, for it is temporizing, putting off the crisis, and justifies his waiting for "five years." He attempts to consider the matter as settled. "The fact is that I am in love with her, and I want to be in love, just as in love as she is with me, and that's why I can wait five years in anticipation of wrapping her shining tresses about my neck one night."

Actual union with the anima-figure would mean, naturally, the beginning of a transformation: a new life of wedded happiness. This is the meaning of her appearance in the form of a bride, or *novia*. And so the Old Man challenges the protagonist to identify her as such. When the Young Man refers to her as his "girl," the Old Man says, "Call her your bride. I dare you!" But the Young Man shrinks from this, for it would require him to think of the union as the beginning of a transforming process, whereas he labors under the fear of embarking upon the quest which would require of him the courage to cut loose from the tenuous hold on "reality" which his feebly developed ego-consciousness represents.

The initial conversation is terminated by the Old Man's final words of encouragement:

> . . . we will . . . remain here . . . and wait. Because anything else is to die on the spot, and it's more beautiful to think that tomorrow we will still see the hundred horns of gold with which the sun raises the clouds.

This confirms the Young Man's belief that one can lead a satisfactory life on an anticipatory basis—a piece of temporizing which has the small merit of relieving his anxiety, for which he is exceedingly grateful. He holds out his hand to the Old Man and exclaims by way of bidding him farewell, "Thank you! Thank you! For everything."

The lacrymose Typist makes another brief appearance, followed immediately by the arrival of the orgiastic First Friend. Because he represents an aspect of the Young Man's own psyche, it seems to me that his entirely uninhibited conversation—obsessively lewd—and his behavior—he is given to handling the Young Man (rubbing noses, tickling, wrestling)—allow us to conclude that he embodies the autoerotic tendencies of the protagonist. He notices that certain pictures are not on display, and asks, "Whereabouts in the house are the pictures of the girls you go to bed with?" and then playfully threatens to cane the Young Man. This episode seems to allude clearly enough to the erotic fantasies which inevitably accompany autoerotic activity (beating with a cane). Further, to judge by the First Friend's description of his "conquests," it would seem that the autoerotic play is obsessive: "Yesterday I made three conquests, and, since the previous day I had made two, and one today, well. . . ."

The Young Man, in spite of his initial disgust at the appearance of the First Friend, is inevitably drawn into his sphere of influence and begins to wrestle playfully with him. The Old Man reappears briefly and the scene makes him furious. He says that he has returned because he will forget his hat—and then corrects himself: he *forgot* his hat. This momentary reappearance in the midst of the playful wrestling is akin to admonitory feelings of guilt. The protagonist "remembers" that he has a thinking function (i.e., it comes back into the room) whose sound influence is at this moment being threatened with extinction (he "will forget" his hat)—rather, it has in fact been extinguished for the nonce (he *forgot* his hat).

This autoerotic activity, which can awaken a profoundly disturbing sense of guilt, is brought to a crisis: offstage a great crash of breaking glass is heard. Bearing in mind that "offstage" means "deep within the unconscious," we can understand the Young Man's desire to seal himself off from chaotic disturbances of this kind, keeping himself safe by means of repression. His response is automatic: he orders his valet to close the windows.

The First Friend looks forward to the gathering storm—an attitude consonant with his Dionysiac, or counter-Apollonian, character. He has aligned himself with forces which he would see unleashed willy-nilly. The Young Man tries to shut out the storm, saying, "This house is mine and no one is going to come in." The First Friend recognizes, however, that simple determination is of no avail. "Anybody" who so desires will come into the house—"not here," he says, meaning the library, "but under your bed," which is to say, in the absence of willful and conscious control.

We continue to hear the peals of thunder, and as they grow louder the First Friend demands that repressive mechanisms be abolished: "Open the window!" he says. We hear a final crack of thunder, and the stage is suffused by a "bluish luminosity," signifying the eruption into consciousness of deeply repressed material. It has gathered to itself enough libido to dominate the psychic stage autonomously, and the other psychic functions are repressed (they retire behind the black screen).

The extraordinary scene which follows is played out between the Dead Child and the Blue Cat. In our discussion of the Grimm story "The Miller's Boy and the Cat," we have already suggested that the cat is the embodiment of the relatively undifferentiated instinctual energy of the feminine unconscious. If we say "relatively" undifferentiated, it is by comparison with the highly differentiated ego-consciousness only; for by comparison with the "blue storm"—disorganized, chaotic energy—the Cat represents a specific constellation.

The Cat is dying and the Child is dead, by which we may understand (what we already knew) that what they represent is inaccessible for use by ego-consciousness. Unlike the miller's boy, the Young Man has not known how to remain in friendly contact with instinct. The Child and the Cat have both suffered destruction, each at the hands of a force a step above him in the hierarchy of the psyche: the Cat has been attacked by children, and the Child has been "attacked" by adults—since we are evidently to conclude that there is a relationship between the Child's First Communion suit and the fact that his heart stopped. That is to say, his "collectivization" via initiation into organized religion is here seen negatively as part of the process whereby primitive libidinal potential is "civilized"—i.e., depotentiated—little by little.

These two figures, like the cicada of Lorca's early poem, are elementary chthonic symbols, which means that they are opposed to the uranic spirituality represented by the Church. The Child longs to live with Mother Earth,

> . . . not heaven. Hard earth,
> filled with crickets that sing,
> with grasses that sway. . . .
> I want to be a child, a child!

The Child and the Cat fall into oblivion once more as the three characters behind the screen emerge fanning themselves. The fan symbol will appear again in the second act, and it is apparent that Lorca attached no small importance to it. "To fan oneself" can be assimilated to the general idea of self-fertilization, or creative interaction between consciousness and the unconscious. That is to say, by my own efforts I can activate a wind (*pneuma*) by means of which my own spirit (*pneuma*) is refreshed. When we see the three characters appear from behind the screen, each of them fanning himself with an appropriately colored fan, we may understand this to be a struggle on the part of each element to maintain its own autonomy, to maintain a share of libido.

The three-way conversation which follows turns into an argument as the First Friend questions the wisdom of "waiting five years." He advocates immediate exploitation of all psychic possibilities: the very moment one becomes aware of a new psychological attitude, one should implement it at the first opportunity, just as a boy (for example) might begin experimenting with heterosexuality at the very onset of puberty. What is the point of letting the fruit ripen? "I would rather eat it green—or better yet, cut the flower to wear in my lapel."

The Old Man, as representative of the collective consciousness, cannot countenance hedonistic gratification of primary impulses. At the same time, however, he cannot be accused of recommending brutal repression as an acceptable alternative:

> All my life I have struggled to bring light into the darkest places. And when anyone has tried to twist the neck of the dove, I stayed his hand and helped the dove to fly.

This is the process of "sublimation," whereby collective spiritual norms are substituted for the unpredictable impulses of the individual. The First Friend counters by saying, "And naturally the hunter has died of hunger!" which he evidently considers to be a crushing reply. (Since the motif of the hunter appears with special significance in Lorca, it will be considered in some detail apropos of the hunting horns in the third act.) When the Old Man defends collective "sublimation" of the individual impulse, the First Friend objects because the individual is thereby "collectivized," or "standardized." An individually unique psychic adventure is denied him: the "hunter"—the one who journeys into the dark forest in quest of food—dies of hunger while the life of the individual is played out within the safe and sterile limits set by the "sublimated" canons of the collective consciousness.

Looking at the matter in this way, it is not difficult to understand why the Young Man says here, "Then long live hunger!" since he himself is loath to undertake the hunting expedition into the dangerous forest. Spiritual inertia is preferable to the risk of losing one's identity entirely in an effort to become something different—an individuated personality.

When the Dead Child and the Blue Cat were raised to consciousness, we pointed out that they were to be seen as symbolic of psychic regression—the return to an archaic and outmoded psychic model. This kind of return, or relapse, is a necessary consequence of spiritual inertia: if I cannot go forward, I will find myself falling back on old habits and ways. It is this sort of regression which is now stimulated by the cry of "Long live hunger!"—stimulated in the form of the Second Friend, the outstanding regressive figure of the play, who enters echoing the last words of the Young Man:

> Yes, long live hunger, when there is toast, oil, and afterwards sleep. A long sleep. An endless sleep. I have heard you.

This is the ultimate expression of spiritual inertia: a life of uroboric bliss.

By his appearance and behavior the Second Friend shows that he occupies an intermediate place between the Dead Child and the Young Man:

> He is dressed in white. He wears an impeccable woolen suit, and gloves and shoes of the same color. If this role cannot be played by a very young actor, it should be played by a girl. The suit should be of an exceedingly exaggerated cut; it must have enormous blue buttons, and the vest and tie must be of ruffled lace.

He indicates by his general demeanor and conversation that he is strongly bound to the mother image, and thinks principally in terms of regression to his source. Chronologically he would seem to represent the early adolescence of the protagonist, the point at which the latter began his "five-year wait."

The adolescent's problem vis-à-vis the female consists, of course, in detaching himself from the mother and establishing a new relation with women. The Second Friend tells of an abortive attempt made by him to isolate for himself, out of the rain, a tiny "rain-woman"; this was when he was only one year old, he says, meaning a year or so preceding the "five years" of adolescence. Woman, to him, is nothing else than a diminutive copy of the Earth Mother from whom he is unwilling to cut himself loose. The song of the little rain-woman becomes "his" song, and it expresses the yearning to return to the source.

It is the Second Friend who, with his rain song, dominates the stage at the end of the first act, as the Young Man sits inertly drumming on the tabletop. This closing scene prophesies the final scene of the play, for (as we shall see) both are dramatic variants of the same idea: capitulation to inertia, and a shrinking back from the fearful chaos with which the task of Becoming threatens to swamp the fragile personality of the Young Man.

As the opening scene of the second act begins, we realize almost immediately that it is built around the idea of immense quantities of libido unleashed and operative in the figures of the *Novia* and the Rugby Player. In our discussion of the *Novia* in connection with the anima figure, we noted that the latter characteristically appears in conjunction with the mythical hero, since she is the *raison d'être* of the hero's existence. It is his goal to rescue her, to release her from captivity; to awaken her; and to make her active in his life. We pointed out at the same time that the Young Man's notion of the *Novia* contradicted the traditional delineation of the anima figure, in that he believed it possible to sit and wait for her to put in an appearance.

A likely source for this attitude is to be found, perhaps, in the anecdote of the Second Friend, who tells how he once "captured" a tiny rain-woman—but unlike the liberated anima-figure (who leads the hero out of the embrace of the mother and into a free and equal relationship with woman) the little rain-woman exercised a regressive influence over the Second Friend and led him to yearn for a return to his maternal origin.

In the present fantasy the hero and the damsel have found each other, and the attraction is irresistible. The whole scene may be seen as a wish fulfillment in which the Young Man assigns to himself the heroically libidinal role, and it terminates when the "real" he (i.e., the inadequate he) intrudes upon the scene.

That the Rugby Player is a fantasy version of the Young Man himself is corroborated by the fact that when the latter attempts to confront the *Novia*, she is taken aback by his appearance, because she had him confused with the virile athlete:

> Novia: Weren't you taller?
> Young Man: No.
> Novia: Didn't you have a violent smile?
> Young Man: No.
> Novia: Didn't you play rugby?
> Young Man: Never.
> Novia: Didn't you ride bareback and kill three thousand pheasants in a single day?[21]

Because of the frankly erotic form taken by her libidinal impulses, we can see that the *Novia* is not essentially different from the libidinal First Friend. While she is part of a wish-fulfilling fantasy, at the same time the Young Man would like to see an essential link between her and the earlier forms of his libidinal joy; for he tells her:

> Suddenly, while I was coming up the stairs, there came to mind all the songs that I had forgotten, and I wanted to sing them all at once.

His approach to her room occasions the release of a sense of life that he has not experienced for years—the song of life which sounds continually in pre-adolescent ears. This suggests her ideal role, that of mediator, the one who places us in contact with vitality itself by meeting us beyond the double barrier of ego and intellect.

This contact with vitality is suggested by the references to life-blood. The *Novia's* maid tells her that she had a boy friend who squeezed her so tightly that her rings cut her and made her bleed, and subsequently the *Novia* applies this to herself. The sadistic bloodletting is a sign of violent passion, but the Young Man's arrival has been cold and passionless, and so she asks him rhetorically, "Where is even a single drop of blood?" The Young Man replies, "I'll spill my blood for you if you like," to which she screams, "I'm not talking about your blood! I'm talking about mine!" The *Novia* cannot "marry" the hero—i.e., become an operative factor in his life —except by being the object of his own liberated libido. He does not give his blood to her, but rather summons all his energy to uniting with her, and releases her vitality. It is she who is destroyed in the consummation, for she is summoned into existence to be incorporated into the personality of the hero:

> The story of the hero, as set forth in the myths, is the history of [the] . . . self-emancipation of the ego, struggling to free itself from the power of the unconscious and to hold its own against overwhelming odds.[22]

The anima-figure is not a "thing," but the symbol of a tendency, or Becoming. The symbol rises up, bringing with it new possibilities from the depths; it gives birth to these, and so fulfills the function of mediator. She does not exist in her own right, as an end in herself. Thus the *Novia* tells the Rugby Player, "There is in your breast a veritable torrent in which I will drown."

It is evident that in this opening scene erotic symbolism is being used to convey the idea of tremendous libidinal energy and discharge. The *Novia*, as an erotic "echo" of the anima-figure, is fantasized as summoning enormous quantities of libido, as transforming the Young Man into the virile athlete represented by the ithyphallic Rugby Player, who possesses an apparently endless supply of cigars.

When the Young Man attempts to intrude his own image onto the scene, the *Novia* "runs away" with the athlete, which is to say that his possession of libido in abundance is likewise only a fantasy, no different from the kind of fantasy characteristic of hard-core pornography.

Pornographic literature is generally conceded to have as its main function the activation of autoerotic images. It is unrealistic only in the sense that fairy tales are "unrealistic." Beneath all the unrealistic fantasy is to be found the expression of a very "real" desire to activate great quantities of libidinal energy. The Kronhausens, in their study of erotic literature, point out that a primary characteristic of "obscene" books

> . . . is the emphasis which they place upon the exaggerated size of the male organ, the largeness of the testicles, and the copiousness of the amounts of seminal fluid ejaculated. It follows that all of these factors add up to the picture of a man whose potency is almost limitless, and whose sex drive is constantly at record strength.[23]

Now while it is true that the cigar-smoking athlete of *Five Years* is an ithyphallic figure, it is also true that he, and the context in which he appears, are symbolic *in a way that transcends sexuality*. A generation of exposure to the symbology of psychoanalysis has popularized the idea that sexuality is the ultimate meaning of symbols. The dream of climbing stairs is "really" a dream of coitus; a cigar is "really" a phallus. The fact of the matter is, of course, that stairways and cigars are no more "symbolic" than is sexuality itself. If a cigar "really" symbolizes the phallus, then what does the lingam "really" symbolize? If a dream of climbing stairs "really" symbolizes coitus, then what does a dream of coitus "really" symbolize? If the spiritual can be understood to be symbolic of the physical, it is not possible to deny the reverse.

Consequently the scene between the *Novia* and the Rugby Player must not inevitably be taken to signify that the Young Man "really" wants to be an irresistible and incredibly potent heterosexual lover "whose sex drive is constantly at record strength." An attempt to maintain that point of view would soon exhaust itself along a tangent of irrelevancies. What *is* of paramount importance to the Young Man, certainly, is the mobilization and expenditure of libido in some way that will enhance his value as a successful liver of life in his own opinion. When he imagines himself to be an ithyphallic hero, he may be reveling in a futile and pornographic fantasy, but the fantasy is not irrelevant to his needs, nor is he unaware of the futility of the fantasy. When he intrudes the "real" image of himself on the scene, the *Novia* rejects him and runs away with the athlete. That the protagonist is alive to the meaning of this event within the dynamics of his own psyche is sufficiently indicated by the fact that the disappearance of those two "energy figures" activates the hollow symbol of the Mannequin.

The Mannequin comes forth singing a mournful song appropriate to her as a symbol which has been emptied of content: "Who will wear my gown? The estuary, in order to marry the sea." It is a song of lost libido, seen as a torrent emptying into the anonymous ocean. She blames the Young Man for the loss of libido: "It is your fault. You could have been like a colt . . . and you are a sleeping lagoon. . . ."

The fact that she is a dummy wearing a wedding dress is a sure sign that Lorca recognized symbols for what they are: general indicators of unconscious tendencies, capable of accommodating any number of specific forms. That the Young Man is now left to confront a symbol emptied of content is a serious diagnosis of his spiritual illness. The meaning has suddenly gone out of his life; it has dropped into oblivion, and he is impotent to summon libido sufficient to reclaim it. He has reached a point of inertia, and is like a "sleeping lagoon": his conscious structure is placid and unstirred by the slightest wave of tidal energy. If he is to continue living at all, he must somehow impart a new meaning to the Mannequin, the hollow symbol of his need to save the remnants of his disintegrating consciousness by commitment to a "bride"—that is, union with a viable element of his psyche which will strengthen his hold on conscious reality before he drowns entirely in the waters of Lethe.

Hence the Mannequin tells him to seek a new bride—the Typist— so that the fertile union may take place. His confidence is restored by her encouragement, and the stage lighting becomes an intense blue.

The Old Man reappears on the scene, and he is greatly upset. The Young Man tells him that his presence is no longer required, and the Old Man replies, "More than ever." This remark may be taken to be correct in a therapeutic sense. The Old Man, as representative of cultural continuity, is in a position, after all, to rescue the Young

Man from his own psychic chaos. What he represents holds forth the possibility of salvation by identification of one's self with the cultural pattern in which one has been bred.

And the Young Man is running out of time: he must find immediately a principle of continuity which will liberate him from the imminent threat of conscious disintegration. Desperately he grasps at the nearest possibility, the persona-figure of the Typist, which represents the most extreme kind of limitation, the most superficial of conscious identities.

When the curtain is raised on Act Three, the stage setting makes explicitly clear the relationship between the house of Act One and the outside—which is not the external reality faced by the persona, but rather the great forest of the unconscious faced by the anima: the great forest where the electric storms originate that the Young Man would preferably shut out.

The opening scenes of Act Three include three characters: Harlequin, the Clown, and the Girl. The first two are evidently denizens of the region, whereas the Girl appears to be a visitor.

This is not the first time that the Harlequin figure has appeared in Lorca. In the poem *Harlequin*, he is depicted as symbolic of psychic duality:

> Red breast of the sun.
> Blue breast of the moon.
>
> Torso half coral,
> half silver and penumbra.[24]

The Harlequin of *Five Years* is not essentially different: he is dressed in black and green, and he sings a song about the antithesis between waking consciousness and sleep.

Waking consciousness is defined within time—sidereal time, which is to say, within the category of Being. The passage of time (and, therefore, the changes which occur in time) is apprehended as a series of units, or segments. Harlequin sings that the two realms are distinct; for sleep (and dreams) is the realm of the unconscious mind, which knows nothing of astronomy nor of sidereal time.

What Harlequin sings is evidently related in some important and essential way with the crisis which ended Act Two. What he says here is, of course, to be applied not exclusively to the sleeping state, but to the unconscious mind in general, first because the sleeping state is dominated by the unconscious, and second because Harlequin is a denizen of the dark forest primeval. When he announces, therefore, that "no one can open seeds in the heart of sleep," he is announcing a basic "law" governing the psyche, which is, that a given direction of growth cannot be deliberately fostered. Stated in a more abstract way, the "law" might read: "no one can take the initiative in the world of the unconscious."

The world of sidereal time, the world invented by intellect, is a world of plodding and predictable cause and effect. Here intellect can produce any mechanical effect it pleases, for the world of Being is an assembly-line world of forms endlessly repeated: "yesterday and tomorrow eat dark flowers of mourning," says Harlequin. In the world of intellect there is no escape from tireless repetition, no chance for transformations into original and liberating dimensions of vitality.

The surging forth into consciousness of new forms is compared to a joyful dawn by whose light we see "icebergs of blue ice":

> How the dawn sings!
> What blue icebergs does it raise up!

We may note here in passing the reappearance of the motif of blue. Here a bright dawn—the dawn of unconscious contents which have been activated, or energized—is compared to a blue iceberg. The iceberg is characterized by the fact that eight-ninths of its mass lies below the surface of the ocean; consequently the image of a "blue iceberg" shining in the dawn conveys a vivid symbol of a psychic condition: the joy of consciousness impelled from below. Libido surges upward, breaks through into a singing awareness, and one is filled with a sense of one's own capacity for being vital. It is not dissimilar to the euphoria of "inspiration."

This is all connected with the chaotic situation of the Young Man at the end of Act Two. There he had deliberately made the decision to foster a given kind of transformation within. He had been forsaken by the *Novia*—i.e., he found himself cut off from contact with the creative unconscious—and so was overcome by a sense of spiritual impoverishment and emptiness. He had lost his identity as a spiritually fertile young man, and his abrupt loss of this self-image makes it imperative that he grasp at a new identity which will afford him even the slightest hope of stable continuity on a conscious level. And so he seeks it in the form of his persona, which can be counted on to furnish a kind of mechanical stability, at the least. Hence he determines to "marry the Typist"—known (significantly enough) in Spanish as the *mecanógrafa* or "mechanographer."

It is then that Harlequin is introduced to declare that no one can deliberately foster an inner transformation. This kind of transformation is under the jurisdiction of the unconscious, and so "no one"—no ego-consciousness—can draw up its agenda. The Young Man has lost the Good Life as described by Harlequin, spokesman for the unconscious (hence a harlequin, a creature unencumbered by the bonds of rationality): a singing dawn in which blue icebergs thrust their sparkling tips above the surface of the fathomless ocean.

We hear hunting horns in the distance, and the stage direction states that we will continue to hear them at intervals *throughout the entire act*. We must make an effort to imagine their presence, for they add an acoustic dimension to the Lorcan meaning of the text.

The motif of *hunting*—particularly in the forest—is for Lorca an image of the penetration into the transpersonal unconscious in quest of life itself—living experiences which can be "captured" in the form of the symbol. The reader will recall that in Act One the Old Man said:

> All my life I have struggled to bring light into the darkest places. And when anyone has tried to twist the neck of the dove, I stayed his hand and helped the dove to fly.

To this the First Friend replied, "And naturally the hunter has died of hunger!" We saw in that passage a reference to cultural "sublimation" of unconscious materials so highly charged that their disruptive threat must be removed by means of social safety valves. Not everyone can be a mystic privately seeking the dove within; but formalized rites can release for most of us the pressures created by repression of tendencies which our culture itself demands of us. Society demands repression and compensates with "sublimation." This collective "sublimation" serves to "civilize" the individual, and to collectivize him, with the result that the lone hunter, the seeker within us who would undertake the solitary task of individuation, "dies of hunger." He ceases to be even a remote possibility in the development of the individual psyche.

In one of his lectures ("A Talk on the Theater") Lorca has characterized poetic inspiration as a "dove wounded by a mysterious hunter."[25] Elsewhere, in his extraordinary lecture on Góngora, he states that Góngora's poetic originality lies "in his method of *hunting* images." The italics are Lorca's, and he uses the Spanish *cazar*, "to chase, to hunt down": "la originalidad de . . . Góngora . . . está en su método de *cazar* las imágenes."[26] Further on in the same lecture he makes an explicit and detailed comparison between the creative act and the chase. Here is the passage, from which we have already quoted, apropos of the remoteness of that forest in which the hunter seeks his game:

> The poet who is going to make a poem (I know from personal experience) has the vague feeling that he is going hunting at night in a very remote forest. An inexplicable fear murmurs [*rumorea*] in his heart. To calm himself, it always helps to drink a glass of cool water and to make black doodles with the pen. . . . The poet is going on a hunting expedition. Soft breezes chill the cornea of his eyes. The moon, round like a hunting horn made of soft metal, sounds in the silence of the highest branches.[27]

"No one," adds Lorca, "was ever so prepared as was Góngora for this internal hunting expedition."[28]

The passage bears a close analogy with the hunting horns in the forest of *Five Years*, the principal difference being that on the one hand Lorca is speaking of creating in a specifically poetic sense, while on the other he is concerned with creating in a psychological sense—the creating of one's Self. The "hunter" in this case is the Girl, who comes seeking her lover who awaits her "at the bottom of the sea."

One cannot help but note a basic similarity between the situation of the Young Man and that of the Girl: they are both youths who are seeking a lost treasure in dual form (he has lost Bride and wedding ring; she has lost lover and thimble) which has been swallowed up by the sea.

She goes on to sing, however, that though she lost something of value, she found it again:

> I lost my crown,
> I lost my thimble,
> and just behind me
> I found them again.

Here Harlequin tells her:

Right now. . . .
You will see your lover
right behind the wind and the sea. . . .
I will give him to you.

The Girl is frightened by this and denies what Harlequin says:

You shall not give him to me.
One can never reach the bottom of the sea.

We might recall here that the Mannequin said the wedding gown would be swallowed up by the sea wherein its train was already "lost."

These thematic similarities are extremely suggestive when we consider that the unconscious is identified with the feminine and oceanic Earth Mother, and the conscious with the masculine solar principle (cf. Harlequin's characterization of joyful consciousness as icebergs sparkling in the sun); for they enable us to support the theory that this Girl who seeks her lover is in fact the Young Man himself, as the seeker who has traversed the realm of his personal unconscious.

In this form the song of loss is completed by the phrase, "I *found* them again," using the past tense and representing the problem as having been solved. This does not apply to the Young Man, obviously, since he lost the Bride and the ring and has not found them again. Indeed, he has not ventured to seek them; rather, he has decided to give up the quest and to resign himself to a life with the Typist—to restricting his identity to a personal and conscious component. The Girl's use of the past tense should not, then, be taken as descriptive of the protagonist's solution to a spiritual impasse. Rather it should be taken, fairy-tale fashion, as a hint, or instruction, telling where to seek:

. . . and right behind me
I found them again.

This is a particularly suggestive hint, in that it characterizes the quest in terms of the direction in which one must face. The persona "faces" the world of external reality, whereas the quest for the treasure within requires that one turn around and face the opposite direction—the direction of the unconscious, which lies right behind one.

When Harlequin presses the issue, insisting that the Girl accompany him forthwith, she draws back, "frightened" and "anxious." We have seen how, in the first act, the Dead Child and the Blue Cat were frightened at the prospect of being "spirited away," and how, similarly, in the opening scene of the play, the Old Man asked the Young Man if the "moment of departure" did not distress him, and he replied, "Yes, yes. Don't speak to me of that." Now, the Girl is frightened by the "moment of departure" and postpones it. It will be useful to keep these passages in mind when, at the end of the play, the protagonist himself attempts to postpone the final "moment of departure."

It is here that Harlequin calls for the fantastic Clown, whose face is reminiscent of a death's-head. Both Harlequin and the Clown are related to the jester or "wise fool." The Wichmann brothers, in their study of the history of chessmen, point out, apropos of the *fou* ("fool"; "chess bishop") that the medieval fool types (later producing a Harlequin offshoot)

> . . . are meant to be regarded as jesters—wise fools. They are mockers, who laugh at mankind and who are laughed at by it because it does not understand them. Since the late Middle Ages a second group had existed, the silly (natural, mentally deranged) fools. It seems obvious that the medieval moral satirists took the description "fool," for an unwise, erring human being, directly from the Bible.[29]

Hence, while rationally and morally the *fou* may appear to us as an object of scorn, symbolically he is something far different; for as a nonrational symbol he is sanctioned by a power superior to reason.

Both the Harlequin and the Clown may be seen as antithetical to the one who was originally their noble patron: the king, emperor, or prince. The wise fool is a fool from society's point of view because he does not pursue power and material wealth; and he is wise for the same reason, though not from the same point of view. The jester is wise too, because his ego is not involved in the worldly matters which are the butt of his jokes. In this sense he may represent a profounder level of life than his lord, who wears himself out in quest of the treasure "out there."

Harlequin and the Clown invite the Girl to join them in the quest for the treasure of which she speaks. The mockery is apparent, for they raise a strong suspicion (by their appearance, behavior, and ironic speech) that a quest under their direction would be uncomfortably ambiguous. As symbolic figures, they indicate that the quest may not be successfully undertaken by the Girl because her fear of it renders her powerless; in short, they represent an image of the seeker's own attitude toward the task. Thus, when it appears to the Girl that Harlequin seems seriously bent on taking her along, she becomes "frightened by the reality" and refuses to go. She puts them off by saying that she is willing to go . . . but "later."

She retires in tears, and Harlequin and the Clown put on a short performance. The Clown says, "Let's do a small boy who wants to change his piece of bread into steel flowers."

This remark is reminiscent of a reference made elsewhere by Lorca to casting "grains of wheat upon a field of steel."[30] The similarity lies, of course, in the opposition between potential growth and sterile conditions. In *Five Years* the child's bread may be seen as his nourishment, which the child wants to trade for (or change into) "steel flowers." Since Harlequin and the Clown symbolically sum up the inner attitude of the Young Man (they dominate the "stage of the unconscious") and since the child must be understood as a child-archetype, it is here evident that Harlequin and the Clown have in mind to represent, or act out, the Young Man's error. If we consider that the *Novia* embodies libidinal Becoming and that the Typist embodies the rigid Being of the persona, the Young Man's willingness to "exchange" one for the other can easily be seen as a defeated willingness to trade spiritual Becoming for spiritual Being. The Typist, being a woman, is a symbolic flower—the image is common-place, and frequent in Lorca—but her poses, her general commitment to social acceptability, make her rigid and sterile. The *Novia* was related to libidinal nourishment and the possibility of growth, for she is a veritable staff of life.

Harlequin and the Clown impersonate the "little boy," and then call upon him to come out, addressing him as *"Señor hombre"* ("Mr. Man"). While the word *hombre* is informally applied to anybody (cf. the popular vocative use of "man" in English), it is nevertheless significant that the epithet is employed here, precisely after the "impersonation" of the Young Man's spiritual situation; for at the end of the play the protagonist, as he expires, will sum up the crisis with one last question: "Is there no man here?" (*"¿No hay ningún hombre aquí?"*). There will be "no man" present in the house, because the protagonist is rapidly regressing, not in preparation for a rebirth but in complete defeat.[31]

In representing this little boy, the Clown sings "sternly":

I lost rose and curve,
I lost my necklace,
and in new ivory
I found them again.

Shortly afterward Harlequin recapitulates the song, singing, ". . . in ivory of clouds I found them again," which clarifies sufficiently the ambiguity of "new ivory" (*marfil reciente*): it means "ivory-white clouds."

Ivory is one of the most durable substances known to man, and is in direct antithesis to clouds, which are transience itself. There is something anomalous, consequently, in the idea of ivory clouds, or of cloud-like ivory. The anomaly not only echoes those steel flowers sought by the small boy, but (even more importantly) emphasizes the antithesis between *ocean* and *clouds*. Previously we have heard the Girl sing of the treasure lost in the ocean (and in the forest); the variant of her song substitutes clouds.

If we try to grasp this idea in less symbolic form, we might say that, in a very general way, *earth* (ocean and forest) has been forsaken for *heaven* (clouds). Defining ourselves further (since "heaven" is exceedingly ambiguous) we might say that the Young Man has forsaken the values of the unconscious (the chthonic) for the values of a restricted ego-consciousness, characteristically thought of as a light from above. Retreating in fear and confusion, he understandably seals himself off from the very difficult world of the unconscious, out of which proceeds not only a promise of spiritual enrichment, but also the threat of insanity. The values of a life restricted to the safe limits of a modest ego-consciousness are like "ivory made of clouds"— not because ivory is durable, but because it is rigid. Like clouds, such values are transient and insubstantial; like ivory they are stony and unbending, and this quality corresponds to the sternness with which the Clown sings of it.

We have elsewhere[32] discussed Lorca's use of the well-known rose symbol, and there is no need to insist upon it here apropos of the line "I lost rose and curve." It might be of value, however, to clarify at this point the very Lorcan use of the *curve*, taken as a psychic symbol.

To get a general conception of the symbolic meaning which can be attached to the idea of a curve, we must bear in mind that such meanings are typically relative, and not absolute. The ocean, for example, is symbolic of one series of ideas when contrasted to the land, but means something rather different when contrasted to the sun. Now in Lorca, the curve must be thought of in contrast to the straight line. The symbolic implications of this contrast are nowhere more neatly revealed than in a passage in *Creative Evolution*, where Bergson uses it as an example of how Being and Becoming differ, even though it is frequently difficult to *see* the difference empirically.

In the passage to which we refer, Bergson is criticizing the "scientific" point of view which would define life as a conglomeration of physical and chemical forces. A purely material concept like this, says Bergson, does not describe life (vitality), but is only a projection of the rigid structure of the intellect itself. The intellect apprehends reality in terms of Being—static forms and states which are strung together like beads on a string. What intellect cannot perceive is the Becoming of vitality, a phenomenon which can only be intuited; i.e., one can grasp it only when the *experience* of it floods one's conscious mind. If living reality were reducible to a series of states, there would be no way in which one state could pass over into the next state. Like Zeno's flying arrow, it would remain forever frozen at a given point. Indeed, only intellect could ever come up with a paradoxical notion of this sort—paradoxical, because intellect is simply not structured to apprehend the phenomenon of Becoming, which is contradictory to intellect's conditions of existing.

Now, says Bergson, let a straight line represent the rigid and unbending world of Being entertained by intellect; and let us draw tangent to this straight line a curve, representing a trajectory (since vitality is always a trajectory whose destination can be perceived only in retrospect by intellect). Bergson's analysis proceeds:

> A very small element of a curve is very near being a straight line. . . . In the limit, it may be termed a part of a curve or a part of the straight line, as you please, for in each of its points a curve coincides with its tangent. So likewise "vitality" is tangent, at any and every point, to physical and chemical forces; but such points are, as a fact, only views taken by a mind which imagines stops at various moments of the movement that generates the curve. In reality, life is no more made of physicochemical elements than a curve is composed of straight lines.[33]

For Lorca, the curve is associated with vitality and typically appears in context with it. In *Poet in New York* (for example), he tells us, in his psychological portrait of the Negroes (= human vitality unrepressed) that they "love . . . the curved dance of the water on the shore."[34] Similarly, in his *Ode to Salvador Dalí* he praises Dalí's art for both its formidable precision and its vitality: intellectual control which he compares to a searing light like the scorching sun that the grapevines of Bacchus fear, and instinctive power: "the chaotic surge of the curved water."[35] In one of his elegiac poems occasioned by the death of the bullfighter Sánchez Mejías he is appalled by the absolute nothingness which the dead body of a man represents; like a rock, it is neither alive nor dead, but is simply stony matter, "with neither curved water nor frozen cypresses."[36]

These examples show clearly what any artist knows—that the curved line is the "natural" line, the line of nature, by contrast with the straight line and the angle, which belong under the jurisdiction of intellect. Lorca himself was not historically far removed from the turn-of-the-century movement known as Art Nouveau, a decorative style inspired in the curvilinear rhythms of growing plants and flowing water. Like flamboyant Gothic, baroque, and rococo, Art Nouveau asserted architecturally once again the vegetative principle in art, the principle expressive of chthonic vitality, by contrast with the geometrical principle (e.g., Romanesque, Georgian, Empire) which portrays conscious intellectual control.[37]

The symbolic significance of the curve, then, is not to be underestimated, since it has a long history as one of the several antithetical pairs of ideas (straight vs. curved) expressive of the opposition between intellect and instinct, conscious control and unpredictable growth. "Curve" is not only synonymous with "vitality," but also alludes to the *trajectory*, the parabolic path laid down by a projectile, and as such calls to mind the idea of Becoming.[38] Thus Lorca, in an early poem, describes a moment of transition in his life: an episode has ended, and he finds himself at a new point in the trajectory being laid down by his movement through life. The poem is entitled *Curve*.[39]

In the play *Five Years* the Clown sings that he lost not only "rose and curve," but also his necklace. This is related to the Girl's loss of crown and thimble, and the Mannequin's loss of the wedding ring, for these are all circular objects identified with the individual person, and indicating his state of wholeness, completion, or spiritual unification. In addition, the thimble is related to a whole series of fertility symbols connected with the creative activities of sewing and spinning (spindle, needle, shuttle, loom, and so forth). Hence when the Clown sings sternly of the loss of rose, curve, and necklace, he is diagnosing with considerable economy the Young Man's spiritual losses: his loss of unifying contact with the creative unconscious.

Harlequin's final words are, "The turning wheel of the wind and the sea." This covers in general the circular symbolism preceding (crown, thimble, ring, and necklace). Syntactically Harlequin's phrase is presumably to be taken as the completion of a sentence begun by the Clown:

> Clown: I am going to demonstrate . . . [exit]
> Harlequin: [as he exits] The turning wheel of the wind and sea.

If this wheel of the wind (spirit, *pneuma*) and the sea (origin, womb) is to be taken positively and as related to the circular symbolism spoken of earlier, then we cannot overlook the fact that Harlequin and the Clown are supposed to speak their last lines *as they exit*. This is important, because "exit" means, in *Five Years*, "repression." After Harlequin and the Clown represent the little boy of the steel flowers (spiritual lopsidedness) they drop out of sight, taking with them their demonstration of spiritual wholeness— the wheel of wind and sea.

At this point the Typist appears, dressed in a tennis outfit, over which she wears a long cape, and she is engaged in conversation with the First Mask, who is described in detail. The general effect of the latter is that of a blaze of yellow against a blue-black background; at the same time, she is decidedly grotesque.

This First Mask, one of Lorca's most extraordinary creations, looms large in the play. Exceedingly complex, her role requires an extended analysis as it unfolds in this scene.

We know that the First Mask and the Concierge (*Portera*) are the same person: the mother of the Dead Child. Now the Concierge (like the *Novia* and the Typist) may be assigned a mediating function, for she is in charge of the entrance to the house, which means, in the context of our play, that she faces toward the world of the "blue storm" and the forest. Further, there seems to be some kind of parallel between the First Mask (= "disguised" Concierge) and the Typist, for she matches the latter's tale of love with one of her own.

The Typist's story is inaccurate, as we know, since she inverts the truth by saying that it was she who deserted the Young Man, and not the other way around; and so perhaps our task at this point should be to attempt to account for the inversion.

In the beginning of the play, when the Young Man still entertained the thought of seeking within for the "treasure," he withdrew libido from his persona, i.e., he accounted it of little value; he rejected it, or (in terms of our play) he "threw her out of the house." Now after the crisis of Act Two wherein the protagonist experiences the truth of his own spiritual impotence, he retreats defeatedly from all attempts to "create himself" from within, and turns back to his limited but trusty persona. This means that he grants new status to it, investing it with a certain value, because in the face of his own defeat, it is all that is left to him. Thus he withdraws libido from the *Novia* and "cathects" it onto the Typist—a tennis player now. (It is worth noting at this point that we can keep track of the Young Man's libidinal trajectory by means of the *athletic motif*, since athletics is as eloquently expressive of libidinal expenditure as is sexuality. We recall that the *Novia* was the object of enormous quantities of libido through the medium of the *Rugby Player*, by contrast to the autoerotic *wrestling* of the first Act, and the amusingly ironic *tennis outfit* of the present act; and Lorca has not yet done with allusions to athletics, as will presently be evident.)

The Typist, then, is the present object of libidinal attachment, and she appears in company with the disguised Concierge: two mediators facing in opposite directions, as it were—the world of external reality (mediated by the Typist) and the world of the dark forest (mediated—in some way as yet to be discussed—by the Concierge). The Young Man's situation is the reverse of what it was previously, since he is now trying to "make do" with his persona: she is the positive value now, whereas before she was a negative value. At the same time, this attempt to identify with the persona brings with it a concomitant *devaluation of unconscious values.*

The Concierge, mother of the Dead Child, and a blazing (numinous) denizen of the world of the unconscious, has undergone a transformation, for now it is she whom the Young Man must reject, together with the unconscious material of which she was in charge, as keeper of the door. Consequently this devaluation takes the form of a grotesque appearance.

Let us remember that we are involved with a psychological experience of no uncommon occurrence. The Young Man (like Lorca himself) is the type of person for whom material from the creative unconscious means everything in this life. It was the lifelong devotion of Lorca, who had himself undergone the shock of repression during his terrifying sojourn in New York City. The creative unconscious was suddenly transformed into an ugly and destructive force, which he portrayed under the name of New York. It is evidently out of this experience that Lorca created the protagonist of *Five Years*, the principal difference being that the Young Man's spiritual impotence must be understood as a permanent disablement. The adventure into the depths of the unconscious requires a personal stability immune to destruction by the encounter "down there"; this is what the Young Man does not possess, and we have seen how he—in the guise of the questing Girl—recoils in fear and anxiety from Harlequin's invitation: she is "frightened by the reality" of it.

It is essential to bear in mind that none of these attitudes and reversals of attitudes is deliberate. When the Typist and the Concierge appear together in their new outfits, we are witnessing a piece of "honest" self-deception on the part of the Young Man. He *must* believe that the Typist serves a valuable function; he *must* lead himself to see as acceptable the union with her. After his ignominious experience with unconscious forces, he does not find her really looking so bad as he had once fancied. He has made the shocking discovery that he does not have the resources needed to become an "inward man," and so he sees the persona in an entirely new light—and it is here that the self-deception begins. His new opinion of her allows him to say to himself, in effect, "I guess I must have always loved her down deep, even though I refused to admit it. Had I loved her as she deserved, she wouldn't have stopped functioning in my life." It is by this kind of ostensible reasoning that the Young Man can convince himself that he did not reject her, but rather the other way around. If he is to retain a modicum of self-esteem, he must not view the persona as a piece of discarded rubbish which he has decided to reclaim; hence the Typist's reversal of the truth: *he* did not desert *her;* on the contrary—*she* abandoned *him*. It is only natural that this reconstruction of the image of the Typist should be accompanied by the debasement of the Concierge, who is now the unworthy one, preposterous and grotesque—an opinion of the unconscious mind which is not uncommonly held.

We have noted that the First Mask is the mother of the Dead Child, who is symbolic of the loss or death of unconscious possibilities, just as growing up represents the loss or death of one's childhood— and with it, one's feeling for life as a shimmering experience: blue icebergs rising up into the dazzling light of dawn. Since the Dead Child belongs to the psyche of the Young Man, we must conclude that the Child's mother derives ultimately from the mother of the Young Man—and so she is dated ("c. 1900"), since the time of the play is "modern" (c. 1930).

As the Concierge, she was posted at the entrance to the house, which is now seen to be nothing more than a baroque toy theater. This is analogous to the position attributed now to the First Mask, who tells us that she was "posted" (i.e., that was her sphere of action) in the foyer of the Paris Opera; for the "toy" theater gives onto a dark forest, while the foyer of the Opera House (according to the First Mask) gives onto the ocean. In either case we have a theater from which one communicates with the vast world of the unconscious (forest, ocean).[40]

We might note Lorca's characterization of the First Mask as *cosmopolitan*. The mistress of a count (Arturo of Italy), she is of Italian origin (she speaks with an Italian accent and uses Italianisms); she moved in the most exclusive circles, attended the Paris Opera, and had a Russian gentleman friend who made her the gift of a whippet. At the same time, it is clear that Lorca wants to combine this with a pretentious and mannered way. Nothing reveals her affectation better than her use of the expression *"¡Oh, qué dulcísimo tormento!"* The phrase is heavy with connotation, and the extent to which it vividly characterizes the First Mask can be demonstrated by a brief study of its semantic background.

We are dealing with a cliché from eighteenth-century baroque opera and drama. The Italian *tormento* (or French *tourment*) was at that time a favorite word, used to describe the sufferings occasioned by love and grief—exactly as the First Mask uses it in *Five Years*. Here are some random examples:

Metastasio, *Didone abbandonata* (1724).
　　Non posso scoprire il mio tormento. (I, i)
　　(I cannot reveal my suffering.)

　　Ma saper che m'adora e doverla lasciar, questo è il tormento!
　　(I, ix)
　　(But to know that she adores me, and that I must abandon her—
　　　this is the torment!)

　　E qual sarà tormento . . . , se questo mio non è? (I, xvii)
　　(And what, then, is grief . . . , if this [grief] of mine does not
　　　merit the name?)

　　Tormento il più crudele d'ogni crudel tormento, è il barbaro
　　　momento, che in due divide il cor. (II, ix)
　　(The cruelest suffering of all cruel suffering is the frightful
　　　moment which breaks the heart in two.)

　　Va crescendo il mio tormento. . . . (III, viii)
　　(My grief grows apace. . . .)

Pergolesi, *Il prigionero superbo* (1733).
　　. . . il mio cor nel suo tormento non desia che il tuo contento. . . .
　　　(III, Aria, "Vedi, ingrato")
　　(. . . my heart in its grief desires only your happiness. . . .)

Olimpiade (1735).
　　Oh tormento maggior d'ogni tormento! (I, Recit., "Stranier, chi
　　　mi sorprende?")
　　(Oh grief, greater than any grief!)

Gluck, *Orphée et Euridice* (1762) (Italian version).
　　Tal pianto, tal lamento raddoppia il mio tormento. (I, i)
　　(Such weeping, such lamentation redoubles my grief.)

Alceste (1767).
　　Rien n'égale mon désespoir, mes tourments. . . . (I, ii)
　　(Nothing equals my despair, my sufferings. . . .)

Haydn, *Il Mondo della Luna* (1777) (adapted from Goldoni).
　　Ahi, che tormento, qui che morì! (I, xi)
　　(Oh, what grief, for now he is dead!)

Cherubini, *Medea* (1797).
　　A morte, a morte l'esecrato autor del mio tormento! (III, Aria,
　　　"Del fiero duol")
　　(Death to the hated author of my suffering!)

By the nineteenth century, *tormento* had become a low-frequency cliché, and librettists managed to write entire texts without having recourse to it, though it does crop up occasionally. In *Lucia di Lammermoor* (Donizetti-Cammarano, 1835), Lucia declares, "Vivo ancor per mio tormento!" (II, iv)—"And yet I live, to my great grief!"— and she is assured: "Quante volte ad un solo tormento mille gioie succeder non fa!" ("How often does it not happen that a thousand joys follow a single grief!"). And in *Aïda* (Verdi-Ghislanzoni, 1871), Amneris and Aïda sing the duet "Amore, amore! Gaudio tormento. . . ." (I, i): "Love, love! Joyful torment!"

The connotations of the word *tormento* are significant, since Lorca's use of it contributes considerably to the characterization of the First Mask as an essentially theatrical and melodramatic figure— affected, "stagey," and unnatural. *Tormento* belonged to a tradition of operatic and dramatic diction used to depict members of the nobility, who were supposed to possess a sensitivity both exquisite and larger than life. More than once it has happened that the dramatic conventions of theater (and radio and television) have actually trained social classes to adopt the stereotyped behavior and diction originally intended to portray them. The essential absurdity of the stereotypy is fully revealed when the dramatic convention being aped has itself become esthetically outmoded—as in the example afforded by the figure of the First Mask.

It may be here that we can find a significant reason for the fact that she is associated with the Italian nobility; for if our analysis of her role in *Five Years* is accurate, the First Mask represents an outmoded, pretentious, stereotyped, and "collectivized" *European*. The nobility as portrayed in Italian opera had become a type familiar to the middle and upper classes throughout Europe. A single phrase— "*¡Oh, qué dulcísimo tormento!*"—suffices to fix the First Mask within a European context, through the diffusion of Italian opera; which is to say that the First Mask portrays a "typical European," rather than a "typical Italian." Her cosmopolitanism supports this notion, while her grotesqueness implies rather forcefully a devaluation of the collective consciousness—an anonymous, chalk-white mask, here carrying on an amicable conversation with the individual "mask" (L. *persona*) of the Young Man. The Concierge faced inwardly, while now, in her "disguise," she faces outwardly—a reversal of attitude

implied by her fantastic story about the Paris Opera and her largesse
to the Count.

She describes a scene which used to occur "in the foyer of the
Paris Opera House": there are, she says, balustrades giving onto the
ocean; Count Arturo and his child (both of whom she had deserted)
would approach in a little boat; "but I would close the curtains and
throw them a diamond."

In order to get at the connotations of what the First Mask says
about the opera, we must reconstruct a cultural milieu. Here we have
mainly to do with the idea of the *foyer* which, by the end of the nineteenth century, had accumulated a good deal of significance in the
world of music—especially that world centered around the work of
Wagner at the time of the famous Bayreuth Music Festivals.

Throughout the nineteenth century the opera house functioned as
a center where subscribers met to socialize against the musical background of an opera in progress. The auditorium was always built in
the shape of a horseshoe with tiers of boxes, so that the spectators
were oriented toward each other. The house lights were not dimmed
during the performance for the simple reason that opera-going was
popularly enjoyed, not as an esthetic but rather as a social activity.

In the 1870s Wagner's plans to create a new kind of opera experience were realized. The theater at Bayreuth was of a radically new
design, for it resembled a modern concert auditorium, directly confronting each member of the audience with the action onstage (this
being the real and only reason for the presence of anybody at the
Music Festivals). Thus was created the modern, well-behaved opera-
goer to whom it would be unthinkable to carry on an animated conversation throughout the performance of an opera.

Pre-Wagnerian audiences, however, considered the opera house
to be part of their social life, as much so as the casino. Hence it was
normally expected to contain game room, restaurant, and foyer. An
attempt was made to change all this at Bayreuth:

> There were no boxes or balconies except for a small gallery at the
> rear. . . . Neither were there any billiard rooms, gaming tables,
> or grand foyers, and the restaurant was in a separate building. . . .
>
> Wagner from the first intended the Festival to be an experience
> not an event. One of the attractions for him of Bayreuth was that
> the audience would have to assemble well in advance. It could not
> rush in at the last minute. . . . In every detail of his planning he

deliberately fostered an atmosphere of intense absorption, even of dedication. As he had explained earlier in a letter to the King [Ludwig II of Bavaria], he did not want "the lounging opera public, accustomed solely to the trivial, but only those who hitherto have remained aloof from these shallow entertainments."[41]

Esthetically then, "opera" means a darkened auditorium filled with a hushed audience absorbed in what occurs onstage. Socially "opera" finds its final *raison d'être* in the foyer, i.e., in an elegant and exclusive atmosphere deliberately created to gratify the social demands of the upper classes. This antithesis was a very real fact of European life during the latter years of the gaslight era. It created passionate sympathies and antipathies, such as the riot occasioned at the premiere of *Tristan* in 1897 at Turin, when Toscanini attempted to conduct in a darkened auditorium.[42]

In *Five Years* it is clear how the Mask is characterizing her presence at the opera: she was a socialite, and to her the opera meant gaslights, foyer, and an occasion to shine. All of this degrades the Mask by identifying her—and the Count by association—with the collective life of the Young Man's nineteenth-century elders, for whom spiritual wealth (dramatic art) was subordinate to the collective game-playing which preceded the First World War.

From what the First Mask says, it can be inferred that she and the Count are different aspects of the same phenomenon. The scars which Arturo bears, made "on her account," are the very scars which she exhibits to the Typist.

Psychic injuries leave psychic scars: a given event brings about permanent changes in the makeup of the ego-consciousness, while at the same time the specific causes of the injury may be repressed. This means that the personal unconscious is similarly reshaped by the addition of new material. Thus it is that we can say that events which "scar" ego-consciousness will also "scar" the personal unconscious. It was this phenomenon to which Freud directed most of his attention, as a matter of fact: the relationship between a sick consciousness and a sick subconsciousness, or personal unconscious. Hence there arises the possibility of seeing Count Arturo and the First Mask as representatives of the degenerate determinants both conscious and unconscious of European civilization at the turn of the century. Whatever wounds he suffered "on her account" scarred them both.

In considering the role played by Count Arturo (a not inconsiderable one, in view of the fact that he himself does not appear on stage), it is just possibly worthy of note that the name "Arturo" (except for the letter *u*) appears reversed in the name for the Concierge—*Portera*: ART(u)RO. This anagrammatic coincidence is not so complex that it could not even be unconscious on the part of Lorca; at any rate it may account for the fact that "Arturo" happens to be the particular name chosen for the mate of the First Mask—the *Portera* in disguise. Just as the First Mask is produced as the "opposite" of the Young Man (i.e., when he abandons the creative unconscious and the *Novia*, a compensatory debasement occurs) so that the two of them are contrasted by virtue of the colors associated with them (the complementary blue and yellow) so, orthographically, are the *Portera* and Arturo "opposites": that is to say, the orthographic antithesis reflects the substantial fact that she and the Count represent spheres which are in neurotic opposition to each other.

When the Typist and the First Mask engage in their amicable colloquy, we know that the Typist is inverting the truth. The First Mask responds by saying that precisely the same thing has happened to her; and later, her reappearance in the play will be marked explicitly by a hysterical inversion of the truth ("See how I'm laughing?" she sobs); hence we must consider the possibility that in her conversation with the Typist, she too may be reversing the situation.

It should be noted that Count Arturo and the *Portera* are not only in orthographic contrast; they are also in social contrast. He is a count, while she belongs to the category of domestic help. They are in a master-servant relationship. Nevertheless, the two of them are parents of the Dead Child; and so if we take "Child" in a symbolic sense (birth out of the union of the conscious mind and the unconscious) the Concierge would here have to be assigned the role of psychopomp—the one who guides or leads the way; specifically, the one who has discretionary powers over the door by which the conscious and the unconscious spheres are in communication.

Similarly, the Typist fulfilled a service function (hired help). Now, however, she appears in an elevated form, wearing a long cape over a tennis outfit, associated (more so in the 1920s than at present, of course) with the socially privileged, while the *Portera* is decked out with the appurtenances of the higher social castes—in debased form.

The devaluation of the unconscious in the form of a *Mask* is curiously revealing. While the protagonist is trying to elevate the Typist (persona, or mask), at the same time the worst thing that he can think to say of the unconscious is that it is pretentious and ridiculously insincere, like . . . a mask. His flight from the unconscious into the security of his persona leads him to heap scorn upon the unconscious, but his exaggerated representation of it as a grotesque mask reveals to us his real opinion of the Mask he is trying to convince himself that he loves. Likewise, the provincial ego-consciousness, for whom the "alien" unconscious is only grotesque, projects this alien quality as European—i.e., non-Spanish.

Finally, the Mask freely admits herself to be a harlot (she is sleeping promiscuously with the stevedores who unload coal at the docks), a new and degrading reference to the "edge-of-the-sea" motif. Rather than cleave to her lover (the Count, as "master of the house") and the Child, she kept aloof whenever they appeared to her at the foyer. Subsequently she learned that Arturo had married a "great Roman lady."

We recall that the Child was dressed as if for his First Communion, which suggested a causal relation between his formal entry into the Church and his demise. The ritual of entry, as a matter of fact, is commonly known to be symbolized as a death of the old and a birth of the new; and among preliterate peoples the initiate is elaborately "killed" and "buried" symbolically.[43] Here, however, only the fact of death is pointed out; no rebirth is attributed to the "collectivization" of the Child by an institution.

Now the Mask says that her lover allowed this same Child to die of frostbite and that he then married a "great Roman lady." It is difficult not to see here a personification of the Church: the Child celebrates his First Communion and then is represented as dead; the Count abandons the Child to the frost (vitality immobilized)[44] and goes off to marry a "great Roman lady"—surely two different versions of the same event.

Both the Mask and her lover, as parents of the Child, are depicted as regressive figures (the Mask is dated "c. 1900") representative of the *psychic heritage* of the protagonist. The Child, after all, does not voluntarily decide to become a member of the Church; it is his elders who are responsible for that, and here it is represented negatively as a conservative instrument of civilization, which does not enrich the spiritual life of the Child, but rather limits it—seals him in a little coffin—by means of psychological repression. The unconscious, instinctual side, when recognized at all by civilization, tends to become stereotyped as a thing remarkably similar to the "evil" allegedly inherent in man. As an institutionalized ritual, then, First Communion can be described as a burial of the instinctual side, which is sealed off as a function that could only cause trouble if not effectively repressed (or "sublimated"). In this stereotyped form, it *is* grotesque like the First Mask, and the "collectivized" man deserts it in favor of an institutionally recognized spouse.

The Typist, after viewing the scars of Count Arturo (which are carried by the First Mask), makes a reply which catches us off guard:

> . . . how lovely to await confidently the moment of being loved!
> . . . That's why we'll laugh. When I was small, I used to save my candy in order to eat it later.

This amounts to what can only be called a dramatic *déjà vu;* for the Typist leads into the subject with which the play began (the joy of anticipation), and her remark, which strikes us with no warning, gives us the sensation that this has all happened before—and indeed enables us to foretell the Mask's reply: "That's true, isn't it? It tastes better."

When the Young Man first made this remark to the Old Man, he was alluding to the *Novia,* an inner value; when the Typist repeats his words, she is alluding to union of the protagonist with herself— an "external" value, as it were, a value oriented toward the social world outside. The devalued symbol of the First Mask is made to give her cordial approval to the union: "That's true, isn't it? It tastes better."

In the conversation between the Young Man and the *Novia,* we recall that the *Novia* was disappointed by his unprepossessing appearance ("Weren't you taller?"). By comparison with values hidden deep within the unconscious, the personal psyche is a paltry thing indeed. But by comparison with the relatively superficial social persona, the personal psyche gains considerably in stature; indeed it seems a terrible waste of spiritual potential to invest the better part of one's energy in the elaboration and care of one's persona. The Typist, however, is delighted by the prospect of union with the "tall" Young Man. "If my boyfriend shows up," she tells the First Mask, "a very tall fellow with curly hair—curly in a special kind of way—act as if you didn't know him." Her taste in masculine beauty evidently attracts her to "cute fellows," as opposed to the formidable virility of the *Novia's* lover.

Hereupon the Young Man appears, dressed in knickers (a restatement of the sporting motif) and wearing blue-checkered, knee-length socks (a restatement of the blue motif). He is looking for the way home (since he is retreating from this dark region), and Harlequin reappears to tell him that he cannot continue in the direction in which he is going because the way is blocked by "the circus," "filled with spectators who are definitely quiet." And then, softly, insinuatingly, he invites the Young Man to join the circus crowd. The Young Man declines, whereupon Harlequin declares "emphatically":

> The poet Virgil made a golden fly, and all the flies died which were poisoning the air of Naples. In there, in the circus, there is some soft gold, enough to make a statue the same size . . . as yourself.

Our discussion of this significant passage should begin perhaps by recalling the goodly number of legends surrounding the name of Virgil, popularly remembered (from the Middle Ages on) as a magician, or necromancer. There are in existence many stories according to which Virgil was a master of the *talismanic art,* the art by means of which the city, one's house, or one's person is preserved from danger. Thus Virgil "freed Naples of a plague of poisonous bloodsuckers by throwing into a well a leech made of gold."[45] He constructed a copper grasshopper "which relieved a plague of these insects,"[46] and a copper cricket which "drove other crickets away from Naples."[47] He "enchanted a fly into a piece of glass, and no flies entered Naples. . . ."[48] Elsewhere it is told that ". . . at Naples Virgil set up a brazen fly . . . which . . . permitted no fly to enter the city."[49] Our immediate source for these stories recalls that according to Pliny the Elder "whenever plagues of flies brought pestilence to the people of Elis, they invoked Myagros, 'the hunter of flies,' by means of sacrifice, and at once the flies died."[50] Similarly Pausanias tells of how the city may be ridded of pestilential flies by prayers to Zeus Averter of Flies.[51]

The talismanic art is analogous to the kind of witchcraft (known best to us in its voodooistic form, perhaps) which involves the mutilation of doll-like effigies: whatever happens to the image will happen to the person whom the image represents. The old stories about Virgil do not usually say whether anything was actually done to the metal figures made by him, though one of the legends cited in the foregoing does state that a talismanic leech of gold was thrown into a well. It may be that it was sufficient simply to recite incantations over the talisman. In any case, the principle behind talismanic magic is evidently related to the general belief that possession of an image gives to one a magic power over the thing represented.

Central to the symbolic significance of flies is their connection with pestilence and putrefaction. A well-known example establishing the psychological meaning of flies is William Golding's novel, *Lord of the Flies* (1954). Here a number of English boys have been isolated on an island, and the novel portrays their gradual reversion to a primitive state as the hygienic veneer of civilization wears away. They gradually become surrounded by dirt and decay, both physically and morally. They learn to kill for food by overcoming a revulsion for slaughtering; and so the decaying head of a pig, ". . . grinning amusedly in the strange daylight, ignoring the flies, the spilled guts . . . ,"[52] comes to symbolize the "Lord of the Flies," the instinctual impulse within us, which, when released by the collapse of ego-consciousness formed according to the canons of order dictated by society, appears as the *decay* of something. E. L. Epstein, in his "Notes on *Lord of the Flies*," points out that the epithet itself ". . . is a translation of the Hebrew *Ba'alzevuv*," our Beelzebub: ". . . [his] name suggests that he is devoted to decay, destruction, demoralization, hysteria and panic. . . ."[53]

Here it is germane to recall that Jung has pointed out how, psychologically, insects in general may

> . . . represent autonomous . . . units that tend to break away from the psychic hierarchy. . . . these little creatures, . . . if control should fail, would reappear as those well-known *insulae*, or personality fragments.[54]

It is clear that *Five Years* is a play whose various characters represent psychological tendencies and "personality fragments" which plague the Young Man and which lead him progressively farther away from the hygienic order of his own house. He becomes the inert spectator of an inner drama, and when he wishes to return home, he is told that the way is blocked by "the circus." Harlequin further suggests that if the Young Man wishes to rid himself of the plague, he should employ the talismanic art. If Virgil could rid Naples of a plague of flies by the use of a golden fly, so can the Young Man rid himself of a plague of personality fragments by means of a "golden Young Man."

The construction of a golden man is strongly reminiscent of the alchemical task which was, precisely, to transmute "base" human nature into spiritual gold. Baynes points out that

> . . . the symbolic value of gold (viz., grains of the sun) was treasured by early civilized man long before it had currency value. . . . the divine man, the King, was either a child of the sun or had in some way partaken of the splendour of the sun.[55]

The secret of finding the mystical gold lay in the discovery of a conversion principle which the alchemists called the Philosopher's Stone, or *elixir* (Ar. *al-iksīr,* "the philosopher's stone"). The Stone, or *elixir,* conferred immortality which (for the Christian alchemists) was the "gold purchasable of Christ."[56] Psychologically the alchemical aim may be defined as the desire to achieve contact between consciousness and the creative unconscious, and Baynes even sees alchemy as "the first, somewhat abortive, attempt to create a Western Yoga."[57]

While there is no need to insist specifically on the golden man of the alchemists, it is useful to bear in mind that the notion is prominent in the history of Occidental culture. Harlequin's declaration that there is enough gold "within" to make a self-image is ironic (since it is Harlequin who makes the statement), but we must range this "soft gold" alongside the other symbols relating to the inner treasure: the *Novia* herself, the wedding ring, the thimble, and the crown.

The Young Man does not even acknowledge Harlequin's mention of the gold within. He is bent only on returning home safely, and so he asks, "Is Poplar Street blocked also?" The wording of this question might be noted, for one does not expect to find a street (*calle*) situated in or about a forest; nonetheless it evidently exists in the psychic landscape of the Young Man, and helps to corroborate our interpretation of the passage in Act One where the protagonist complains of the noise, dust, heat, and offensive odors of "the street." There we pointed out the need to see this street as belonging to the world of the unconscious, and not to the realm of external reality. It will shortly be clear that the library of the first act is literally surrounded by the great forest, and that references to the "outside" of the house therefore mean "beyond the threshold" of conscious life. To forget this explicit meaning which Lorca gives to the "inside" and "outside" of the house is to introduce an element of confusion into a play which is already difficult enough.

In his bewilderment the Young Man tries to explain that he was going "home," but it is evident enough that he does not really have a very clear idea of what this home might be: "I was going to my house —I mean, not *my* house; to another house, to. . . ." He leaves the sentence unfinished, and the Clown breaks in to end the statement, not with the expected noun, but with a verb: "—to seek." And then he advises the Young Man to "turn around and you'll find it." The psychological meaning of this has already received our attention; we should note, however, that the Clown, when he says that the Young Man will "find it," is not talking about any house (*casa*). He says, "*lo encontrarás*"; and since *casa*, being feminine, cannot be the antecedent of the masculine or neuter *lo*, we may conclude that the "it" of the search is the "treasure hard to find"—which is revealed when one seeks within by "turning around" to "face in the opposite direction." One must escape the limits of one's house by crossing the threshold which separates the conscious precinct from the great forest of the creative unconscious.

This is implied by the Typist, whom we now hear singing:

> Where are you going, my love,
> with the air in a glass
> and the sea in a windowpane?

Harlequin has already made reference to the "wheel" of the wind and the sea, the *pneuma* and the unconscious, and now the Typist characterizes the Young Man as a small, limited vessel (glass) or area (windowpane) containing the vastness of the air and the sea.

A certain ambiguity in this passage makes it necessary to examine it in brief detail. I refer to the expression "with . . . the sea in a windowpane (*vidrio*)." A windowpane represents a point of view even more limited than that of the entire window. Elsewhere Lorca has used *vidrio* in this symbolic fashion, for in his lecture on Góngora he distinguishes between popular and courtly poets by saying that while the popular poets were persons who wrote poetry while mingling abroad in the traffic of the great world, the "intellectual" courtly poets composed while seated indoors at their desk, "looking at the roads through the leaded panes (*vidrios*) of the window."[58]

The psychological meaning of a window view is strongly suggested by a remark in Lorca's prose poem *Saint Lucy and Saint Lazarus,* where the speaker, looking out the window at the night sky, says, "there is nothing lovelier than to see a star taken by surprise and fixed within a frame."[59] Here the reference is to the perception of something valuable (a star) within the window framing one's view into the immense blackness of the night sky.

In *Five Years,* to have "the sea in a windowpane" is presumably parallel to having "the air in a drinking glass," and the two of them carry a negative connotation quite unlike that of having "a star in a window." The passage is sufficiently vague, so that we cannot reasonably see in it anything beyond the depiction of personal limitations in the form of inhibition: the inhibition of what are actually immense natural forces, thwarted and confined within the person of the Young Man.

There now follows a love scene with the Typist, at the end of which the curtains are opened on the miniature baroque theater, and to our surprise we see the library of the first act, reproduced on a small scale. Enter the First Mask, hysterically upset. She continually sniffs smelling salts, as if to keep from fainting. She announces that she has deserted Count Arturo, and the two lovers appear to be on the verge of consummating their union when the Typist suddenly breaks the spell by telling the Young Man that it will be necessary to wait five years more.

The Young Man has waited patiently while the *Novia* was off "traveling" during his years of adolescence; she reappears briefly and superficially, only long enough to reveal her capacity to activate great quantities of libido (the Rugby Player) which she subsequently accompanies back to the anonymity of her origin, leaving behind a drained and impotent ego-consciousness. This latter, in an effort to stabilize itself, reforms around the persona, which results automatically in the appearance of a new representative of the unconscious: the First Mask. This Mask appears as part of a play of opposites (yellow-blue)—the Jungian "enantiodromia"—for she represents the unconscious now as something unattainable, and necessarily grotesque, therefore. The five-year wait must begin again in the manner suggested by Jung:

> Unless the conscious mind intervened, the unconscious would go on sending out wave after wave without results, like the treasure that is said to take nine years, nine months, and nine nights to come to

the surface and, if not found on the last night, sinks back to start all over again from the beginning.[60]

We have noted that while the Typist and the Young Man are making love, the Dead Child crosses the stage of the miniature theater. It is here that the protagonist relates the Child to the child-archetype within himself (the possibility of a new spiritual growth within), and he asks his presumptive helpmate to assist him: ". . . it is my son. He is alive within me, like an ant alone in a closed box. A little light for my son. Please." This is, of course, a futile plea, for the persona has nothing to do with these inward matters. The Typist is concerned solely with communicating outwardly, and she reacts to the Young Man's plea by demanding of him, in an "authoritarian and harsh" manner: "Have you written the letters?"

Their relative places onstage situate her above him—a fact which she comments upon—indicating symbolically her momentary superiority. She offers to join him, and it is here that the Clown and Harlequin call for an appropriate music expressive of unrealized potential, "a music of years, of unopened moons and oceans." Psychic death leaves behind it only "the shroud of the air."

While the Young Man is anxious to consummate the union with the Typist, anxious to arrive at a safe stasis, his attempt to picture this as some kind of longed-for fulfillment is vitiated by the realization that spiritually he is sealing his doom. He says to the Typist, by way of describing the love nest awaiting them, that "up there . . . you can hear the nightingale sing," which is idyllic enough; but then he urges her to accompany him forthwith, "even if you can't hear it; *even if the bat should fly against the windowpanes*. . . ." In the chamber of the house in which the union should take place, the Young Man reveals his awareness of the fact that the union implies repression. Again we see that the "outside" (the bat against the windowpane) is actually the great nocturnal blackness which surrounds the conscious mind—with which the bat has well-known symbolic associations; for this "biological renegade"[61] represents what is to ego-consciousness an "alien motive or impulse":

In mediaeval legend the bat is a classical form of the Devil, representing the insidious power of an evil thought. What is implied . . . is the presence in the mind of certain ideas which are renegades from reason in the same uncanny fashion as the bat is a renegade mammal.[62]

The Young Man is trying to convince himself that he can successfully invest sufficient libido in the Typist to maintain a level of consciousness adequate to the task of living. He is trying to make her "matter" to him; for when we say that something "matters" to us, we are saying that it attracts a quantum of libido. Thus, when he passionately clutches her by the wrists she chides him with hurting her; and he replies, "That is the way to make you be aware of me."

This dialogue approaches its conclusion at the point where the Young Man believes that the union has been agreed to. The Typist declares that she will be his, he replies that he will be hers, and then she adds "timidly," "When five years have gone by!" The protagonist is stunned, but accepts the verdict of the Typist, who tells him, in effect, that his spiritual future does not lie with his ego-consciousness, for it is powerless to plan or construct. At one time he had fancied that his goal lay in the direction of the individuation process. He had hoped for self-transcendence through the agency of the unconscious, and the first part of the play took psychic inventory, so to speak, only to reveal that the task which he had set for himself was beyond his powers. He had no psychic center from which to act effectively; indeed, if we can speak of a "psychic center" at all, it is the center of the "blue storm" which threatened to break throughout the first act.

Abandoned by the *Novia*, the "keeper of the treasure," he attempts to negotiate a union with the Typist, who treats him no differently, for once again he is reduced to a passive *waiting*. Probably no reader of this play will have failed to note that *waiting* (*esperar*) is as much a dramatic motif as is the color blue, which is not surprising, in view of the fact that the title itself alludes to a five-year wait.

"Waiting" can be either a positive or negative thing, depending upon whether a *maturation* is taking place. In the first act the protagonist begins a dialogue concerned with waiting when he says to the First Friend, ". . . you can't understand that a person might wait five years for a woman, overflowing with and burned by a love that grows every day." The Friend replies that "there is no need to wait," as if to say that one must cut the Gordian Knot, act ruthlessly, commit oneself to a course of action, and let the Devil take the hindmost. The moment a psychic element is raised to consciousness, one should experiment with it, even if this be on a gross level. Who cares about waiting for the fruit to ripen? "I would rather eat it green—or better yet, cut the flower to wear in my lapel."

But the Young Man, we recall, defends his passivity; there are too many psychic elements clamoring for recognition, and there must be, somewhere deep within himself, a common denominator which will serve as a principle of unification. He is beset by the realization that he carries within an endless variety of potentials, and that he cannot select any one of them without cancelling out the others. Discovering the direction in which one confidently feels that one ought to develop is what we call "finding oneself"; the Young Man cannot make up his mind to commit himself spiritually once and for all, for he is loath to accept the spiritual limitation that a choice necessarily entails. The First Friend assures him "egotistically," "*You* come before the others"—which is to say that ego ought to be prized above all other psychic elements.

This is the "egotistic" point of view which seems to have an inordinate attraction for metropolitan, civilized man. It is his hybris, the wanton violence which ego commits on all other psychic functions. Ego is King and ought to be venerated by all. The fact that the Young Man can question this point of view is, of course, symptomatic of the storm gathering within. Like Lorca himself, the Young Man intuits a profound spiritual fact whose existence characteristically goes unrecognized by civilized Occidental men. Most of us appreciate that certain select, creative human beings—our "culture heroes," as it were—have had a rich and full spiritual life, but we like to account for this by attributing to them a special "talent," or "genius," letting the matter rest there, obscured by the application of a label. It hardly occurs to us that these special human beings were tapping a source of creativity common to all men. The man we consider to be "normal" is doing well merely to establish once and for all a dependable ego-structure and to get through life with a minimum of harassment from the unconscious. It is as if we were saying, "Repression is the secret of successful living."

The Young Man has "waited" five years. He is now on the threshold of adulthood, and the thought occurs to him (in the form of the First Friend) that "ego comes before all else." He counters this argument with the thought born out of a valuable intuition, that "by waiting, the knot comes untied and the fruit ripens." This reveals his recognition of the fact that life cannot satisfactorily be thought of merely as a process by which the ego comes to dominate the psyche. The psyche is an organism which fulfills its destiny by growing—if we can treat it as a product of nature, and not as a cast-iron weapon capable of shooting in a single direction: the weapon whose only purpose is to conquer the world outside.

Precious as this intuition is, the Young Man has not as yet made it effective, for he bears within a counter-tendency to grow impatient with waiting—the First Friend is evidence for this, convinced as he is that "*you* come before the others."

Returning to the last dialogue between the Young Man and the Typist, we must consider the implications of the remark that he wait another five years. It appears that the significance of this lies not in the fact that *five* years are involved, but rather that the waiting period corresponds roughly to adolescence, the period of life during which the *Novia* was expected to return. It is obvious enough that the waiting did not produce a "ripened fruit," for a period of his life has come to a close, and he has nothing to show for it. What should have been a period of spiritual expansion has turned out to be a progressively limiting experience centering finally upon the Typist. But she is not so easily seduced: the union must be put off for five years (= "nine years, nine months, and nine nights"). One notes that in the emotional scene immediately preceding this pronouncement, the Young Man had whipped himself into a frenzy of passion over the Typist, very much as if he were protesting too much. In the end, however, he cannot bring off this piece of self-deception. The Typist is no fit substitute for the long-awaited treasure. The new direction which he would like to give his life cannot, finally, be convincingly invested with any libido; she says "timidly," like a profoundly rooted suspicion which will always intrude itself ever so slightly, "Go back to waiting."

Now this "waiting" can be, as noted, either positive or negative, and only the dramatic context can tell us which affect applies here. When the Typist informs the Young Man that he must wait five more years, the energy and passion with which he had managed to work himself up is instantly dissipated. He claps a hand to his brow, says, "Ah!" and begins slowly to descend the stairs connecting the two stages. He has just been told to do the same thing he has already done, which is to say that the final realization presents itself that he cannot deliberately choose to cut himself off from the area inhabited by the *Novia*. He cannot willfully enclose himself with the Typist in that chamber "upstairs" and expect to dwell happily while the nightingale sings joyfully "outside" his window—for he knows well that the bat will come flying against the pane.

Up till now it was possible to hope that "waiting" would be rewarded by the harvest of a ripened fruit; now it transpires that he bided his time in vain, for he is no more oriented at present than he was five years ago. Though his adolescence is irretrievably gone, though he is on the threshold of adulthood, he has done nothing more than give himself a future restricted to the small circle of ego-consciousness. His enthusiastic attempt to invest his persona with some vitality is patently false; she will not absorb the proffered libido, but instead shrinks back and tells him to wait some more. His enthusiasm is instantly deflated, and as he turns away from her she remains where she is, on the stage of the miniature theater, frozen into an "ecstatic" attitude.

This stage direction deserves some attention, for it gives us our final view of the Typist: it is how we (and the Young Man) will finally remember her. The "ecstatic" attitude has two notable characteristics: (1) it is immobile, and (2) it conveys, naturally, the idea that the subject is in a trance, meaning that the soul is absent from the body. When the Typist turns the Young Man away, she strikes an attitude which reveals not only the rigidity that is characteristic of her but also *withdrawal*. She is elsewhere, spiritually absent from the stage of the miniature theater which represents the Young Man's personal psyche in its proper perspective. This is, no doubt, an appropriate delineation of the persona, which is, by definition, directed outward and away from matters which concern the intimacy of the psyche. An efficiently operating persona is (like a good stenographer) absorbed in taking care of our "correspondence" with the world around us. It carries us out of ourselves, and we fall into a role —a mask or attitude remarkably invariable which could indeed be described as a "pose"—except that the word "pose" suggests a fundamental insincerity which ought not to be attributed to the persona. The persona represents, rather, a trance-like attitude, "sincerely" absorbed in the external business at hand—and so is, at last, quite as alien to the Young Man as the First Mask. Hence the appearance of

John, who emerges to cover the Typist with a "large white cape." This symbolic act is not essentially different from the act of "traveling," for they are both assimilable to the idea of dissociation. The function which "goes on a trip" or is "covered by a cape" is being depotentiated or repressed.

As the Young Man goes down into the dark forest, the First Mask speaks up: "The Count kisses the picture of me in my riding habit." This is the final use of the athletic motif, which we have now seen in the form of rugby football, wrestling, tennis, and (golf) knickers. At the very moment when union with the Typist is revealed as impossible, the First Mask announces that her lover still values her as a libido-object. In spite of the undesirable qualities imputed to her by the Young Man, she still finally appears, not like the "ecstatic" Typist, but as a horsewoman; that is the way the Count remembers her, and it is that memory he values—the memory of her as a "libidinal expert."

We should recall that at the end of the scene between the Young Man and the Mannequin, the Mannequin "faints" as the protagonist rushes off to seek his new treasure. In the following act occurs the dialogue between the Typist and the First Mask; subsequently the Young Man hears the Typist singing, "Where are you going, my love, with the air in a glass and the sea in a windowpane?" This little song accusing him of being hopelessly limited, or repressed, is reminiscent of the Mannequin's song, in that they both express the notion of the sea as an area with which there is no hope of dealing. The Mannequin's treasure is lost in the sea, and to this the Typist adds the idea that the Young Man is spiritually so confined that he is trying to glimpse the ocean within the limits imposed by a windowpane.

Now these two scenes, ending with the two songs, have a curious relationship: when we last see the Mannequin, she ends her mournful little song and collapses in a faint; and after the Young Man has made his first unsuccessful attempt to approach the Typist, she repeats her own mournful little song, at which point the First Mask reenters, "sniffing incessantly a vial of smelling salts." At the same time she must deliver a relatively long, hysterical speech, telling us how she has finally deserted the Count for good. According to the stage directions then, this speech must be repeatedly interrupted by her need for the smelling salts.

We have already seen that there are certain similarities to be remarked between the Mannequin and the First Mask: the one is gold, the other yellow; the one is a wooden figure whose only purpose is to exhibit, or keep in protective readiness a symbolic garment—in a sense, she *is* the garment; the other smothered in clothing which, according to Lorca's directions, must belong to the fashion of the turn of the century. Further, the First Mask is identified precisely by that very mask of hers, and she wears what is obviously a wig of yellow silk which falls about her "like a mantle." This highly conspicuous and artificial appearance of hers is very reminiscent of the Mannequin, for the two of them are sharply differentiated from all the other characters by their extraordinary dress and their singularly nonhuman features. Further, if we recall that a third character—the effeminate Second Friend—is likewise required to be extravagantly dressed (his suit must have an "exceedingly exaggerated cut"), it begins to appear that the three of them form a series which shows the unconscious as its image undergoes a progressive transformation. The Second Friend is regressive, and desires only to return to his feminine source. The needed consolidation of his "lower masculinity," or youthful virility, does not take place, and thus the Young Man, at the end of his adolescence, has no standing ground which would enable him to establish any kind of safe relationship with woman. For the Second Friend, woman was Mother (source); for the Young Man, it is a voluptuous but unattainable *Novia*. When she abandons him, the situation of which the Second Friend is symptomatic is reactivated as a Mannequin mourning its lost treasure. The Mannequin finally collapses in a faint. Still later, the Typist tells of the hopeless limitations under which the Young Man labors, at which point the First Mask appears, striving to avoid fainting by the use of smelling salts.

"Fainting," like "traveling" and "cloaking," means repression: falling into a state of unconsciousness, involuntarily dropping into the unconscious. The First Mask, frankly hysterical, falls to the floor weeping ("Can't you see how I'm laughing?") and says that her deserted lover will search everywhere for her. She is going to hide, she says, "in the blackberry bushes." She announces this intention to conceal herself, and then, like a child who really wants to be found (for hiding is just a game) she repeats loudly, *"In the blackberry bushes,"* as if to make sure that her hiding place will eventually be discovered. She adds hysterically that she is shouting because she doesn't want her Arturo to hear. What it is that is being lost to consciousness here can be inferred, to an extent, from the reference to blackberry bushes.

There are two other references in the play to blackberry bushes: (1) in the scene of the Dead Child and the Blue Cat, where the Child says that he used to go off and eat blackberries and apples, when he was a living, happy child; and (2) the scene immediately following the exit of the Rugby Player, when the *Novia* says that she would like to be so strong and resistant that she could even take hold of a blackberry bush without feeling the thorns.

The blackberry bush appears elsewhere in Lorca's work, in contexts which are explicitly symbolic. Before glancing at these, it might be useful to recall the characteristics associated with the blackberry bush which are responsible for the symbolic role which Lorca assigns to it; for the blackberry bush grows wild, and (like the thorny rosebush) bears something desirable which cannot be attained without risk of painful injury.

The poem *Blackberry Bush with Gray Trunk*[63] consists of a dialogue between the speaker and the bush:

> Blackberry bush with gray trunk,
> give me a cluster of my own.
>
> Blood and thorns. Draw near.
> If you love me, I'll love you.
>
> Leave your fruit of green and shadow
> upon my tongue, blackberry bush.
>
> What a lingering embrace would I give you
> in the penumbra of my thorns.
>
> Blackberry bush, where are you going?
> To seek a love that you do not give me.

The speaker asks the bush to give freely of its fruit, but it replies that he will have to undergo the physical pain of gathering it. He will have to sacrifice blood, and in the dark shadow of its thorns it will embrace him. The speaker has nothing to say, faced with the prospect of the excruciating embrace, and so the bush "turns away," in search of a love that the speaker will not (or cannot) give.

Here the speaker's desire for something for nothing is represented as an attitude deserving of dismissal, since the treasure which lies hidden in the dark shadows of the bush cannot be retrieved without danger. Taking this as a psychological metaphor, we can see that the danger is a necessary evil, since ego-consciousness is essentially conservative and can come into possession of new contents (the coveted fruit) only through transformation—i.e., destruction—of the old, which it tends to resist. New inner knowledge, like a secret, requires of necessity a fresh psychological equilibrium; it cannot merely stand idly within one's consciousness. It is *assimilated,* and the old conscious structure gives way to the new. One's consciousness has been expanded, and the scars (as if left by the thorns protecting the shadowed fruit deep within the bush) bear witness to the destruction wrought.

In 1928 Lorca delivered a lecture on the subject of creative imagination, and developed there (as might be expected) the idea that poetic creation is the result of creative interaction between the conscious and the unconscious; and there he characterizes the poetic search for the "treasure" as requiring that one cross a dangerous threshold barred by blackberry branches "so that seeking hands will be injured by love of it."[64]

These passages indicate clearly enough, then, the symbolic role which the fruit-bearing bramble occupied in Lorca's mind; it is basically the guardian of an inner treasure, and so not qualitatively different from the dragon which must be vanquished by the knight. In *Five Years,* the Child was given to eating blackberries; the *Novia* expresses the wish that she were capable of grasping a blackberry branch with her bare hands; and finally the First Mask announces loudly and emphatically that she intends to hide herself among the blackberry bushes. Symbolically these passages all refer to an instinctual value far below the threshold of consciousness. One must expose one's conscious structure to the risk of plunging into the "penumbra" of the lacerating thorns. The First Mask, when she announces her intention to hide in the blackberry bushes, is telling the Young Man hopefully that if he (i.e., Count Arturo) wants to find her he must be willing to expose himself to a blood sacrifice—for the bush will defend itself; its thorns are strong, and they pierce painfully like so many small stilettos.

We have already seen how the Dead Child is symbolically related to the Second Friend (they are both dressed in white and associated with blue), and so we can add him to our series of images representing the Young Man's apprehension of the unconscious, as it is transformed in his eyes: Child, Second Friend, Mannequin, and First Mask. The Mask is going to hide herself in the blackberry bushes which the Child was wont to frequent, and so the series comes full circle.

The scene depicting the final break with the Typist ends as the Young Man "desperately" seeks a way back to his house. The "ecstatic" Typist calls out to him one last time: "I'll wait for you, love! Come back soon!" This, as the Young Man wanders about, "trembling," confused by contradictory and ironic instructions. In the depths of his instability, it is the last call he will hear from the world of conscious stability.

The setting for the second part of the last act is the library of Act One. The Young Man has returned from a trip, and open luggage lies scattered about the room. The Valet and a Maid are gossiping about the Concierge, whom they identify as the former lover of Count Arturo.

The Young Man enters, showing signs that he is about to faint—a fact which must be related, of course, to the fainting of the Mannequin and to the smelling salts of the First Mask. The Mannequin was a depotentiated symbol (who is at present headless and inert); the First Mask was a debased symbol; and the two of them were fainting.

"Fainting" is the nearest thing to a "symbolic pun" that can be imagined, since it means "to lose consciousness" or "to become unconscious"—and hence expresses the idea of repression or involuntary forgetting. The *Novia,* as a value, was repressed by the Young Man (she fell into the unconscious); she left behind a hollow symbol (the Mannequin) which in turn was repressed: it collapsed into a faint. Subsequently, after the Typist sings that the protagonist is like a tiny vessel containing the air and the ocean, the First Mask appears, on the verge of fainting. Throughout the play the Young Man's principal problem seemed to lie in seeking the road to psychic wholeness; but his conscious resources were so few that, as he became progressively aware that the route to the treasure lay closed to him, a new problem took shape. It is not now a question of finding psychic wholeness; it is, rather, a question of maintaining a precarious foothold in the realm of conscious orientation: he himself is now on the verge of fainting.

The Young Man engages his Valet in a conversation which reveals that he is suffering an alarming regression, a confused and frightened retreat from the riddle of consciousness. The world of his childhood floods his mind, and he is struck by the fact that everything seems so much smaller than it once did. He gives himself up to the spiritual well-being of that forgotten world and sets aside the insoluble problems posed by the phenomenon of ego-consciousness. His regression to familiar paths makes him feel like a fountain flowing freely, or a weather vane turning with the wind. "But what about the wind itself?" the Valet asks, in effect: "Does the wind feel all right?" And the Young Man replies, "I am fine"—as explicit a use of the *pneuma* symbol as one is apt to find.

The Young Man must change into formal dress, and the Valet tells him that his tailcoat is laid out on the bed. The extent of the Young Man's regression is here indicated by the fact that he resists the idea of the tailcoat (i.e., his grown-up, "formal" self) laid out on his present bed—which is "so big" and "so empty" by contrast with the little bed he used to sleep in:

> How comfortable it was. I remember that when I was a child, I saw an enormous moon rise behind the railing at the foot of the bed . . . or was it through the grille of the balcony? I don't know.

The text here requires a brief commentary on Lorca's use of the word *barandilla* ("railing," "balustrade"), since it has for him a special significance.

Barandilla (along with *barandal,* elsewhere used by Lorca) is derived from *baranda,* which is cognate to our *verandah.* Lorca writes variously of the railings of porches, bridges, piers, and balconies (cf. the "balustrades" of the foyer at the Paris Opera) as expressive of a *standpoint,* or *observer's point of view.* In Spain the ubiquitous balcony characteristically has a protective railing by which one sits (as on the old-fashioned American front porch) to watch the passing parade and to be seen; hence the remark in Lorca's play *Doña Rosita the Spinster:* "A girl who doesn't want to get married doesn't sit day and night at her balcony rail."[65]

The protagonist of *Five Years* says that he confused the railing at the foot of his bed with the railing of the balcony, as he saw the moon rise. He here confuses the railing of his own little bed with the railing of the balcony fronting on the great moonlit night "outside." The one is personal, while the other—part of the house itself, and opening directly onto the great forest-world beyond—transcends

the purely individual in the same way that the transpersonal unconscious constitutes a vast, nocturnal world beyond the diminutive
precinct (little bed) of our own personal unconscious.

The passage seems aimed at suggesting that the Young Man, when
a child, confused the contents of his personal unconscious with
material from the collective unconscious. The "confusion" is not
meant negatively, of course, but suggests, rather, that when the
Young Man was a child an avenue was open to the transpersonal unconscious which has since then been closed. Once there was a "confusion"—i.e., mingling—of personal and collective contents. Subsequently however, the Young Man "gave the bed away"—to his
Typist. That is to say, a psychic shift has occurred; material from
the transpersonal unconscious no longer rises into view like a great
moon seen through the railing of one's bed. The personal unconscious
has become nothing more than a function of the conscious mind, just
as the little bed is now in the possession of the Typist.

Subsequent to this the Young Man voices a curious complaint:
"How is it that the air in this house is always so rarified?" While it is
evident by this remark that he is experiencing difficulty in catching
his breath, his explanation for the discomfort ("the air is too thin")
is symptomatic of his primary illness—loss of contact with the creative, feminine unconscious.

This neurotic complaint has been documented clinically, and is
discussed by Gerhard Adler in his study of a patient suffering from
claustrophobia: "She had had very occasional attacks in her middle
thirties, and they had always occurred when she was staying at some
mountain inn or hotel."[66] These attacks were accompanied by the
feeling that she was no longer in contact with her earth-rooted instincts: she succumbed to the horrifying belief that she was living in
a void. Consequently, whenever she sojourned in the mountains, her
material surroundings seemed to symbolize a separation from the
earth "below." She was isolated on a mountain height: "height with
all its symbolical significance of 'spirit,' the '*thin air*' and 'light' of
the masculine attitude as compared with the 'earthiness' of the
feminine attitude."[67]

The Young Man's loss of creative contact with the unconscious
through fear of it results in a rarified atmosphere and, at the same
time, in the hysterical sensation that his house is being "invaded" by
the botanical realm to which the great forest belongs:

143

How is it that the air in this house is always so rarified? I'm going to cut down all the flowers in the garden—especially those cursed oleanders that grow over the walls, and that grass that springs up by itself at midnight.

The Young Man leaves to dress just as the three Card Players arrive. The time has come for the protagonist to stake his lifeblood on a game of cards. While this "game" appears to be a mere symbolic formality, it is evident from anecdotes told by the Players that on occasion it has actually happened that the intended victim did indeed win.

As the Players relate these anecdotes, we may note that they are accustomed to playing with the French (or English) deck—our standard bridge deck—rather than with the deck normally used in Spain. For our present purpose it is sufficient to point out that the principal difference lies in the matter of suits; for instead of our hearts, spades, diamonds, and clubs, the Spanish deck retains the suits of the ancient Gypsy tarot cards: cups, swords, pentacles (gold coins), and wands, respectively. It retains also the picture-symbols for the four suits, quite unlike the highly stylized pips appearing on the English deck. Thus the four of swords, for example, is marked either by four actual swords or by four daggers; the four of wands usually bears four realistically drawn clubs of Hercules; the four of pentacles bears four gold coins; and the four of cups—corresponding to our hearts—displays four chalices or Grails.

In *Five Years* this last correlation is explicitly made by the First Player, who recalls that he once played cards with a young man in Venice who appeared to be on the point of throwing in his *as de coeur* (ace of hearts) *which was filled with blood*. The Player was about to appropriate it when the young man fled, drinking from the ace of cups which he held. Though the Player thought he would win by taking the young man's ace of hearts, he unexpectedly lost because his opponent was able to produce its equivalent in the form of a blood-filled Grail from which he drank new life. Here we should note that the commonplace symbolism of the Grail (or chalice) corresponds to what we have been considering to be the primary theme of our play: the quest for the treasure (self) hidden in the feminine unconscious. The disappearance of the *Novia* coincided with the loss of libidinal energy (the Rugby Player), intimately associated with the flow of lifeblood. The collapse of the ego-structure and the failure to individuate here is "death"; the victim grows "pale" as the blood drains from his face, and he will surely die unless he can (as it infrequently happens) activate a new and unexpected source of energy with which to nourish the expiring conscious structure.

The Third Player tells of an old man of India who, like the young man of Venice, suddenly reversed his fortune and escaped with his life:

> In India I played with an old man who had not a single drop of blood left on the cards. I was awaiting the moment to hurl myself upon him, when he took a special aniline dye and dyed all the cups red and managed to escape among the trees.

We recall that in the second act mention is made of two fans which the Young Man had given to the *Novia:* a blue one depicting "three sunken gondolas," and a white one with the head of a tiger painted on it. (It would be profitable here to draw attention to the associative connections between the two fans and the two card games just recounted, for the association of *gondolas* and *Venice* is inevitable, while that of *tiger* and *India* is hardly fortuitous.) The *Novia* made much of the fact that the Young Man was bloodless, whereas she was filled with hot blood. He had presented her with two fans, one evidently associated with a dominant feminine unconscious (boats sunken in watery depths), and one with a dominant masculine consciousness (the destructiveness, courage, strength, self-confidence, and so forth of the tiger). Both fans had been broken and "lost"; they were both dissociated from the *Novia*, who subsequently "disappeared" with the libido figure.

Now we hear that a pale young man very nearly succumbed to one of the Card Players, but at the last moment he was able to activate a sufficient quantity of libido to enable him to escape his "fate"— for he ran away with two girls. Applying this anecdote to the Young Man himself, we might understand it as a retrospective allusion to his attempts to save himself by transferring his allegiance first to the Mannequin, and second to the Typist.

The second card game was played against an "old man" of India. We may recall that the Young Man's attempts to save himself from destruction ended by "wounding" the Old Man; but that eventually the latter appears all dressed in blue, or sufficiently invested with libido to witness (oversee) a final split between the Young Man and the Typist.

We might note here that a deck of cards is very much like an allegory of the psyche, for it is made up of a large number of interrelated units (the fifty-two cards) which, like the many different psychic functions,[68] change in value and significance according to the game being played (my psyche and your psyche are each playing different games; therefore my cards do not have the same combinative meanings as yours). But cards are not used exclusively to play games. They are used to tell fortunes, and the fortune-telling pack par excellence—the tarot—is normally considered to be a potential representation of the psychological makeup of the querent. Fortune-telling is not essentially involved with predicting the future; rather, it is intended to reveal to the adept the spiritual dynamics of the querent, who will then gain some measure of control over his future by attuning his attitudes and behavior accordingly.[69]

In the play, then, the two card games—one with a young man in Venice, another with an old man in India—are associated symbolically with two broken fans, by virtue of the fact that both cards and fans carry symbolic images related to the psyche of the Young Man, who is himself a querent, or "seeker." He is now struggling to maintain a certain autonomy in the face of domination by the feminine unconscious—a situation suggested by the image of the sunken gondolas. The tiger depicted on the other fan must be seen as symbolic of the logos function, as masculine power and confidence in its ability to usurp for its own purposes extraordinary amounts of libido—"his own purposes" being those related to the control of all major life situations by ego-consciousness.

The Young Man himself is certainly no tiger vis-à-vis his circumstances, as is clearly demonstrated by the fact that he ultimately proposes to identify with an unsuitable persona image. This identification cannot finally be brought about; the Young Man cannot, in the end, commit himself to a self-imposed exile from his own instinctual nature. The human being possessed by a deep-seated sense of the need to find a new psychic pattern may sooner regress into what is hopefully a temporary chaos rather than give up the quest entirely by surrendering to the rigidity of a sterile ego-structure that promises to be nothing more than a spiritual straitjacket confining him for the rest of his life. The crucial moment arrives when perhaps only one tremendous effort would save him from drowning in the unconscious —but the price is too great, that terrible tension required to maintain a conscious pattern of life that has no discernible purpose beyond that of perpetuating itself so that one can present a "sane" façade to the world outside. A life that uses all one's energy in the single purpose of perpetuating a meaningless "sanity" is a bleak prospect indeed, just as is the life of the reformed alcoholic who exhausts himself in the effort to remain sober; what should have been a point of departure has become a torturous goal. And from the conversation of the three Players, it is apparent that the Young Man has lost all determination to maintain a significant level of consciousness: "His life is escaping through his eyes . . . and staining his shirt front blue."

The Second Player tells a third anecdote, this time concerning an abortive card game with a "boy who, in Sweden . . . , and on the point of dying," escaped not by playing a trump, but by emitting a powerful stream of blood that nearly left them blind.

If we are to seek a symbolic pattern in these anecdotes, we must surely make note of the fact that the three intended victims were (1) a child, (2) a young man, and (3) an old man, each of whom managed to mobilize enough libido to retain a foothold in conscious reality. That is to say that their relative ages seem to allude to the very real fact that the problem of maintaining conscious organization in the face of threatened disintegration is one that remains potential throughout life, and which must be solved by means appropriate to one's years. According to the first anecdote the young man in Venice had available enormous amounts of psychosexual libido by means of which he effected his escape. At that stage of life the internal enemy may be countered or outflanked by a flight into the charged activity of the "lower masculinity": ". . . he had an ace of cups [i.e., the chalice] overflowing, and drinking from it, he fled by way of the Grand Canal, with two girls."

Technically, the Grand Canal of Venice is known in Spanish (by analogy with the Italian) as the *Canal Grande*. In our text, Lorca calls it the *Gran Canal* which, while it could be a colloquial variant, suggests (as proclitic adjectives characteristically do in Spanish) a metaphorical value. (Compare in English the meaning of royal, in the expression "the Royal Palace," with its metaphorical meaning in the expression "the royal road to riches.") Certainly sexuality is popularly treated by young men as the *Gran Canal* of the libidinal flow, as libido's mainstream of self-affirmation, as the "royal road" to egocentric felicity.

The old man of India, we learn, averted psychic disintegration by another means. The text does not specify precisely how, but tells us that it was by means of "a special aniline dye" which he was able to produce at the last moment. This is very suggestive, for it means that the old man, by contrast to the youth in Venice, did not have recourse to any spontaneous natural means (e.g., burgeoning sexual libido); rather, he saved himself by means of a substance which had to be synthesized; and, indeed, consolidation of psychic structure after the middle years must be the result of labor. It is not given to one "naturally," as the automatic consequence of maturation.

The third of the intended victims, the boy in Sweden, did not save himself by means of any special tactic. He did not resolve an internal problem by transferring it to another sphere (e.g., the psychosexual), nor did he "synthesize" a solution; he simply asserted an all-powerful élan—that naked vitality which Lorca was wont to impute to children. He did not "escape," but rather depotentiated the forces which threatened him. His opposition was irreducibly direct and obviated the necessity of playing out a "card game." The child's answer to psychic threats is simple and aggressive, for he still participates generously in the realm of the unconscious, like a fish in water. The child simply "turned on" his vitality, and in so doing negated the entire problem of the need for a consciously centered psychic structure—the problem implied by questions such as Who am I? and What is my place in life?

We have already commented on the fact that two of the three places named—Venice and India—bear what seems to be a deliberate reference to the two fans given to the *Novia* by the Young Man. The introduction of *Sweden*, however, raises a greater interpretive problem, and perhaps it is not possible to achieve anything beyond a general surmise.

The three places named hint at a certain universality, just as the three intended victims suggest a life span; for we have India, Venice, and Sweden—three life-styles, three cultural world views: the Mediterranean ("sunny south"), Scandinavia ("frozen north"), and India ("mysterious Orient"). Rather than *Sweden*, could Lorca as well have said Norway, or Iceland? We could hypothesize on the basis of other Lorcan references[70] that the north and the south were for him stereotypically symbolic of two complementary halves of human vitality: the introverted, smoldering "metaphysical" profundity attributed to northern peoples, and the alleged extraverted, passionate vitality of Mediterranean peoples. The argument would, however, be impertinent at this point, since it would lead us far afield solely on the basis of a hypothetical connection between Sweden and the north. For the present, however, there seems to be no discernible evidence which would permit us to amplify the allusion to Sweden.

At this stage of our analysis we ought to point out that the three Players are complete strangers to the drama, by contrast with all the other characters; as such, they cannot well be seen as components of the Young Man's *personal* psyche. Rather, they (like the three Fates) are the personification of the final triumph of forces from the deepest layers of the psyche—the "objective" psyche, which ". . . is impervious to the critical and ordering activity of consciousness; in it we hear the voice of uninfluenced primal nature. . . ."[71]

Any human being who feels himself driven by forces deep within, forces which he feels himself powerless to oppose, will be tempted to objectify their existence as fate, or destiny.[72] Hence the conversation of the three Players may be considered in much the same way that we consider the "external" voices heard by the mentally disturbed, who feel themselves falling further and further away from the threshold of adaptation to empirical reality. The following clinical description of a schizophrenic patient bears a suggestive analogy to the "destiny" of our protagonist, and will serve to clarify the issue:

> . . . there was an insistent but unclear notion of a journey with her father in the Pacific. The whole situation was tinged with guilt, people accusing her and being about to punish her. These are typical representations of the regressive flow of the libido away from the role of conscious adaptation to the outer world and toward the unconscious. . . .[73]

The close similarity between psychotic withdrawal and bodily death should also be noted, since it has its origin in the mind of the patient, and is not merely a metaphor invented by the clinical observer:

> . . . [the patient] said that she had already died and was resurrected and living in the afterlife, which is to say that the ego had died to the world of reality and found itself in the "other world," the "beyond," the "land of spirits," the inner world of the unconscious. . . . that other world like an odorous vapor invaded the life of the here and

now, which then became an intermingling of the world of time and the world of eternity or of conscious and unconscious.[74]

The passage from one stage of life into another involves a spiritual death and rebirth, a transferal of libido from one powerful attachment to a new one (as from "mother" to "the elders"), a fact that is abundantly evidenced by primitive rites of initiation, where the initiates are made to dramatize some form of demise, burial, and resurrection.[75] This is a massive withdrawal from the obsolescent adaptation to reality in order to regroup one's psychic resources: the boy must "forget" his childhood and be reborn into a new psychic world, e.g., the world of the warrior.[76] This withdrawal, ritualized in primitive cultures, appears to be symptomatic of what may occur in severe cases of mental disturbance among civilized adolescents, as Perry suggests:

> Catatonic schizophrenia abounds in symbolism of the initiation process, and it occurs characteristically in adolescence, either during the second decade or, if the psychological work of this period of life is delayed or prolonged, in the third or even fourth decades.[77]

While the protagonist of *Five Years* is not a clinical case but rather a fictional creation of Lorca's (who had no formal knowledge of psychopathology), it would certainly seem that he is portraying a schizophrenic process leading to catatonia. By the end of the drama our Young Man evinces symptoms clinically described by Plokker[78] as characteristic of such a condition: he has lost all "affective contact" with the community of people, and in the final moments he confronts only archetypal "strangers," components of his own being who clearly cannot become parts of a functioning structure, but who appear only as personifications of the fated end. Similarly, we have seen in the "blue storm" and in the "rarified air" a dramatization of what Plokker describes as the patient's unrest and anxious expectancy of approaching disaster:

> . . . there is a different atmosphere surrounding things, the old familiar surroundings have a strange "charge," there is something in the air. The patient is, however, unable to say what is threatening him. The simplest things acquire symbolic significance.[79]

The three Players may well be a hallucination, for, as Plokker observes, "the patient vaguely feels his own mental destruction, the change and disappearance of his familiar world. He now projects this feeling on to the world around about him."[80]

Finally, the protagonist appears to reproduce the last stage of withdrawal, a falling into the void, where the disturbance ceases to evolve:

> The patient no longer seems to be aware of this objective stagnation, the inner emptiness and coldness are no longer experienced as being painful. . . . There is no longer any "becoming," only a limited "being." The symbolic process is past and has left behind it a deserted region. It is as if a typhoon had swept over a landscape. The wind has now dropped again, but everything is destroyed, collapsed, flattened to the ground.[81]

All this appears to be the nearest thing to a "documentary description" as we are likely to get of what ails the Young Man. He has attempted to return from his journey into the great forest, only to discover that he must finally confront the three Fates, three total strangers who invade his house, completely assured that this is one victim who will not escape them; which is to say that his own sense of defeat is definitively externalized, and it only remains to go through the motions of a formalized surrender.

The three Players dominate the stage of the house, and when they confront the Young Man formally attired, they taunt him; for his costume, cognate to the persona-function (social role playing) fits him well. The Third Player remarks that "there are times when our clothes look so fine on us that we wish we might never—"

"—that we can no longer tear them from our back," interrupts the Second Player.

In these two remarks is summed up the dilemma of the Young Man who had hoped to establish a minimal foothold in reality by identifying his conscious personality, or sense of conscious continuity, with the image of the "Mechanographer." For one Player says, in effect, that sometimes our "social garment" fits us so well that we should like never to doff it. This is the comfortable security of a social role—but the danger of such a role is obvious: for once we allow ourselves to become too closely identified with the role, then we suffer the consequences of locking ourselves into it. We mummify, and all other spiritual potentials wither. So well does the garment fit that it is no longer a question of *desiring* to remain in it; rather, so well does it fit "that we can no longer [even] *tear* it from our body."

The notion suggested here is no different from the extraordinary (and unintentionally sinister) statement made at the turn of the century by William James, apropos of *habits*, and expressed likewise in terms of clothing:

> Habit is . . . the enormous fly-wheel of society, its most precious conservative agent. . . . It alone prevents the hardest and most repulsive walks of life from being deserted by those brought up to tread therein. . . . Already at the age of twenty-five you see the professional mannerism settling down on the young commercial traveller, on the young doctor, on the young minister, on the young counsellor-at-law. You see the little lines of cleavage running through the character, . . . the ways of the "shop," . . . from which the man can by-and-by no more escape than his coat-sleeve can suddenly fall into a new set of folds.[82]

All this, which impresses us as a sentence of doom for the individual, is meant by James to show the value to society of straitjacketing its members. The conclusion which James writes to this paragraph and the fact that he seems to find in it no cause for pessimism clarify for us, I think, why the Young Man should choose to cut himself off from the bleak, mechanical future awaiting him; for even though a man becomes enslaved to his persona-function from which he "can by-and-by no more escape than his coat-sleeve can suddenly fall into a new set of folds," James says,

> On the whole, it is best he should not escape. It is well for the world that in most of us, by the age of thirty, the character *has set like plaster, and will never soften again.*[83]

To speak and feel like this, it would seem that one must possess a mentality which values the society over the individual—the unfortunate individual, who has no choice but to yield, or to return to his source. The Young Man of *Five Years* has made his choice and has "invited" the three Players to oversee the final surrender.

They, as we have noted, are taunting the Young Man, for the garment he now wears is his "burial garment," which he donned expressly to meet them; and so well does it fit him that he will never again be able to remove it, since, in reality, there will be no "he," no consciously acting subject capable of desiring or willing its removal.

Card play commences, and (since the outcome is inevitable) the Young Man, gripped by his fear of the impending change, attempts

to postpone it. He offers drinks and recommends especially the chartreuse, which is like (he says) "an immense night with a green moon,
within a castle inhabited by a young man with algae of gold." This,
as his agony begins. He is falling into his "fated" living death, and I
take the suggestive description of the chartreuse to be a pathetic
and wishful vision of the final "nirvanic" state in which he would
like to float painlessly forever.

He succumbs to "fatal" necessity. His "heart" is destroyed, the
thread of life is cut, and the three Players leave precipitately. The
Young Man is fast falling into the other world, and he calls out to
his valet:

> Young Man. John. John. One must live.
> Echo. John. John.
> Young Man. [dying] I've lost everything.
> Echo. I've lost everything.
> Young Man. My love . . .
> Echo. Love.
> Young Man. [On the sofa.] John.
> Echo. John.
> Young Man. Is there . . .?
> Echo. Is there . . .
> Second Echo. [More distant.] Is there . . .
> Young Man. . . . no man here?
> Echo. Here . . .
> Second Echo. Here . . .
> [The Young Man dies. The Servant appears with a lighted can-
> delabrum. The clock strikes twelve. Curtain.]

Lorca's use of the *echoes* (first one, then two), besides bearing a
curious (and probably fortuitous) similarity to the schizophrenic
symptom known as "echolalia,"[84] is surely intended to render dramatically the acoustic effect of *emptiness*: the reverberating emptiness
of a cave, or the emptiness of an abandoned house, which characteristically resounds, hollow, when all the furnishings are removed.

The final appearance of the Valet is indicative, I think, of the last
vestige of life remaining to the Young Man; for here, where John
enters carrying a candelabrum (= minimal illumination), he re-
inforces a suspicion which is raised from his very first appearance
in Act One. He always walks on tiptoe, is unobtrusive, and silently
obeys commands—all of which suggests that the role assigned to

him is that of the motor function; and at the final moment, as the clock strikes midnight, the Young Man expires—and the barely mobile valet is the only sign of life left in the house.

The play ends, then, at the stroke of twelve midnight, and so it is finally appropriate to consider the question of the elapse of time with respect to the dramatic action. Certainly there is a quesion to be considered, though it need present no serious interpretive problem, as long as we understand that Lorca's references to the clock are not related to sidereal time. Rather, they are symbolic, as is every other element of the drama. We are concerned with a chain of psychological events which are outside the time continuum, as are the succeeding "events" of a dream which, while impressing the dreamer as occupying several minutes or hours of sidereal time, can be measured only by the stop watch. Most of us have probably experienced this in such a way that the actual time consumed by the dream could be verified: as when an elaborate dream episode culminates in the sound of an auto horn awakening us; between the time that the sound waves impinged upon the ear, and the time that they were converted into an acoustic impression, the sleeper may have lived out several "hours" of an oneiric fantasy *culminating* in the sensory impact of the original stimulus.[85]

Such is the compression of time in *Five Years*. We are given to understand that Act One consumes only seconds, since the clock strikes six shortly after the curtain goes up, and John tells us that it is six o'clock just before the end of the act. This must be taken to mean, then, that the passage of sidereal time has nothing to do with the dramatic action, since this takes place within the matrix of the unconscious mind—in the realm of Becoming, of "mythological time."

The question of time in Act Three is quite the opposite, for the last scene begins at the same point in time occupied by Act One. That is to say that the Dead Child has *just been buried*. Indeed, this burial is a datum that binds the entire action together beyond the threshold of sidereal time. If we were to attempt to interpret these time indications sidereally, we would reach the untenable conclusion that the final scene occupies *six hours*, since its beginning coincides with the burial of the Dead Child (six o'clock), whereas the final curtain is rung down at the stroke of twelve. Any consideration of the time element as being other than symbolic must lead nowhere.

A reading of the play as if it were constructed according to the demands of logic must run afoul of itself, and the attempt to extricate oneself by the application of further logic only worsens matters, as is evidenced by the following commentary:

> . . . [The Young Man] is alone. His last desperate words are answered only by a strong echo. . . . Juan crosses the room with a candelabrum as the clock chimes six times. The echo repeats the six strokes. The time is the same as at the start of the play. . . .[86]

This represents an attempt to reject the time indications, while accepting them simultaneously. We reject them when we say, "But six hours could not possibly have elapsed in the last scene"; and we accept them when we say, "Obviously it is *still* six o'clock." The stage direction does not say that an echo "repeats the six strokes"; it says that "the clock strikes twelve" (*El reloj da las doce*).

In the world of "mythological time" the clock is just as symbolic as everything else, as is obvious in the following hypothetical dream:

> Sundown. I am alone on a great prairie. Gradually I become aware that a shadowy figure is approaching me. I turn to flee, but then I see that my way is barred by a high wall. Suddenly I am not on a prairie at all; I am entirely surrounded by a high wall! All is dark and gloomy. Panic-stricken, I look up to the top of the wall: can I climb over? But there, at the top, I see a clock; the hands are pointing to twelve! It begins to strike. I awake in a cold sweat.

Now I think that nobody—not even persons who have no knowledge of dream interpretation—would think that such a dream presented any problem in time sequence, i.e., that it was needful to "explain" the fact that "six hours" had elapsed between the beginning of the dream (sundown) and the end (midnight). Taking it to be a dream concerning death, "sundown" would mean "your day is ending"; and "midnight" would mean "your hour has come!"

If our text indicates, therefore, that the Young Man dies at midnight, we must understand this to be a reference to the strong symbolic associations which attach to the midnight hour, as when we read in the Book of Job: " In a moment shall they die, and the people shall be troubled at midnight, and pass away. . . ." (34:20) Midnight is not inevitably the "last hour," of course, but rather the *turning point*, "the time when the power of the unconscious is at its greatest height."[87] Midnight, as symbolic of psychic destiny, may suggest death, or it may suggest death and resurrection, since symbolic values originate in a "pre-scientific" part of us for which the daily rise of the sun can by no means be taken for granted. In describing the journey of the sun-hero ($=$ ego-consciousness) Neumann points out that whereas

> . . . the first half of the night, when the westering sun descends into the belly of the whale, is dark and devouring, the second half is bright and bountiful, for out of it the sun-hero climbs to the eastward, reborn.[88]

Hence it is that midnight is the crucial turning point which

> . . . decides whether the sun will be born again as the hero, to shed new light on a world renewed, or whether he will be castrated and devoured by the Terrible Mother, who kills him by destroying the heavenly part that makes him a hero.[89]

Symbolically it is not at all obvious that the sun will return after midnight—for mayhap the sun-hero "shall be troubled at midnight, and pass away."

The fact that the midnight hour symbolically marks the maximum power of the unconscious can be abundantly documented in folklore, which proliferates with Goyesque apparitions:

> Everything was quiet . . . till midnight, when all at once a great tumult began, and out of every hole and corner came little devils.[90]

> She slept quietly till midnight, and then there was such a noise in the house that she awoke. There was a sound of cracking and splitting in every corner, and the doors sprang open and beat against the walls.[91]

> At the same moment the clock struck twelve midnight, and the earth shook under the boy's feet.[92]

> It happened once, at midnight, that all the bells started ringing in Hamar cathedral, and the organ started playing by itself.[93]

> Precisely on the stroke of midnight the window flew open and a large black bird alighted on the window-sill.[94]

In the Japanese folktale "The Old Men Who Had Wens," midnight signals the appearance of ogres.[95] And in the Grimm tale "The Golden Bird," it is at midnight that the fantastic creature comes to steal an apple from the king's garden.[96]

In the play *Five Years,* it is obvious enough that the symbolic midnight with which it ends marks the extinction of the Young Man's ego-consciousness. He falls back into the anonymous darkness whence we all came; and we know that he has renounced any further attempts toward conscious differentiation: "There is no man here."

The ending of this drama is, in one sense at least, no different from that of Lorca's other tragedies. Like *Yerma, Blood Wedding,* and *The House of Bernarda Alba, Five Years* ends when the destructive inner storm is unleashed. Impulses that can be neither contained nor integrated erupt into chaos, and the effective life of the individual is terminated. The protagonist of *Yerma,* like an enraged spinster, strangles her husband, whose lewdness symbolizes (in the form of a projection) an impulse within herself, which she has repressed throughout the drama. In *Blood Wedding* the instinctual impulse runs wild; the bride gives it full vent, and the resultant chaos cannot be set into order again—it can only be peremptorily terminated. In *The House of Bernarda Alba,* Adela, the youngest daughter, yields to an illicit passion; and when it appears that her lover has been killed, she hangs herself.

In those three tragedies the ultimate destructiveness is the result of sexuality run wild: it is an instinctual drive that envelops the principals and dashes their lives to pieces. It would be much too limiting, however, to read *Five Years* as a play rooted in erotic passion. Unless we are going to interpret it psychoanalytically, we cannot ultimately reduce everything to sexuality; for sexuality (like other components of the psyche) appears here as a symptom. Any of the forms which it may take—autoeroticism, for example—is not a *fait primitif,* but only a specific manifestation of a larger problem: the problem of finding a means of relating three worlds—the world of ego-consciousness, the collective world outside, and the collective world within.[97]

PART II
THE ARCHETYPAL SYMBOLS OF LORCA

CHAPTER FIVE

The Child-symbol

Narcissus

Child!
You're going to fall into the river!

At the bottom there is a rose,
and in the rose there is another river.

Look at that bird! Look
at that yellow bird!

My eyes have fallen into the water.

Good heavens!
He's slipping! Child!

. . . and I myself am in the rose.

When he got lost in the water,
I understood. But I can't explain it.

Narcisco

Niño.
¡Que te vas a caer al río!

En lo hondo hay una rosa
y en la rosa hay otro río.

¡Mira aquel pájaro! ¡Mira
aquel pájaro amarillo!

Se me han caído los ojos
dentro del agua.

¡Dios mío!
¡Que se resbala! ¡Muchacho!

. . . y en la rosa estoy yo mismo.

Cuando se perdió en el agua
comprendí. Pero no explico.

The Archetypal Symbols of Lorca

Those of us who spend much time reading poems and mulling them over generally take it on principle, I believe, that the poet is one who lives in a world consistently alien to the collective, everyday world of the rest of us. It is a world from whose vantage point it seems natural to say, with Wallace Stevens,

> I love to sit and read the *Telegraph*,
> That vast confect of telegrams,
> And to find how much that really matters
> Does not really matter
> At all.[1]

This is characteristic of the point of view generated by living in the world of the poet, for we must recognize a simple and crucial difference separating us from him: in this everyday world which has (so to speak) impounded our very lives, we seem habitually to be seeking some form of spiritual *stability*, a dependable orientation to guide us along what we like to call the road of life. This is what we think we ought to have. But the poet: for him it appears that the very meaning of life resides precisely in his capacity to *resist* such inner stability. For us, spiritual stability is the means to an end—coping with life at large—while the only "end" available to the poet, *qua* poet, is the writing of poems; and the writing of poems depends upon a fluid, unstable inner atmosphere. The unwritten poem cannot come to be, unless all can come to be. It must be the poet, the dealer in metamorphoses, who senses more keenly than others the value of instability, and who must, like Antonio Machado, conclude:

> Poetry, cordial poetry.
> A builder?
> "Neither in the soul nor in the wind
> Is there a foundation."[2]

The poet cannot be hedged in (however securely) by all those things in our world that "really matter." Or (as Wallace Stevens has elsewhere recalled), "everything like a firm grasp of reality is eliminated from the aesthetic field."[3]

The poet is a man confronting an inner domain that must fall into oblivion unless he will submit himself to the transformations whereby it is rescued into the light of our day. It is for this reason that the poem, besides being esthetically all that it is, is simultaneously the sign of a sacrifice; for the poet's own stability has been sacrificed to the birth of a new configuration.

The inner domain can little by little be born into the light of our day, then, if the poet will submit himself to the lifelong task—a gratuitous task that no man ever asked another to undertake. The years of the man are bound to the life of his muse. He carries within him One that is greater than himself. Lorca did not esteem the continued existence of himself as more worthy than that of the girl drowned in the well. How could he? It is the larger part by far that lies beneath the waters, and so it has been written:

> . . . you, sleeping down there
> Face down in the unbelievable silk of spring,
> Muse of black sand,
> Alone.

> . . . look at me.
> How can I live without you?
> Come up to me, love,
> Out of the river, or I will
> Come down to you.[4]

The poet lives a life of continual gestation and birth. To find "stability" would mean the death of him as poet, for it would be the stability of a stagnant backwater.

The Lorcan texts which we have examined offer plentiful evidence that Lorca was himself keenly aware of what we have been saying here; and with respect to our last point—the sense of inward gestation and birth that lies upon his mind with the nagging insistence of a vocation—any descriptive analysis of Lorca's poetry must call attention to the repeated appearance in it of the *infant* and of the *child*. Because this, as symbolic of his own inner life, is the image both of emergent poetry and potential fertility. The newborn child is what Jung, in his essay on this subject, called "potential future,"[5] which we need to understand as a future large with *potency*. The little child is a fresh creature whose birth already implies the successful fusion of forces, and he promises a fresh world about which our stable and repetitious intellect can predict nothing. The appearance of the child-image constitutes an inward assurance of what Baynes described with characteristic aptness as a "forward extension of psychic continuity."[6]

The child-symbol best known to us as such, and as no mere figure of speech is, of course, the Christ Child. His meaning for Occidental man was once all that the inner vision of the newborn child can mean for the individual. The Christ Child was once a collective image symbolizing a new future, a new Law, a new kingdom on earth: a new reality, let us say. Meister Eckhart, writing at some time early in the fourteenth century, observed the psychological analogy, and insisted that the historical birth in the manger was no guarantee of anything, unless the Child could be born in the mind of each Christian:

> As surely as the Father by his simple nature begets the Son innately, so surely he begets him in the innermost recesses of the mind, which is the inner world.[7]

"If thy heart is heavy," says he, "thy child is not born."[8] Presently we shall see how, six centuries later, one Christmas in New York, Lorca will ponder this idea and come to the same conclusion.

It is really difficult to exaggerate the importance of the child in the works of Lorca. Even the most casual reading of his poetry discloses that the child confronts us at every turn, both as an object of discourse and as a symbolic image. Had we never read a biography of Lorca, it would still be evident that he was never very far from the world of children, and that he gave it every consideration. For him the child was, as he put it, "Nature's foremost spectacle."[9] The reality inhabited by small children is a reality largely uncompromised by intellect. It is a world which is extraordinarily intense, because it— like our own dreamworld—is a *symbolic* reality. It elicits Wordsworth's "natural piety," because it is tremendous, that is, it has the power to make the little one to tremble. Says Lorca:

> We have only to observe his earliest games, before he is confused by intelligence. . . . With a button, a spool, a feather, and the five fingers of his hand the child builds a complex world alive with primordial vibrations. . . . He lives within an inaccessible poetic world closed off to rhetoric, imagination (*that* go-between!), and fantasy; with his nerve centers exposed, he inhabits a region of horror and profound beauty, where a shining white horse—half nickel and half smoke—suddenly falls wounded, blinded by a swarm of furious bees.[10]

The unconscious, then, is the child's natural habitat. He can immerse himself in it at will, it seems, like John Crowe Ransom's little Max, who sets off into Fool's Forest:

> "Become Saint Michael's sword!" said Max to the stick,
> And to the stone, "Be a forty-four revolver!"
> Then Max was glad that he had armed so wisely
> As darker grew the wood, and shrill with silence.[11]

And so the child-symbol must mean, above all, contact with the realm of living symbols, which is the poet's only real promise of creative fertility. The conscious psyche of the poet is like a nest: it is a structure built to shelter the tender young creatures while they grow strong enough to make their own way in the world.

This is precisely the idea behind one of Lorca's early poems, entitled *Nest*, which describes a period of spiritual sterility, i.e., a period during which effective contact has been lost with the creative forces of the unconscious. No nest (in spite of the title) actually appears in the poem; but Lorca already knows that he dwells in the world of the poets:

> What vigil is this that I keep
> in these moments of depression?[12]

He is vigilant because he intuits the imminent appearance of a creature which has been born, but not yet delivered into his arms:

> What brambles are hiding from me
> something newly born?[13]

We are back to the poem, characteristically twentieth-century, which has itself as its own subject. In the form of a birth-symbol the creative act becomes an instinctual obstetric feat.

The same symbolism appears in much greater detail in another poem, *Presentiment,* written at about the same time as *Nest.* Here a presentiment is the feeling that the *niño futuro,* the child to come, is about to fill the house of the psyche with his presence. He will grow and give of himself only to the extent that we nurture him, after the manner of the selfless mother:

> . . . the child to come
> will tell us a secret
> when he is playing in his bed
> of stars.
> And it is easy to deceive him;
> therefore
> let us offer him tenderly

our breast.
For the silent mole
of presentiment
will bring his rattles
while the child sleeps.[14]

We may note in passing how the child's point of origin, the feminine unconscious, is already inhabited by the little chthonian animal, the mole, which will bring the infant of futurity his rattles to play with. "Rattles" here probably has a symbolic relationship to speech; i.e., when a new value evolves into conscious form, it becomes possible to articulate it, to speechify. The comparison degrades language, which is the petrifaction of what was previously a kind of protean vitality.

In his lecture on *duende,* the name which the Spanish Gypsies give to the vital impulse underlying their own creative powers, Lorca describes for us the psychic region in which symbolic transformations take place:

> Through the empty archway there comes a mental breeze that blows insistently over the heads of the dead, in search of new landscapes and unknown accents; a breeze that smells of baby's saliva, of crushed grass, and of the velum of jellyfish; a breeze which heralds the constant baptism of things just created.[15]

Here the threshold of consciousness is an empty archway presumably fronting on the edifice of the personal psyche, which is surrounded by the vast region of the collective unconscious. Again we note an association of the child-motif with a chthonic symbolism appropriate to the world of the unconscious; for as in the poem *Presentiment* the infant was served by the mole which dwells in the subsoil, so here it is born in a world of "crushed grass" and "velum of jellyfish," archaic indicators of a primordial atmosphere.

This same chthonic child appears in the poem *Heaven Alive* from *Poet in New York.* Here the speaker finds himself "stuck," at a spiritual impasse, sealed off from the creative unconscious, and so he swears that he will seek out

> . . . the first landscape
> of clashes, liquids, and murmurings
> from which there seeps a newborn babe. . . .[16]

What we have called here "murmurings" are actually "rumors"—*rumores,* an idiosyncratic word in Lorca describing the living sound

of libido at work. When the speaker here seeks a "landscape of murmurings," he is thinking of the "region of vital Becoming." It is the
same region that sends forth the breeze laden with the odor of infant's
saliva, the only region that holds out a redeemable promise of transformation.

The "psychic infant" appears in association with the Christ Child
(after the manner, mentioned above, of Meister Eckhart) in another
poem from *Poet in New York*—*Christmas on the Hudson River*—
which represents the spiritual sterility of the poet confronted by the
unassimilable culture of New York City. While *Christmas on the
Hudson River* is too complex to study here in detail, Lorca's use of
the child-motif in it can be discussed adequately without doing
violence to the context.

These are the relevant passages:

> . . . everyone was singing Hallelujah,
> Hallelujah. Deserted heaven.
> It's all the same. All the same! Hallelujah!
>
> It makes no difference that each minute
> a newborn babe waves his little branchings of veins. . . .
>
> What *does* matter is this: hollow. A world alone. Outlet.
> No dawn. Inert fable.
> Only this: outlet.[17]

The title itself—*Christmas on the Hudson River*—is significant to
our present purpose, of course, since the symbol of the Christ Child
ostensibly represents man's spiritual renewal for the Occident. As
Lorca sees the symbol, however, in its institutionalized, American-
ized, Protestant form, it is meaningless, a form long since emptied of
content: "Deserted heaven."

The title in Spanish is *Navidad en el Hudson,* and so *Navidad*
(Christmas) is never very far from the idea of "nativity." The
Nativity of which Lorca speaks has primarily a psychic significance
(as it did for Meister Eckhart), and it is that with which the passage
quoted is concerned. The reader of Lorca's New York poems will do
well to remember throughout that the City becomes a carrier of a
psychological projection. Lorca's sudden transplantation to the alien
megalopolis produced what was evidently a massive shock; indeed,
it was a traumatic experience which unleashed all sorts of sinister
material from below. The New York poetry is in the form of a

volcanic eruption, a vomiting forth, and the entire book is dominated by symbols of destruction and disease. This, as a matter of fact, is the principal difference between *Poet in New York* and everything written by Lorca previously. The New York poetry represents an *invasion* by the unconscious, a struggle to assimilate material which is unassimilable; whereas his previous poetry characteristically represents the gradual integration of unconscious contents according to a chthonic rhythm dictated by the metabolism of the poet's own nature.

New York City becomes the carrier of a pathological projection possibly because it shows to Lorca a world dominated by a neurotically afflicted ego-consciousness. When we read the New York poems we see a man who is spiritually paralyzed, disoriented, and lost to the magic circle wherein he has been accustomed to conjure up safely material from below. This kind of sterility—loss of contact with the Becoming of the creative unconscious—and the chaos of New York evidently come to represent the same thing, so that *whatever he says about New York City applies with equal force to himself.* Thus, when he says:

> It makes no difference that each minute
> a newborn babe waves his little branchings of veins. . . .

he is not only indicting the Waste Land; he sees into that Waste Land as into a mirror, and it is this that makes it so fearful. The creative process as he knows it is frustrated; the "psychic child," the newborn babe, comes and goes unattended. The infants doomed to die within are hardly different from the little children mourned by the contemporary American poet James Wright:

> How many scrawny children
> Lie dead and half-hidden among frozen ruts
> In my body, along my dark roads.[18]

If within Lorca's body a newborn babe makes an abortive appearance each minute, what of the *annual* Nativity, the Child remembered but once a year in the City?

In our discussion of the poem *Cicada!* we noted that Lorca identified the libido-symbol (cicada) with the Christ figure. The latter was removed from its specifically historical and Christian context, and reinterpreted as a chthonic numen. Man's "salvation," consequently, was to be found chthonically, within libidinal creativity. To "sublimate" the numen, to project it beyond the biosphere, beyond the reach of the Earth Mother, is to turn it into a psychic nonentity. This, in effect, is what institutionalized Christianity has done to the Christ figure, if we read rightly the implications of Lorca's poetry, both in *Cicada!* and in *Christmas on the Hudson;* for Christmas, as celebrated in the American megalopolis, has no significance except as an empty commercial enterprise.

The Christ Child has for Lorca, however, its deepest significance as a symbol for psychic rebirth through repeated confrontation with the chthonic realm within. In New York the poet is lost in a world which recognizes only the letter of the Gospel and not its spirit. If this has occurred, it is because the megalopolis, civilization rampant, is a world dominated by ego-consciousness, whose highest values are supplied by logos. So by definition the "civilized" man characteristically places no conscious value upon, has no conscious interest in or sympathy for, the individuation process—the search for a spiritual center other than ego. His highest values are to be found in his empirical reality. He has turned the Nativity—the Child-symbol—into an annual commercial event, and in this degraded form it has no symbolic standing as the representation of spiritual renewal. For the civilized man, the Nativity simply represents a historical "religious" occurrence signifying that man can live forever in Heaven after he dies. Civilization has worked long and hard at the job of psychological repression, and finds greater value in that moment of its glorious history called "The Age of Enlightenment" than in the moment of the Manger.

Another use of the psychic child: the poem *Book* is a summary of the poet's impressions upon rereading poems composed by him in the distant past. Each poem, he says, represents the birth of a child, the raising to consciousness of a symbol complex which was fixed in the form of a poetic composition—after which it ceased to play an effective role in the creative Becoming of his own psyche:

> Like children pressing their little noses
> against the opaque windowpane,
> thus the flowers of this book
> against the invisible pane of the years.[19]

We have already seen this image used in the play *Five Years*, toward the end of Act III—although with a slightly different meaning. The reader will recall that the protagonist is psychologically "stuck" and that he reacts with severe anxiety. He describes himself as if he were with child: within he carries a psychic content of which he has a presentiment, but which, somehow, cannot break through into consciousness:

> Yes, my son. He runs around inside me, like an ant alone within a closed box. . . . A little light for my son, please. He is so small. . . . He presses his little nose against the windowpane of my heart, and yet he has no air.[20]

In the passage quoted from the poem *Book*, the poet's verses represent children which were actually born, and when he recalls them, it is as if they had gone forth from the house of his psyche, as if they were pressing their faces against the window and looking in at him. In the passage from *Five Years*, however, the protagonist is not talking about artistic creativity as such, but rather about spiritual rebirth— the attainment to a new level of fulfillment which, for Lorca, appears to be naturally expressed by the child-symbol.

We should note in passing that the "psychic child" mentioned in the passage from *Five Years* is described chthonically, in the manner that one comes to think of as characteristically Lorca's. In *Presentiment,* the mole was charged with supplying a stimulus; in the lecture on *duende* we are told that the winds of creativity come laden with the odor of infant's drooling and jellyfish; and now the child is compared to an ant ("He runs around inside me, like an ant alone within a closed box"), which, like the mole, is a chthonian creature: the ants appear to be the "lords of the sub-soil,"[21] "the myrmidons, the 'nimble nurslings of earth.' "[22] The ant expresses the "earth-born nature of life and particularly of man,"[23] and the "psychic child" described in *Five Years* is nothing less than a Myrmidon, that is to say, a psychic component whose significance lies in the fact that it is a product of the chthonic realm. It is *autochthonous,* of the nature of the soil in which it dwells.

It is thus far evident that Lorca possessed an intuitive understanding of the child-archetype as symbolic of spiritual transformation produced by a return to the telluric realities of the psyche. The "spiritual rebirth" promised by such a transformation is not dissimilar to the kind of "rebirth" implied by the term *Renaissance,* as conventionally used by historians when they speak of that era characterized by an attempt to recover the spiritual values of pagan antiquity.

Lorca himself understood that pre-Christian myth is produced by a preconscious state of mind, and that spiritual "rebirth" must mean a reestablishment of contact with the preconscious realities of the psyche. This is nowhere more evident than in the remarkable poem, *Narcissus* reproduced at the beginning of this chapter; for in *Narcissus* Lorca reinterprets the myth as expressive of spiritual transformation in terms of the child-symbol.

To make his point, Lorca transforms Narcissus into a little child, since the myth has for him a dynamic psychological meaning— essentially the same meaning which Erich Neumann was to find in it some thirty years later:

> Narcissus, seduced by his own reflection, is really a victim of Aphrodite, the Great Mother. He succumbs to her fatal law. His ego system is overpowered by the terrible instinctive force of love over which she presides.[24]

Lorca understands that Narcissus "dies," in the sense that his ego-consciousness is overpowered by the forces of instinct, and that this represents a "childish" regression. If civilized man considers ego-domination to be the hallmark of maturity, it is precisely because the immaturity of the young child is marked by an absence of such control. The child is characterized by his tenuous ego-system which repeatedly succumbs to instinctual impulses. His consciousness is largely a lighted stage upon which the forces of instinct act out numberless engrossing dramas.

Thus to Lorca, *Narcissus* is equivalent to "regression"—but in the positive sense. Narcissus becomes a child on the bank of a river, gazing with fascination into its waters. An alarmed adult shouts a warning: "Watch out, child! You're going to fall into the river!" The child can take no heed, because within the river he spies a rose, and within the rose he spies another river.

Now the rose is well known as a symbol for one's psychic center, "the center of the being and of the power of growth within the human psyche."[25] Lorca, in his *Prayer of the Roses,* explicitly identifies the rose as man's spiritual center: ". . . all of them [i.e., the roses] when they were born, imitated the color and the form of our heart."[26] In other words, the rose carries a good deal of the same symbolic significance as does the child-symbol itself as when, in the poem *Useless Song,* Lorca describes the process of spiritual transformation as a "rose-to-be, a confined vein."[27] The bloodstream is the carrier of libidinal energy which, when liberated into consciousness, will bloom like a rose—or be born, like a child. The rose-to-be (*rosa futura*) is not essentially different from the child-to-be (*niño futuro*) of the poem *Presentiment*. Lorca himself clearly understood their interchangeability, as is evidenced in his *Double Poem of Lake Eden*, from *Poet in New York*, where he says, "I want to weep, speaking my name: rose, child, and fir."[28]

The narcissistic child, then, gazes into the living waters and sees a rose—and within the rose, another river. It would be difficult to find a more apposite example than this of Lorca's ability to capture in image a symbol within the realm of Becoming—i.e., his ability to enforce the notion of symbols as representative of processes, and not of things. In *Narcissus* we are confronted with the multiple image of a child in a stream in a rose in a stream.

The child characteristically lives in intimate contact with the Earth Mother. In *Narcissus*, the physical proximity of the living waters activates in the child a sense of well-being—he is in his natural element—and produces in him a feeling of unification with the Mother. This gratifying sense of wholeness manifests itself as a symbol floating up into consciousness: the symbol of the "river-rose." Libido is a flow of energy "comparable to a steady stream which pours its waters broadly into the world of reality,"[29] and so symbolically assimilable to the pulsing flow of the bloodstream: the "little branchings of veins," the "confined vein." Deep within me I contain a river-child at the center of a red rose; if I can turn my consciousness inward, if I can direct my vision away from the outer world and project it downward into the depths of me, then my eyes will "fall into the water," and I will be transformed into a child in a river in a rose in a river: a symbol of potential futurity within the liberated flow of libido which takes the form of a red rose as it circles around and around the center—all of which is induced by the hypnotic gazing into the flowing waters of the Earth Mother.

This kind of "drowning," or regression, described by Lorca, does not carry the negative implications emphasized by Neumann in the passage quoted above, where we read that Narcissus is a "victim" of Aphrodite, and that he "succumbs to her fatal law." Lorca's Narcissus clearly achieves a kind of *atonement*, which is to say, at-Onement, by being drawn into the rhythm of nature. Ego-consciousness itself may be negatively described as a striving away from Mother Earth, whereas the child who would "drown" has only to weaken ever so slightly his slender grasp on world reality. Lorca's notion of the Narcissus transformation is sympathetically inclined; for though the manner in which it occurs remains a mystery to him, he can naturally understand that it would happen:

> When he got lost in the water,
> I understood. But I can't explain it.

As a final note to this poem, we might point out that the alarmed adult who speaks out would arrest the child's "regression" by diverting his attention to a "yellow bird." If the child's attention can indeed be successfully diverted, it will flow outward and upward, as a proper ego-consciousness ought to, rising away from the dangerous influence of the chthonic realm. Though the gesture is futile (since the child "slips" and falls into the water), the adult clearly does not take this to be a disaster, but rather a natural turn of events which he "understands." For if the whole episode is seen as an event occurring within the psyche of the poet himself, it only means that his "adult" ego-consciousness was unable to prevent the flow of libido back to its chthonic source.[30]

CHAPTER SIX

The Ocean-symbol

Fable

Unicorns and Cyclopes.

  Golden horns
and green eyes.

Upon the coastal rocks
in a mighty rush
they illustrate the
glassless quicksilver of the sea.

Unicorns and Cyclopes.

  A pupil
and a power.
Who can doubt the terrible
efficacy of those horns?
Nature,
hide thy targets!

Fábula

Unicornios y cíclopes.

  Cuernos de oro
y ojos verdes.

Sobre el acantilado,
en tropel gigantesco,
ilustran el azogue
sin cristal, del mar.

Unicornios y cíclopes.

  Una pupila
y una potencia.

Ocean-symbol

> ¿Quién duda la eficacia
> terrible de esos cuernos?
> ¡Oculta tus blancos,
> Naturaleza!

In our examination of *Preciosa and the Wind* we saw that the notion of mythology is not to be lightly taken in Lorca's work. To speak of his "mythological grasp of reality" is not to use a metaphor, since *Preciosa* is concerned precisely with the dynamic origins of myth.

Our discussion of that poem was ultimately concerned with the mythological significance of the figure of St. Christopher, since that is what the poem is about; at the same time, however, the terms of the narrative required us to elucidate the psychological meaning of ocean and land divided by a threshold, which may or may not have impressed the reader as being incidental to the "story." The principal point to be brought out now, however, is this, that in the poetic cosmos of Lorca the ocean can never be of only *incidental* importance, because it was never a *mere* metaphor to which he "happened" to allude. In *Preciosa* we have seen how the ocean-symbol is a working part of the narrative machinery, but presumably it would have been possible for Lorca to use other symbolic contrivances to set in motion his story of Preciosa. So how was it that he chose the ocean? How was it that he began by setting his protagonist on the dangerous threshold dividing the land from the water?

Insofar as the question can be answered, we must say that Lorca chose the ocean because it was for him the ultimate genesis-symbol. It was a symbol which he grasped and with which he lived in all its primal genetic significance.

It is the inner world of nonego with which Lorca was always concerned. Indeed, we can say without exaggeration that *the inner world of nonego was Lorca's vocation.* In the chapter on the child-symbol we were concerned specifically with Lorca's apprehension of what has come to be known generally as the "creative unconscious." There we saw how the Narcissus of old "turns"—i.e., is transformed—"becomes as a little child," and so enters unto the kingdom of the creative unconscious, thus producing the generative symbol of the child in a stream in a rose in a stream. Up through the stream of libido there floats, like a hypnagogic vision, a "picture" of the creative activity going on in the realm of nonego.

Preciosa, however, is concerned with another "picture," a hallucination: a veritable monster spawned by the Gypsy-ocean—if by
"monster" we mean a creature larger than ego whose appearance
frightens the subject out of her wits. The world of nonego is prolific
as is nothing else—unless it be the primordial "assembled waters" of
Genesis. It is that world which made Lorca a poet, as it is that world
which makes anyone a poet, of course; but the point here is that the
fertility inhering in nonego itself became something like an obsession
with Lorca, and in his work it is projected in all its oceanic com-
plexity: its seemingly infinite size, its massive fluidity, its tidal surge,
its depths, its anonymous darkness, its proliferation of myriad forms
lurking unseen within, its "devouring" action, and so forth. What
may appear to the casual reader of *Preciosa* as merely one of several
elements in the poem—I mean that murky zone

   . . . where the ocean roars and sings
   its fish-filled night

—is for Lorca the archetypal symbol of life itself in all its forms,
whether constructive or destructive, anabolic or catabolic, paleozoic
or post-impressionistic, phallic or cerebral, fleshly or symbolic. Lorca,
who tells the Reclining Woman that to see her naked "is to understand
the fever of the sea,"[1] and who compares the erotically exciting nude
to the squid because like some pliant, enveloping mollusk she pulls us
down into the deep waters where she "blinds with ink of perfume";[2]
this is the same Lorca who says to the Holy Wafer, "It is thus, O
Anchored God, that I wish to have Thee."[3] When Lorca holds a sea-
shell to his ear, his heart "fills up with water" and "with little fishes
of shadow and silver."[4]

When his friend, the bullfighter Sánchez Mejías, is fatally gored,
Lorca writes: "the ocean also dies."[5] He compares the early years of a
poet to "the childhood of the sea."[6] In one of his public lectures he
declares that the true measure of the dramatist is whether he knows
how to express "the anguish of the sea in a character."[7]

The list of examples could be extended to statistical proportions,
but it is not our aim here to make a statistical contribution to the
study of Lorca. What we would like to pursue is Lorca's open awareness of the oceanic nonego as the source of all that we may hope to
be and all that we may fear to be; not only his own awareness of it, but
his capacity to create in us the same awareness if we will read and
think on his poems.

What we can become is intimately bound up with *how* we go about it, of course; here the means determines the end in spite of ourselves. An attempt to attain spiritual heights through disavowal of "bestial" instincts, for example, can only countermine our plans, since ego-consciousness cannot presume to be the undisputed lord and master of instinct.

What goes on in the realm of nonego, and how the unconscious can slay its own monsters—i.e., furnish its own therapy—are embodied by Lorca in the strange sea-poem *Fable,* reproduced at the beginning of this chapter. What we wish to offer is not an accumulation of examples (which, taken out of context, could really have no convincing cumulative effect) but rather a symbological exploration of an archetypal poem about the ocean. It is the very ocean that spawned St. Christopher for Preciosa—a monstrous St. Christopher never seen by any of us—and it is also the same ocean which generated the cyclopes and the unicorns—creatures which, though invisible to us, have populated the minds of many generations of men, and therefore seen by Lorca as two races that have come down with us through the ages along with our dogs and our cats.

Most of us (if we think of the matter at all) no doubt imagine the unicorn as living in a remote forest or mountain, while the cyclops survives dimly as an uncouth troglodyte. It now becomes necessary, however, to join with Lorca in seeing them as images cast upon the ocean—*because the unicorn and the cyclops are nothing else than expressions of our attitude toward the unconscious itself.* These creatures tell you not what the unconscious is like, so much as what your attitude toward it can be like, and it is this that leads to the remarkable result in Lorca: an unprecedented piling together of pelagic unicorns and cyclopes. As far as Lorca is concerned, they come from the ocean.

Let us pursue the implications of this, first by reviewing the character attributable to Lorca's ocean in the zoomorphic and humanoid guises of the poem *Fable,* and second, by considering why it is that they should make an unprecedented joint appearance.

We will begin by recognizing that prescientific man senses the animal kingdom to be made up of "good" animals and "bad" animals, i.e., those which are well disposed toward man, and those which seem bent on doing him harm. It is a sort of spontaneous Zoroastrianism that perceives a moral significance in the phenomenon of natural enemies—the perpetual struggle between a "noble" principle and a "base" principle, as, for example, the traditional enmity thought to exist between the stag—what I will call the *proto-unicorn*—and the serpent: an enmity freely recognized by all naturalists from Pliny to Topsell. The noble hart, because it "seeks freedom and refuge in the high mountains," came to be a symbol of "solitude and purity of life,"[8] opposed by nature to the serpent principle.

> The bestiaries agree in attributing to stags the fairest qualities: their physical beauty, their grace, agility, sociability, and love for one another are natural gifts which adorn them. Though shy at first, they possess an indomitable bravery; they know the medicinal virtues of plants; they terrify serpents.[9]

Aelian tells us that the stag terrifies serpents "by an extraordinary gift that Nature has bestowed,"[10] and describes how it seeks out the lair where the "venomous creature lurks," magnetizes it as it were with its breath, and eats it alive. This "extraordinary gift" was bound to make it appear to be the natural enemy of the Adversary:

> There was an old belief that the stag, though a timorous creature, had a ruthless antipathy to snakes, which it laboured to destroy; hence it came to be regarded as an apt emblem of the Christian fighting against evils.[11]

Now the unicorn, like the stag, was thought of as a frequenter of high places, especially the upper reaches of Tibet and the Mountains of the Moon in Abyssinia. Similarly, he was an aristocrat by nature, and it is of passing interest to note that Topsell, writing in the seventeenth century, remarked that the hart was yearly decreasing in numbers "because Democracies do not nourish game and pleasures like unto Monarchies, and therefore they are daily killed by the vulgar sort. . . ."[12] The commoner who kills the stag (or the unicorn) symbolizes an attack by the "lower" against the "higher."

Certainly part of the natural nobility of the stag was connected with the mana inhering in staghorn; for, as Topsell informs us,

> Authors do generally affirm, that when a Hart hath lost his horns, he hideth them in some secret place, because he understandeth some secret vertues are contained in them, which mankinde seeketh for. . . .[13]

These "secret vertues" are symbolically akin to the *potencia* which

Lorca's poem attributes to the unicorn: *potencia* or "generative virtue" (*virtud generativa*), as the Royal Academy defines it.

We have been suggesting here, of course, some of the cogent reasons for calling the stag a *proto-unicorn* (by way of characterizing the unicorn), and one symbologist even reports a legend in which we catch a glimpse of an actual transformation:

> In the first century A.D., the daring unbeliever Wang Ch'ung . . . said that . . . the stag in times of widespread prosperity takes the form of the unicorn. . . .[14]

The essential quality of the unicorn is naturally the one which gives him his name; for the unicorn's horn is really the *raison d'être* of the legend. If man needed to invent the unicorn, it is because he needed an animal which bore the wonderful *alicorn*.[15] The alicorn is composed of a substance whose attributes are clearly derived from those of all horns and antlers. These bony excrescences have always been looked upon with circumspection and a certain amount of awe. They are associated with strength and aggressiveness, and all horned animals are so defined—by their possession of horns. They represent the essential physical (and "moral") quality of the animal in somewhat the same way that a man may be defined as the phallus bearer. All that makes one a man—his "virility," aggressiveness, courage, maturity, and so forth—all this is attributable to his possession of a phallus; and it is hardly possible to doubt the phallic associations accruing to horns and antlers as an outward manifestation of *aggressive libido:* the so-called male principle, which may be exhibited by anybody, of course, regardless of sex.[16] In fact it is enlightening to the symbologist to realize that horns and antlers constitute a precise link uniting the ideas of "physical libido" and "spiritual libido." The young stalwart who tames the shrew and the conductor who tames a hundred-piece symphony orchestra are exhibiting the same force in different ways, but only the young stalwart is engaged in what is essentially a phallic activity—unless we are to accept uncritically the Freudian hypothesis of "sublimation," whereby one denies differences by closing his eyes to them.

From the primitive point of view it would appear that horns are something like *cranial phalli,* which is to say that they represent *phallic power not directly involved in sexual activity.* Only men can possess the phallus, but both sexes possess libidinal aggressiveness equally, a fact especially obvious among primitive people,[17] just as in the animal kingdom horns are not the exclusive possession of the male.

Since horns are the most conspicuous characteristic of animals possessing them and since they grow out of the head, they are apprehended as a *physical projection of the mind:*

> Recent studies of Indian religious thought have indicated that horns have been widely regarded as containing projections of the brain-substance, and that in the primitive man's mind this is identified with the *seed* of the creature.[18]

The horn is concentrated life-essence emanating from the brain—the brain, which is the organ of ego-consciousness, sees, understands, and is opposed to darkness and chaos. Here is where we find, then, a source for the universal belief in the prophylactic virtues of horn, and its widespread use in the form of amulets and medicinal powders.

The unicorn is nothing so much as the carrier of a "superhorn." All natural animals have a complicated life-cycle to which the possession or nonpossession of horns is incidental, so to speak; but the unicorn is free of all such natural entanglements. Its life is unencumbered and pure; it exists for one great moral purpose, to bear the magic horn.

In its natural state, the unicorn functioned as a water purifier, for it was well known that the evil serpent daily poisoned the water of life, and so the beasts of the forest depended upon the unicorn to undo the damage:

> . . . when the animals assemble at evening beside the great water to drink they find that a serpent has left its venom floating upon the surface. . . . They dare not drink, but wait for the unicorn. At last he comes, steps into the water, makes the sign of the cross over it with his horn and thereby renders the poison harmless.[19]

This was the outstanding trait of the unicorn, the virtue for which it was sought by men: for the possessor of an alicorn could never be harmed by poisonous substances—an advantage to be prized particularly by the Renaissance nobleman, it appears, who went to special pains and expense to acquire an alicorn of his own.

It is well known that the unicorn could be taken only through the mediation of a virgin, in whose presence it immediately grew tame, for it would lie down beside her and rest his head in her lap, so en-

abling the hunter to approach and capture or slay it. Hence throughout the Middle Ages the unicorn was understood to be an allegorical
figure representing Christ, since it was through the lap of the Virgin
that God became approachable by man.

The unicorn, then, is the purifier of poisoned waters, the shield
protecting man from the venomous serpent. His horn is the life-essence
concentrated not in the genitals, but above, in the mind: it is the
essence of the mind as the preserver of life equilibrium and the
shield against the forces of darkness and chaos.

In the poem *Fable* the unicorns share the scene with a number of
cyclopes, and it can hardly be doubted that the symbolization of an
opposing principle is here intended, since the cyclops is everything
that the unicorn is not. The unicorn is beneficent, whereas the cyclops
is malevolent; he is destructive of man, since he is nothing less than a
man-eating monster, and possesses the attributes of the "micro-
cephalic giant," the "archetypal low-brow, hating everything which
challenges thought."[20] The possession of a single eye is indicative
of Cyclops' subhumanity, a brute force which can overwhelm any one
of us in the form of rage, "devouring" in a moment our painfully
developed and precariously maintained higher humanity. Cirlot, in
his discussion of the Ojancanu, the Basque version of the cyclops,
calls this figure "a symbol of the evil and destructive forces behind
the primary or regressive side of Man."[21] The cyclops is undiluted
instinct.

The giants of Lorca's *Fable* are given a green eye, a chthonic eye:
an eye harking back to the vegetative realm. There is a strong symbolic contrast between the green eye of the cyclopes and the golden
horn of the unicorns, for it is the difference between the sympathetic
nervous system and the cerebro-spinal system; the darkness of the
swamp, and the shining light of the sun. And the material earth-form
of the sun is gold, the "supreme ripening"[22] of the earth-substance,
its perfecting, its ideal transmutation into spirit, a transmutation
envisioned by the mystical alchemists, as noted in the discussion of
Five Years (where it is pointed out to the protagonist that the
"plague on his house" can be driven off by the construction of a self-
image out of the "gold within").

Lorca has brought together, then, in a symbolic representation the
two principles of human nature as envisioned for centuries: the subhuman giant and the noble unicorn. They appear, however, in a

curious way, for we do not seem to be looking directly at them. According to the poem

> Upon the coastal rocks
> in a mighty rush
> they illustrate the
> glassless quicksilver of the sea.

This is a difficult passage, for the reader will observe that in the original the first line of this verse says, *"Sobre el acantilado . . . ,"* which I have translated "upon the coastal rocks." *Acantilado* is derived from *cantil* (and ultimately from L. *cantus*, "rim"),[23] which is "ocean shelf," or "(rocky) cliff." Theoretically these unicorns and cyclopes could be upon a coastal promontory, or they could be upon the continental shelf, either wading, or actually submerged, since the shelf achieves a maximum depth of about five hundred feet. In attempting to reconstruct the image in our own mind, so that it passes before our eyes like a film episode, we have to know whether these creatures are rushing along a promontory, a reef, or whether we glimpse them beneath the surface of the water at some distance out from the beach.

This requires us to adjust our sights on the second half of the image:

> they illustrate the
> glassless quicksilver of the sea.

The optic effect here reminds us of the myriad "crystals" of moonlight dappling the surface of the sea in *Preciosa and the Wind*. By day the sunlight, in similar fashion, spreads a tremulous, metallic sheen upon the surface of the sea, and it is this compound quality, tremulous and metallic, that evokes the image of quicksilver. Here, however, we are dealing with a fertile evocation, because this quicksilver in turn calls forth the idea of a mirror.

We do not observe directly the unicorns and the cyclopes, but seem to look at their images as in a mirror. They are reflected, precisely, because the text says that they "illustrate" the mercurial surface of the sea. Now in Spanish *ilustrar* has a connotation which "illustrate" cannot have in English, because the Spanish for "light" is *luz*. The primary meaning of *ilustrar* is "to give light (*luz*) to." To find a comparable semantic situation in English we would have to resort to the word "illuminate," as when we speak of an "illuminated manuscript." Keeping in mind this meaning of the word, we could understand the passage this way:

> with their own images
> they illuminate
> the glassless quicksilver of the sea.

The mercurial surface of the sea is a luminous effect of the sunlight, and the sea is illuminated in both senses, viz., as an object lying in the sun, and as a folio out of a manuscript (back in the days when unicorns and cyclopes trod the earth!). These images are seen as in a mirror—*azogue* ("quicksilver") is sometimes used popularly in the sense of "mirror"—but they are not reflections, because we have to do with a paradoxical "glassless mirror."

The mirrors that most of us use are provided with a glass surface, the purpose being to give us a reflection of the phenomenal world. The mirror *gives back* an image of whatever is placed in front of it. Now to observe the specular reflection of a unicorn or a cyclops, it would obviously be necessary to place the creature before the glass. We would have to begin in the manner of the ancient recipe for rabbit stew: "First catch a rabbit."

The mirror of *Fable*, then, is really the essentially fabulous part of the whole episode, for how can one have a mirror without a glass? It sounds like one of those formulas typical of the fairy tale: If you would see the unicorn, you must look into a glassless mirror. The hard part is to find the magic mirror; the rest is easy.

We know, however, that the glassless mirror does exist: it is the scintillating surface of the illumined ocean—and when you look into it, you don't see reflections of the phenomenal world. You don't even see a reflection of the blue firmament. You see "illustrations," "illuminations": images of a reality which does not belong to the phenomenal world.

From the foregoing considerations, then, it would seem that we ought to conclude that the unicorns and cyclopes are not rushing along some cliff high above the surface of the ocean, but that they have their existence somewhere else, and that they appear to us not in the flesh, but as images flickering across the glassless quicksilver of the sea.

Normally we think of the symbol as an image taken from empirical reality, and expressive of a psychological situation—such is the dream-symbol, for example. Now mythological figures are symbols—

of this there can be no doubt—but they are not faithful reflections of the phenomenal world. Obviously they are *based* upon the phenomenal world, but the finished products of mythology have their origin elsewhere. Nor are we free to believe that mythological creatures are deliberate and conscious inventions. Rather than intellectual constructs, they are intuitions: they express a grasp of the human condition in the same way as the poem—for the poem itself is not *primarily* a linguistic phenomenon, but rather a symbolic act. The words of the poet convey a symbolic intuition, and (like the mythological creature) it is a primary example of the creative powers of the unconscious mind. From the depths of the oceanic unconscious images rise to the surface, the threshold, the point of contact where there is enough illumination to make such an image visible. Like a hypnagogic vision, the picture is suddenly there: we suddenly become aware that it has presented itself to view, and that we have been watching without knowing when it first rose into consciousness; something within has used the glassless mirror of our microsea in order to "give an illustration." *And the unconscious "reflects" our attitude toward it.*

If our exposition will tolerate here an interpolation from another poem, we can demonstrate quickly how Lorca draws an explicit contrast between the cyclopean attitude and that of the unicorn: attitudes which have also "illustrated" themselves in the form of Satan (as Lucifer) and Venus. This occurs in a poem titled *Sea,* where the ocean is compared to Lucifer:

> The sea is
> the Lucifer of the blue.
> The sky fallen
> for wanting to be light.[24]

This fallen sky is filled now not with stars, says the poem, but with glaucous mollusks. The sea has come to be thought of as satanic, and Christ the Master walked upon it. But "pure" Venus is the goddess of its depths. "Miserable man is a fallen angel," but who can doubt that Earth is the "probable lost Paradise"?

We have to do here with a reevaluation of the unconscious mind. The sea, a "formidable Satan" now, is a creature of "glorious spasms," ruled over by an immaculate goddess: Venus. The poem states that this "immaculate" sphere is man himself (both are fallen), and it wrestles with the two different views of the unconscious which we have actually seen develop in the evolution of depth psychology: the Freudian and the Jungian, which tend in rather different directions. That is to say that psychoanalysis represents the "subconscious" (personal unconscious) as primarily a realm of repressed material— material repressed because it is unacceptable to consciousness. Analytical psychology represents the psyche as an organism tending toward wholeness—a view sometimes called "holistic"—and which seems to have a built-in goal, a teleology, that transcends the limited goals of ego-consciousness. The psyche would realize itself by realizing its Self, by finding a center other than ego. Ego, however, would fain be king of the psyche. This is especially true of civilized man, whose very hallmark is the extraordinary degree of ego-differentiation realized by him. It is perhaps the primary difference between us and the preliterate man, and we even go so far as to equate ego-consciousness with reality: what is untrue or irrelevant to ego-consciousness loses ontological status. This makes us particularly susceptible to the destructive onslaughts of repressed material. We tend to identify instinct and the unconscious with the forces of darkness; we oppose it as the enemy, as bestiality. That monster called the Freudian subconscious is a modern myth which describes our attitude as tellingly as any ancient myth ever told us what the men of old were like. The subconscious is a beast whose determinants must be sought in the subhuman id, and it would appear that its principal activity consists in harassing ego-consciousness, which can engage in constructive behavior only by "sublimating" tendencies which are "really" destructive. The symbology of psychoanalysis always shows us the beast that lurks within; it is a grim rationality that forces us unrelentingly down a dark passage:

> My right hand was clutched
> in a vicelike grip.
> "You will come with me." And I went forth in my dream,
> blinded by the red glare.
> And in the crypt I heard chains rattling,
> and the stirring about of caged beasts.[25]

Thus Antonio Machado described the fruits of the subconscious. When we descend into that "crypt," we are confronted by the unblinking stare of the subhuman eye—the eye of the cyclops that threatens to hold us prisoner in his gloomy cave where we will be torn to pieces and devoured.

> A pupil
> and a power.
> Who can doubt the terrible
> efficacy of those horns?
> Nature,
> hide thy targets!

Here then are the adversary and the champion, the single eye *versus* the power. We have noted that *potencia* is defined as "generative virtue." Man can adopt either a positive or a negative attitude toward the ocean within, but he cannot rid himself of his unconscious, much less escape its destructive potentiality by "forgetting" it. We cannot escape from the cave of the cyclops by pretending it does not exist. What we must do is to follow the example set by Ulysses, who destroyed the threat when he stabbed out the eye. We can do the same thing, not with a pointed shaft of wood, but with the golden lance of the unicorn.

How can we believe in the cyclops and yet deny the reality of the unicorn? Why were we once so ready to accept as real the monster called subconscious? Our belief in it is our own sickness, our own punishment. We read the poets and admire their work without realizing the contradiction: Cyclops cannot write poems! It is only the golden, generative virtue of the alicorn which can liberate us from the monster. When we look into the glassless mirror of the sea, we can make out whatever "illustrations" we like; but we cannot look upon the cyclops while denying simultaneously the latent existence of the unicorn. The one necessarily implies the other, and here is the miracle: for acceptance, as an act of faith, of the unicorn is our own salvation, because the unicorn bears the weapon whereby we may stab out the fearful green eye. We cannot kill the cyclops, but we can depotentiate him, inflict upon him the terrible efficacy of blindness.

The alicorn is like a magic lance made to fly surely to the center of all natural targets. It is at once the healer and the fertilizer of ego-consciousness; it is a *potencia*, a generative power that can rise to the surface of the ocean only through the mediation of the symbol. Without the symbol, man dies.

An irony underlies the opposition of the unicorn to the cyclops:

for the repressed state produces the destructive image in the shape of a humanoid figure, whereas integration of unconscious contents in the form of creative activity produces a "higher" humanity— symbolized by the figure of an animal! It is a noble animal, to be sure, but an animal nevertheless, affirming the nobility inhering in man's instinctual side. A denial of this side is not noble—quite the opposite; for, as Topsell puts it, those who disbelieve in the unicorn are a "vulgar sort of Infidel people" (the same who daily kill the stag?) by whose disbelief "it appeareth . . . that there is some secret enemy in the inward degenerative nature of man, which continually blindeth the eyes of God his people, from beholding and believing the greatness of God his works."[26] It would appear that Topsell intuited what the coming Age of Enlightenment was holding in store for its progeny: the sickness of spiritual lopsidedness that was to culminate in the birth of cyclops. The Freudian breakthrough was hailed by moderns as a twentieth-century discovery of the True Cross; but for Lorca, the cyclops was only one of any number of chimerical creatures which one might succeed in calling forth, for the ocean possesses an inexhaustible virtuosity, and there is nothing that it is incapable of producing in response to our attitude toward it.

When Lorca found it necessary to terminate his sojourn in New York, he diagnosed his illness in a way characteristic of him: "I will go to Santiago [de Cuba]," he wrote, for "my coral lies in darkness."[27] Typically, he understood the spiritual nightmare of his New York stay not *simply* as a confrontation with the cyclopean merman lurking within, but rather as a *dissociative process* whereby the beautiful and fantastic structures of his microsea were swallowed up in sunless waters. "The sea is choked with sand," he wrote; "I will go to Santiago."[28] The passage to the West Indies would be a spiritual renewal: again the golden sun would fertilize the waters of a tropical sea. The cyclopean symptoms would pass away and the poisoned waters would be decontaminated—for who can doubt the terrible efficacy of faith in the unicorn?

The following abbreviations have been used for works by Lorca. All references are to the 13th edition of his *Obras completas* (Madrid, 1967).

CJ	*Poema del cante jondo*
DT	*Diván del Tamarit*
Five Years	*As Soon As Five Years Pass*
Libro	*Libro de poemas*
Llanto	*Llanto por Ignacio Sánchez Mejías*
NY	*Poeta en Nueva York*
OC	*Obras completas*
PC	*Primeras canciones*
PS	*Poemas sueltos*
RG	*Romancero gitano*

Notes

1. Quoted in Jorge Guillén's Introduction to the *Obras completas,* p. lvii.
2. For the primitive concept of property, see Paul Radin, *The World of Primitive Man,* pp. 115-18.
3. Erich Neumann, *The Origins and History of Consciousness,* p. 275.
4. See Mircea Eliade, *Shamanism: Archaic Techniques of Ecstasy,* pp. 168-76.
5. Jean-Paul Clébert, *The Gypsies,* p. 114.
6. Ibid.
7. Ibid., pp. 161-62.
8. In his play *Doña Rosita la soltera,* Lorca uses "crystals" similarly to describe radiancy: "the crystals of the dawn" (II, p. 1404).
9. *Libro,* p. 274.
10. NY, p. 476.
11. PS, p. 638. Precisely the same image appears in Marcus Varro, the grammarian, writing in the first century B.C. He connects the two ideas of "lust" and "garland-plaiting," since the name Venus, he says, is derived from *vincire,* "to bind"—because the garland *"is a binder of the head"* (= Lorca's "Apollo made of bone"). Varro documents his fanciful etymology with a line from Ennius: "The lustful pair were going, to plait the Love-god's garland." (*On the Latin Language,* Book V, par. 62. Italics mine.)
12. As Cirlot points out: ". . . the generic implication of fecundity pertaining to all vegetation-symbols." ("Laurel," *A Dictionary of Symbols.*) In Lorca's tragedy *Yerma,* the protagonist is given a "laurel prayer" as an aid to fertility (III, 1, p. 1330).
13. *Libro,* p. 282.
14. Just as the tidal surge suggests aggressive male libido and not the womb (cf. Neptune and his horses).
15. *Soldado destinado a la persecución del contrabando.*
16. Perhaps the most famous use of this symbolism is to be found in Piero della Francesca's fresco portraying the Resurrection, "where the figure of Christ rises with magical serenity above the figures of the soldiers, held in unnatural sleep." (John Canady, *Metropolitan Seminars in Art,* Portfolio 8, p. 18.)
17. See Diarmuid MacManus, *Irish Earth Folk,* p. 12.
18. See C. G. Leland, *Gypsy Sorcery and Fortune Telling,* pp. 60, 69.
19. *Retrato de Silverio Franconetti* (CJ), p. 320.
20. *Diálogo del Amargo* (CJ), p. 334.
21. We could also say that the singer's art is the *glorieta,* and attribute

the "silence" to the hushed expectation of the audience, though this is a more extrinsic interpretation.

22. *Grimm's Fairy Tales*, I, p. 83.
23. Roland Kent, in his edition of M. Varro, op. cit., I, p. 340n.
24. "Flute" is the primary meaning of *gaita* which, when called a *gaita gallega* (Galician *gaita*), means "bagpipe." Here the association with the pipes of Pan is indicated, especially because the Spanish *gaita* is characteristically accompanied by a small drum, or *tamboril* (as implied by the colloquial expression *tamboril por gaita*, which means that one is indifferent to a proffered choice, i.e., "pipes or drums— it's all the same"). In our poem the "duet" is played by flute and tambourine.
25. *Libro*, p. 272.
26. Ibid., p. 288.
27. John Canady, *Mainstreams of Modern Art*, p. 521.
28. Ibid, p. 522.
29. *Oda a Salvador Dalí* (PS), p. 620.
30. See, for example, *Symbols of Transformation*, pp. 48, 316n; *Psychology and Alchemy*, p. 284ff.
31. *Natural History*, VII, p. 33.
32. Ibid, XI, p. 112.
33. Erich Neumann, *Amor and Psyche*, p. 59.
34. *Natural History*, VIII, p. 166.
35. *On the Characteristics of Animals*, VII, p. 27.
36. OC, p. 1307.
37. Ibid.
38. *Mundo* (PS), p. 632.
39. *Teoría y juego del duende*, p. 118.
40. *Venus* (*Canciones*), p. 385.
41. *Escuela* (PS), p. 628.
42. See pp. 82-83, for a discussion of *blue* as a motif in Lorca.
43. The use of *rumor* as the sound of nature's Becoming is typically Lorca's, just as visually it is a "trembling." (See p. 54, and n26, corresponding.)
44. *Canción de cuna* (PS), p. 548 (3rd ed.). The 13th edition carries the reading "body and earth of snow" (*cuerpo y tierra de nieve*, p. 649). In either case the symbolic meaning of "snow" is unaffected.
45. P. 1266.
46. *Epitafio a Isaac Albéniz* (PS), p. 637.
47. *Five Years*, I, 1, p. 1051.
48. Ibid., II, p. 1104.
49. *Aire de nocturno* (*Libro*), p. 288.
50. *Otra canción* (*Libro*), p. 290.
51. *Teoría y juego del duende*, p. 118. (Italics mine.)
52. See my article "An Analysis of Narrative and Symbol in Lorca's *Romance sonámbulo*," *Hispanic Review*, XXXVI (1968), pp. 338-52.

The *Romance sonámbulo* (*Sleepwalker's Ballad*) contains the most famous use of "green wind."

53. *Burla de don Pedro a caballo* (RG), pp. 461-62.
54. "The moon is very close, / Tranquil in our air. . . ." (*Advenimiento*, in *Cántico*, p. 47.) *Aire nuestro* is also the title of Guillén's collected works.
55. This is the first of four *Nocturnos a la ventana* (*Canciones*), p.368.
56. See II Samuel, 13.
57. RG, p. 465.
58. *Huerto de marzo* (*Canciones*), pp. 417-18.
59. *Canciones*, p. 364.
60. Ibid., p. 414.
61. It is of passing interest to recall that E. M. Forster's *A Passage to India* (published in 1924, and therefore contemporary with *Preciosa*), bears an analogy to Lorca's poem: the young English lady is the victim of a sudden, unexpected encounter between East and West; while visiting a cave-temple her ego-structure is shattered, and in a moment of hysteria she imagines that her Indian guide has attempted to rape her.
62. *The Origins and History of Consciousness*, p. 135.

CHAPTER TWO

1. *"El cante jondo,"* pp. 55-56. (Italics mine.) In earlier editions the reading *"que destrozaron su propia alma"* ("who destroyed their own heart") is *"que desbrozaron su propia alma"* ("who cleared an opening in their own heart"). The earlier reading is possible, given Lorca's penchant for the use of fanciful language in his lectures, but the context seems to demand the later reading.
2. P. 138.   3. Ibid, p. 139.   4. Ibid.   5. Ibid.

CHAPTER THREE

1. Of course the "similarity" may be in some measure contrived, i.e., fictional.
2. Canto II, *The Worker*, p. 51.
3. *Pajarita de papel* (*Libro*), p. 234.
4. *Balada interior* (*Libro*), p. 245.
5. Using Silberer's application of this term. Functionally, the symbol is a "reflected image of intrapsychic processes which lead to symbolization" (Gutheil, *The Language of the Dream*, p. 123). For example, the hypnagogic vision of falling into a lake, whatever else it might signify, reflects the process itself of falling asleep (into the depths of the unconscious).

Notes

6. Compare Cirlot's discussion of the *lake-dwelling* ("Palafitte," *A Dictionary of Symbols*).
7. See pp. 28-31, where Lorca's use of "high" and "low" is discussed apropos of *Preciosa and the Wind*.
8. It should be noted that in the passage here translated, Lorca says not *agua de pozo* (well water), but *linfa de pozo* (well-lymph). *Linfa* and lymph (in Gk. a variant of nymph!) already express precisely the double meaning we are here attributing to water: (1) a "fluid of the human body," and (2) a "fluid of the Earth Mother." (Cf. our discussion, pp. 24-25, of the intrinsic symbolism of the word *pneuma*.)
9. *Casida del herido por el agua* (DT), p. 568.
10. I, p. 1075.
11. II, 2, p. 1322.
12. III, 1, pp. 1334-35.
13. Ibid., 2, p. 1345.
14. I, p. 1450.
15. P. 1601.
16. In general we may say that towns not watered by a river and dependent upon wells for their water supply are considered to be disadvantaged and unpromising. It is probably not insignificant that in Spanish a cesspool is called a "black well" (*pozo negro*). The fact that the same word (*pozo*) refers both to well water and to sewage suggests the opinion in which wells, *as opposed to rivers*, are held. One observes that it is not only the city people who feel that life without "running water" is substandard.
17. "The Psychology of the Child Archetype," *The Archetypes and the Collective Unconscious*, p. 164.
18. Apropos of the weeping girl, see p. 168, for discussion of the doomed "psychic child."
19. P. 472.
20. *Paisaje con dos tumbas y un perro asirio* (NY), p. 510.
21. Lorca's use of the word *porvenir* (rather than *futuro*) connotes "future in store," as when we say, "He has a brilliant future (*porvenir*) ahead of him."
22. On the anima-image as representative of the "inner attitude," see Jacobi, *The Psychology of C. G. Jung*, p. 5.
23. H. G. Baynes, *Mythology of the Soul*, p. 333.
24. "Concerning Mandala Symbolism," *The Archetypes and the Collective Unconscious*, p. 356.
25. Ibid.
26. Lorca characteristically applies the notion of *trembling* (or *vibrating*, or *oscillating*) to life in all its forms: flesh, blood, wind, light, foliage, etc., because "trembling" means *Becoming*.
27. DT, p. 570.
28. "Concerning Mandala Symbolism," *The Archetypes and the Collective Unconscious*, p. 358.

29. *Creative Evolution*, p. 144.
30. The text reads *"Mientras la gente busca silencio,"* *mientras* meaning "during the time that." If a contrast is indicated ("while, on the other hand"), then *mientras que.*
31. *Vientre* means both "belly" and "womb."
32. *Veleta (Libro)*, p. 174.
33. *El diamante (Libro)*, p. 208.
34. As in the *Cry Toward Rome (Grito hacia Roma)* (NY), pp. 520-21, where civilization is depicted as forging chains for the children of the future (ll. 19-20).
35. *Proverbios y cantares (Campos de Castilla)*, no. 35, p. 214.
36. Ibid.
37. The collection contains two poems of this nature, the *Landscape of the Vomiting Crowd* (pp. 487-89) and the *Landscape of the Urinating Crowd* (pp. 489-90).
38. From the poem *Misterio de la fuente, en ti las horas*, reprinted by Dámaso Alonso in *Poesías olvidadas de Antonio Machado, Cuadernos Hispanoamericanos*, nos. 11, 12 (1949), p. 121.

CHAPTER FOUR

1. *Grimm's Fairy Tales*, I, pp. 158-62.
2. Ibid., p. 161.
3. Lévy-Bruhl, *Primitive Mentality*, pp. 35, 55.
4. Baynes, *Mythology of the Soul*, p. 559.
5. Sampson et al., *Schizophrenic Women*, p. 1.
6. The *sol azul* of the poem *Tornasol*, in *Cántico*, p. 76.
7. Baynes, *Mythology of the Soul*, p. 802.
8. *Grimm's Fairy Tales*, I, p. 175.
9. See p. 101, for Lorca's specific stage direction.
10. Not to be confused with the Jungian archetype called the Wise Old Man, "the superior master and teacher, who symbolizes the pre-existent meaning hidden in the chaos of life." (Jung, *Archetypes and the Collective Unconscious*, p. 35.)
11. *Suicidio (Canciones)*, p. 406.
12. *La imagen poética de don Luis de Góngora*, p. 74.
13. *Las nanas infantiles*, pp. 100-01.
14. See Baynes, *Mythology of the Soul*, p. 456.
15. This is the Jungian notion of the archetypes, which are "pictorial forms of the instincts." (Neumann, *Origins and History of Consciousness*, xv.)
16. *Grimm's Fairy Tales*, I, p. 8.
17. Wickes, *The Inner World of Man*, p. 91.
18. I take the "five years" to be symbolically equivalent to the conventional "seven years" of the folktale—the seven-year quest, seven-year servitude, seven-year imprisonment, etc.

19. Neumann, *The Origins and History of Consciousness*, p. 198.
20. Jung, *The Archetypes and the Collective Unconscious,* pp. 19-20.
21. The reference to killing three thousand pheasants in a single day is, of course, meant to imply the possession of extraordinary virility. The figure of *three thousand* is not, however, fanciful, nor snatched at random, and it is of interest to compare statements made by the Count de Beaumont (of France) in a television interview. The Count, an enthusiastic hunter, in describing one of the photographs lining the walls of his trophy-filled den, said, "This is certainly my weekly record of the shooting I made [sic] in Greece. We shot that day about one thousand, five hundred partridges and something like three thousand pheasants in the same day." The Count added: ". . . if you don't walk, if you don't breathe fresh air, if you don't go under the rain and in the cold, you are not a man." (From the documentary *Sixty Minutes,* televised by CBS on March 4, 1969.)
22. Neumann, *The Origins and History of Consciousness*, p. 127.
23. Kronhausen, *Pornography and the Law*, p. 221.
24. *Arlequín (Canciones)*, p. 367.
25. *Charla sobre teatro*, p. 150.
26. *La imagen poética de don Luis de Góngora*, p. 69.
27. Ibid., p. 74.
28. Ibid.
29. Wichmann, *Chess: the Story of Chesspieces from Antiquity to Modern Times*, p. 48.
30. *El público*, p. 1161.
31. Since "regression" can be a withdrawal of libido from the ego-structure in order to burst the boundaries in search of new values, or it can be a chaotic retreat like the fatal fall of Icarus into the depths of the unconscious (cf. Neumann, *The Origins and History of Consciousness*, p. 188).
32. In our discussion of the child-archetype, pp. 171-72.
33. Bergson, *Creative Evolution*, p. 31.
34. *Los negros*, p. 477.
35. *Oda a Salvador Dalí* (PS), p. 620.
36. *Cuerpo presente (Llanto)*, p. 542.
37. See Zimmer, *The Art of Indian Asia,* I, p. 262.
38. It is not unusual to use in Spanish the word *trayectoria* ("trajectory") to mean the course or path that can be discerned in the works of an artist or writer.
39. *Curva* (PS), p. 594.
40. See Lorca's poem *Ciudad* (PC, pp. 350-51) for an analogous image: the city is "invaded" by both forest and ocean.
41. Martin, *The Opera Companion*, p. 147. See also Newman, "Planning Bayreuth," *The Life of Richard Wagner,* IV, pp. 292-319.
42. Martin, *The Opera Companion*, p. 150.

43. See Eliade, *Shamanism,* p. 33; and Perry, *The Self in Psychotic Process,* p. 117.
44. See pp. 26-27, for discussion of this point apropos of *Preciosa and the Wind.*
45. Spargo, *Virgil the Necromancer,* p. 12.
46. Ibid., p. 33. 47. Ibid., p. 84. 48. Ibid., p. 47.
49. Ibid., pp 16-17. 50. Ibid., p. 72. 51. Ibid., p. 73.
52. Golding, *Lord of the Flies,* p. 127.
53. Ibid., p. 190.
54. Baynes, *Mythology of the Soul,* pp. 704-05, quoting Jung.
55. Ibid., p. 225.
56. From an alchemical text by Robert Fludd, quoted by Silberer, *Problems of Mysticism and its Symbolism,* pp. 180-81.
57. Baynes, *Mythology of the Soul,* p. 225.
58. *La imagen poética de . . . Góngora,* p. 63.
59. P. 13.
60. Jung, *Psychology and Alchemy,* p. 84.
61. Baynes, *Mythology of the Soul,* p. 777.
62. Ibid., p. 776.
63. *Zarzamora con el tronco gris (Canciones),* p. 378.
64. *Imaginación, Inspiración, evasión,* p. 91.
65. *Doña Rosita the Spinster,* II, p. 1401.
66. Adler, *The Living Symbol,* pp. 21-22.
67. Ibid., p. 33. (Italics mine.)
68. Naturally I am not using the word *function* in the technical Jungian sense of the "basic four" (thinking, intuition, feeling, and sensation).
69. See Rákóczi, *The Painted Caravan.* Though the author speaks much of the *general* "divinatory" significance of the cards, see his descriptions of the Gypsy adept engaged in *individual* readings ("Examples," pp. 90-105).
70. *Veleta (Libro),* pp. 173-75; *Suite del agua* (PS), pp. 593-96; *La selva de los relojes* (PS), fourth section, p. 612; and *Oda a Salvador Dalí* (PS), fourth section, p. 621.
71. Jacobi, *The Psychology of C. G. Jung,* p. 35.
72. Baynes, *Mythology of the Soul,* p. 326.
73. Perry, *The Self in Psychotic Process,* p. 48.
74. Ibid., pp. 13-14.
75. Schaer, *Religion and the Cure of Souls in Jung's Psychology,* p. 44.
76. Eliade, *Shamanism,* p. 149.
77. Perry, *The Self in Psychotic Process,* p. 117.
78. Plokker, *Art from the Mentally Disturbed,* pp. 15-30.
79. Ibid., p. 23.
80. Ibid.
81. Ibid., p. 52.
82. William James, *Principles of Psychology,* I, p. 121.

83. Ibid. (Italics mine.)

84. See Plokker, *Art from the Mentally Disturbed*, p. 30.

85. See the classic example given by Gutheil, *The Language of the Dream*, p. 5: the sound of a falling book creates an oneiric drama lasting a half-hour (by the clock in the dream) and culminating in a pistol shot—which is the crash of the book against the floor.

86. Lima, *The Theatre of García Lorca*, p. 186.

87. Wickes, *The Inner World of Man*, p. 101.

88. Neuman, *The Origins and History of Consciousness*, p. 165.

89. Ibid.

90. "The King's Son Who Feared Nothing," *Grimm's Fairy Tales*, I, p. 46.

91. "The Hut in the Forest," *Grimm's Fairy Tales*, I, pp. 141-42.

92. "The Battle Between the Sea *Draugs* and the Land *Draugs*," *Folktales of Norway* (Christiansen, ed.), p. 54.

93. "The Sea Serpent in Lake Mjösen," *Folktales of Norway*, pp. 70-71.

94. "The Black Hen," *Gypsy Folk Tales* (M. Vorísková), p. 154.

95. "The Old Men Who Had Wens," *Folktales of Japan* (Seki, ed.), p. 126.

96. *The Golden Bird, Grimm's Fairy Tales*, I, p. 116.

97. Because of his ambiguity within the framework of analytical psychology, I have omitted discussion of the Father of the *Novia*. As part of the manifest content of the text, he is a parody of the Young Man: he is ineffectually "related" to the *Novia*, and he is ineffectually "conscious" (he is an absent-minded astronomer, and astronomy is the least humanistic—i.e., earthbound—of the sciences). But since this is "manifest," it seems gratuitous to inform the reader of the fact—while to analyze his character beyond this would be to indulge in unwelcome guesswork.

CHAPTER FIVE

1. From "Mandolin and Liqueurs," *Opus Posthumous*, pp. 28-29.

2. From *Poema de un día*, in *Campos de Castilla* (*Poesías completas*, p. 187).

3. "The Noble Rider and the Sound of Words," *The Necessary Angel*, p. 30.

4. Wright, "To the Muse," *Shall We Gather at the River*, p. 58.

5. Jung, "The Psychology of the Child Archetype," *The Archetypes and the Collective Unconscious*, p. 164.

6. Baynes, *Mythology of the Soul*, p. 885.

7. Eckhart, *Sermons and Collations Tractates, Sayings*, p. 49.

8. Ibid., p. 34.

9. *Las nanas infantiles*, p. 96.

10. Ibid., pp. 100-01.
11. "First Travels of Max," *Selected Poems*, p. 13.
12. *Nido* (*Libro*), p. 289.
13. Ibid.
14. *El presentimiento* (*Libro*), p. 214.
15. P. 121.
16. *Cielo vivo* (NY), p. 500.
17. *Navidad en el Hudson* (NY), p. 492.
18. Wright, "The Frontier," *Shall We Gather at the River*, p. 34.
19. *Libro* (PS), p. 626.
20. P. 1125.
21. Bergson, *Creative Evolution*, p. 134.
22. Neumann, *Amor and Psyche*, p. 95.
23. Ibid.
24. Neumann, *The Origins and History of Consciousness*, p. 90.
25. Wickes, *The Inner World of Man*, p. 17.
26. *La oración de las rosas* (PS), p. 580.
27. *Canción inútil* (*Canciones*), p. 417.
28. *Poem doble del Lago Edem* (NY), p. 499.
29. Jung, *Psychology of the Unconscious*, p. 194.
30. Rollo May, in his discussion of the Narcissus symbol, points out that Narcissus does not fall in love with "himself." This ought to be obvious, but apparently it is not, since "narcissism" popularly means "self-love." But, as May says, Narcissus "did not recognize himself," meaning that ego-consciousness falls in love (becomes fascinated) with a different part of the psyche. According to the myth, Narcissus had already spurned Echo; and while this element does not enter Lorca's poem, we can easily see the implications of it: "echo" is a duplication of ego-consciousness. (See Caligor and May, *Dreams and Symbols*, p. 122.)

CHAPTER SIX

1. *Casida de la mujer tendida* (DT), p. 570.
2. *Interior* (*Canciones*), p. 399.
3. *Oda al Santísimo Sacramento del altar* (PS), p. 630. (Italics mine.)
4. *Caracola* (*Canciones*), p. 372.
5. *Cuerpo presente* (*Llanto*), p. 544.
6. *Tu infancia en Mentón* (NY), p. 475.
7. *Charla sobre teatro*, p. 149.
8. Ferguson, *Signs and Symbols in Christian Art*, pp. 26-27.
9. Translated from de Pinedo's *El simbolismo en la escultura medieval española*, pp. 79-80.
10. Aelian, *On the Characteristics of Animals*, 2.9.

11. Bayley, *A New Light on the Renaissance*, p. 16.
12. Topsell, *The History of Four-Footed Beasts and Serpents and Insects*, I, p. 97.
13. Ibid., p. 98.
14. Borges, *The Book of Imaginary Beings*, p. 70.
15. Coined (from the Italian *alicorno*) by Odell Shepard to avoid the "cacophonous" term "unicorn's horn." (See his *The Lore of the Unicorn*, p. 101n.)
16. The specifically phallic symbolism of the alicorn is especially noticeable in the belief, sometimes mentioned, that the unicorn had a "mobile" horn "susceptible of erection." Shepard, *The Lore of the Unicorn*, pp. 104-05)
17. See Briffault, *The Mothers*, particularly Chapter Seven, "The Position of Women in Matriarchal Societies."
18. Kenneth Oakley, in the Introduction to Folke Henschen's *The Human Skull*, p. 16.
19. Shepard, *The Lore of the Unicorn*, p. 60, quoting from *Physiologus*.
20. Baynes, *Mythology of the Soul*, p. 723.
21. Cirlot, "Ojancanu," *A Dictionary of Symbols*.
22. Eliade, *The Forge and the Crucible*, p. 52.
23. According to Corominas, *Diccionario crítico etimológico de la lengua castellana*.
24. *Mar (Libro)*, p. 276.
25. Machado, *Y era el demonio de mi sueño*, in *Galerías*, p. 78.
26. Topsell, *The History of Four-Footed Beasts and Serpents and Insects*, I, p. 552.
27. From the poem *Son de negros en Cuba* (NY), p. 531.
28. Ibid.

Bibliography

Adler, Gerhard. *The Living Symbol.* New York, 1961.

Aelian. *On the Characteristics of Animals.* Cambridge, 1958-59.

Allen, Rupert. "An Analysis of Narrative and Symbol in Lorca's 'Romance sonámbulo,'" *Hispanic Review,* XXXVI (1968), pp. 338-52.

Alonso, Dámaso. "Poesías olvidadas de Antonio Machado," *Cuadernos Hispanoamericanos,* nos. 11, 12 (1949), pp. 335-81.

Bayley, Harold. *A New Light on the Renaissance.* New York, 1909.

Baynes, H. G. *Mythology of the Soul.* New York, 1955.

Bergson, Henri. *Creative Evolution.* New York, 1911.

Borges, Jorge Luis. *The Book of Imaginary Beings.* New York, 1969.

Briffault, Robert. *The Mothers.* New York, 1931.

Caligor, Leopold, and Rollo May. *Dreams and Symbols: Man's Unconscious Language.* New York, 1968.

Canady, John. *Mainstreams of Modern Art.* New York, 1959.

———. *Metropolitan Seminars in Art.* New York, 1958.

Cherubini, Luigi. *Medea.* Milan, 1960.

Christiansen, Reidar (ed.). *Folktales of Norway.* Chicago, 1964.

Cirlot, J. E. *A Dictionary of Symbols.* New York, 1962.

Clébert, Jean-Paul. *The Gypsies.* London, 1963.

Corominas, Juan. *Diccionario crítico etimológico de la lengua castellana.* Madrid, 1954.

Donizetti, Gaetano. *Lucia di Lammermoor.* New York, n.d.

Eckhart, Meister. *Sermons and Collations, Tractates, Sayings.* London, 1956.

Eliade, Mircea. *The Forge and the Crucible.* New York, 1956.

———. *Shamanism: Archaic Techniques of Ecstasy.* New York, 1964.

Ferguson, George. *Signs and Symbols in Christian Art.* New York, 1954.

García Lorca, Federico. *Obras completas.* 3rd ed. Madrid, 1957.

———. *Obras completas.* 13th ed. Madrid, 1967.

Gluck, Christoph. *Alceste.* Paris, 1949.

———. *Orphée et Euridice.* New York, n.d.

Golding, William. *Lord of the Flies.* New York, 1959.

Grimm's Fairy Tales. Louis and Bryna Untermeyer (eds.). New York, 1962.

Guillén, Jorge. *Cántico: Fe de vida.* 4th ed. Buenos Aires, 1950.

Gutheil, Emil. *The Language of the Dream.* New York, 1939.

Haydn, Joseph. *Il mondo della luna.* New York, 1958.

Henschen, Folke. *The Human Skull.* New York, 1966.

Jacobi, Jolande. *The Psychology of C. G. Jung.* 6th ed. (revised). New Haven, 1962.

James, William. *Principles of Psychology.* New York, 1896.

Jung, C. G. *The Archetypes and the Collective Unconscious.* New York, 1959.

———. *Psychology and Alchemy.* 2d ed. New York, 1968.
———. *Psychology of the Unconscious.* New York, 1957.
———. *Symbols of Transformation.* 2d ed. New York, 1967.
Kronhausen, Eberhard and Phyllis. *Pornography and the Law.* New York, 1959.
Leland, Charles G. *Gypsy Sorcery and Fortune Telling.* New York, 1962.
Lévy-Bruhl, Lucien. *Primitive Mentality.* London, 1923.
Lima, Robert. *The Theatre of García Lorca.* New York, 1963.
Ludlow, Fitz Hugh. *The Hasheesh Eater.* New York, 1857.
Machado, Antonio. *Poesías completas.* 4th ed. Madrid, 1936.
MacManus, Diarmuid. *Irish Earth Folk.* New York, 1959.
Martin, George W. *The Opera Companion: a Guide for the Casual Opera-goer.* New York, 1961.
Metastasio, Pietro. *Tutte le opere.* Milan, 1953.
Neumann, Erich. *Amor and Psyche.* New York, 1956.
———. *The Origins and History of Consciousness.* New York, 1954.
Newman, Ernest. *The Life of Richard Wagner.* New York, 1946.
Palamás, Kostís. *The Twelve Lays of the Gipsy.* London, 1969.
Pergolesi, Giovanni. *L'Olimpiade.* Rome, 1942.
———. *Il prigionero superbo.* Rome, 1942.
Perry, John W. *The Self in Psychotic Process: its Symbolism in Schizophrenia.* Berkeley, 1953.
Pinedo, Ramiro de. *El simbolismo en la escultura medieval española.* Madrid, 1930.
Pliny (Gaius Plinius Secundus). *Natural History.* Cambridge, 1938.
Plokker, J. H. *Art from the Mentally Disturbed.* Boston, 1965.
Radin, Paul. *The World of Primitive Man.* New York, 1953.
Rákóczi, Basil. *The Painted Caravan.* The Hague, 1954.
Ransom, John Crowe. *Selected Poems.* New York, 1963.
Sampson, Harold, Sheldon Messinger, and Robert Towne. *Schizophrenic Women.* New York, 1964.
Schaer, Hans. *Religion and the Cure of Souls in Jung's Psychology.* New York, 1950.
Seki, Keigo (ed.). *Folktales of Japan.* Chicago, 1963.
Shepard, Odell. *The Lore of the Unicorn.* New York, 1967.
Silberer, Herbert. *Problems of Mysticism and its Symbolism.* New York, 1917.
Sixty Minutes. CBS Television Documentary. March 4, 1969.
Spargo, John. *Virgil the Necromancer.* Cambridge, 1934.
Stevens, Wallace. *The Necessary Angel.* New York, 1951.
———. *Opus Posthumous.* New York, 1957.
Topsell, Edward. *The History of Four-Footed Beasts and Serpents and Insects.* Facsimile reproduction of the 1658 ed. New York, 1967.
Varro, Marcus. *On the Latin Language.* Cambridge, 1938.
Verdi, Giuseppe. *Aïda.* London, n.d.
Vorísková, M. *Gypsy Folk Tales.* London, 1966.

Bibliography

Wichmann, Hans and Siegfried. *Chess: the Story of Chesspieces from Antiquity to Modern Times.* New York, 1964.
Wickes, Frances. *The Inner World of Man.* New York, 1948.
Wright, James. *The Branch Will Not Break.* Middletown, Conn., 1959.
————. *Shall We Gather at the River.* Middletown, Conn., 1960.
Zimmer, Heinrich. *The Art of Indian Asia: its Myths and Transformations.* New York, 1955.

Index

Index

Index